Steeple

VOLUME 2

THE SILVERY MOON

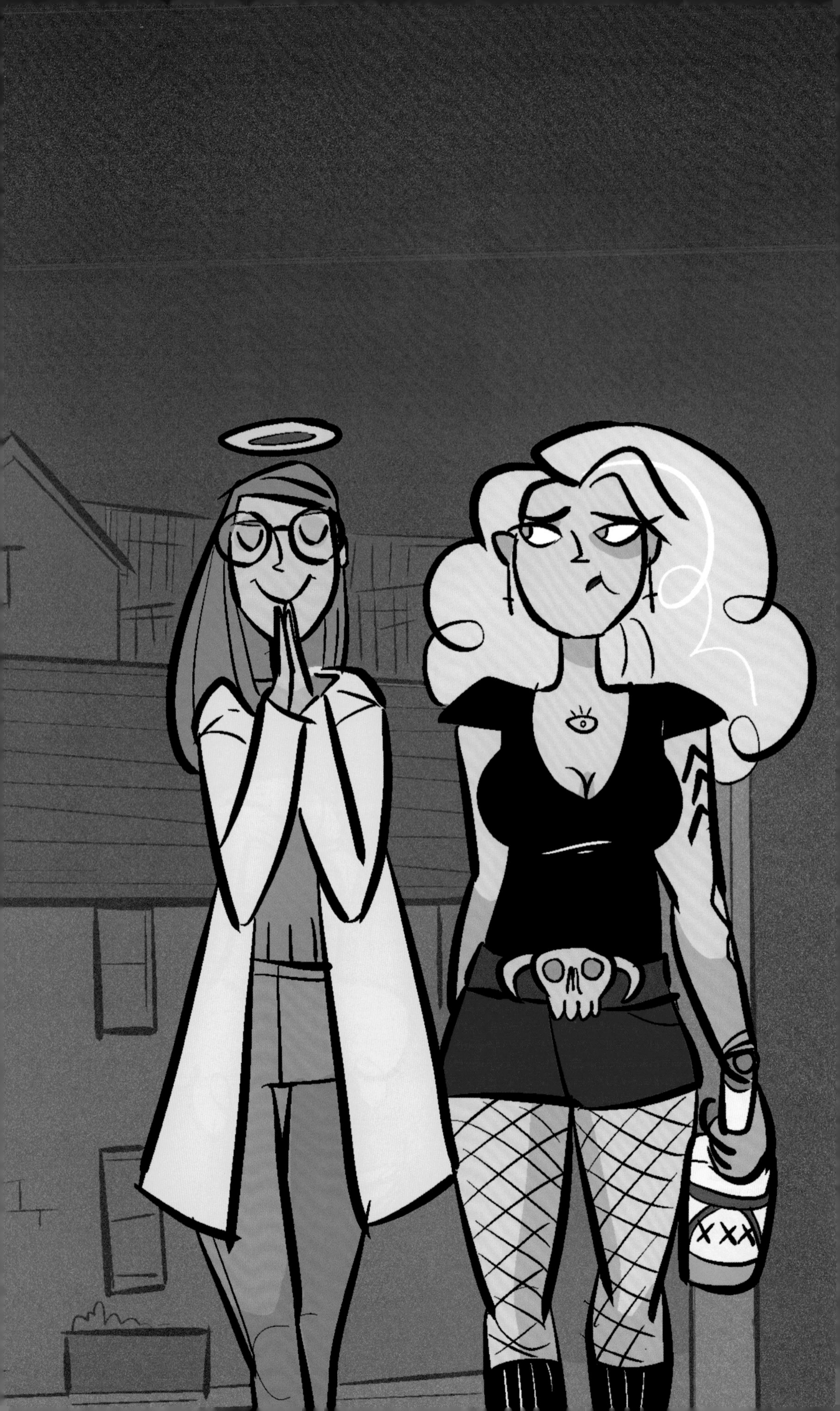

STEEPLE

VOLUME 2

THE
SILVERY MOON

SCRIPT, ART, AND LETTERS:
JOHN ALLISON

COVER BY
MAX SARIN

STEEPLE CREATED BY
JOHN ALLISON

DARK HORSE BOOKS

President & Publisher **MIKE RICHARDSON**

Editor **DANIEL CHABON**

Assistant Editors **CHUCK HOWITT** AND **KONNER KNUDSEN**

Graphic Designer **KATHLEEN BARNETT**

Digital Art Technician **ANN GRAY**

Steeple Volume 2: The Silvery Moon

Collects a new OGN *Steeple* volume 2.

Published by Dark Horse Books | A division of Dark Horse Comics LLC | 10956 SE Main Street, Milwaukie, OR 97222

DarkHorse.com
To find a comics shop in your area, visit comicshoplocator.com
First edition: August 2021
Ebook ISBN 978-1-50672-475-1
Trade paperback ISBN 978-1-50672-474-4

1 3 5 7 9 10 8 6 4 2
Printed in China

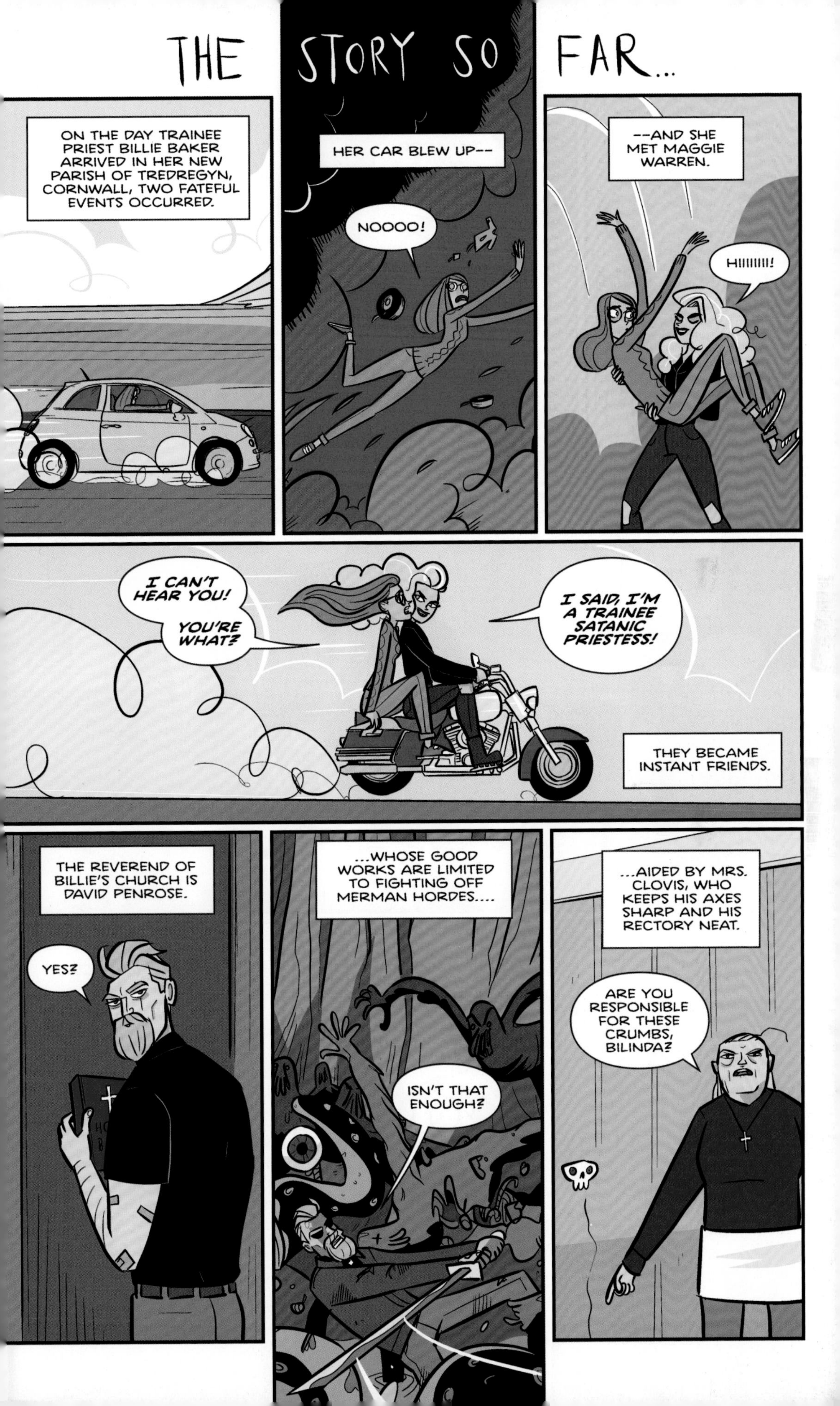
THE STORY SO FAR...
ON THE DAY TRAINEE PRIEST BILLIE BAKER ARRIVED IN HER NEW PARISH OF TREDREGYN, CORNWALL, TWO FATEFUL EVENTS OCCURRED.
HER CAR BLEW UP--
NOOOO!
--AND SHE MET MAGGIE WARREN.
HIIIIIII!
I CAN'T HEAR YOU!
YOU'RE WHAT?
I SAID, I'M A TRAINEE SATANIC PRIESTESS!
THEY BECAME INSTANT FRIENDS.
THE REVEREND OF BILLIE'S CHURCH IS DAVID PENROSE.
YES?
...WHOSE GOOD WORKS ARE LIMITED TO FIGHTING OFF MERMAN HORDES....
ISN'T THAT ENOUGH?
...AIDED BY MRS. CLOVIS, WHO KEEPS HIS AXES SHARP AND HIS RECTORY NEAT.
ARE YOU RESPONSIBLE FOR THESE CRUMBS, BILINDA?

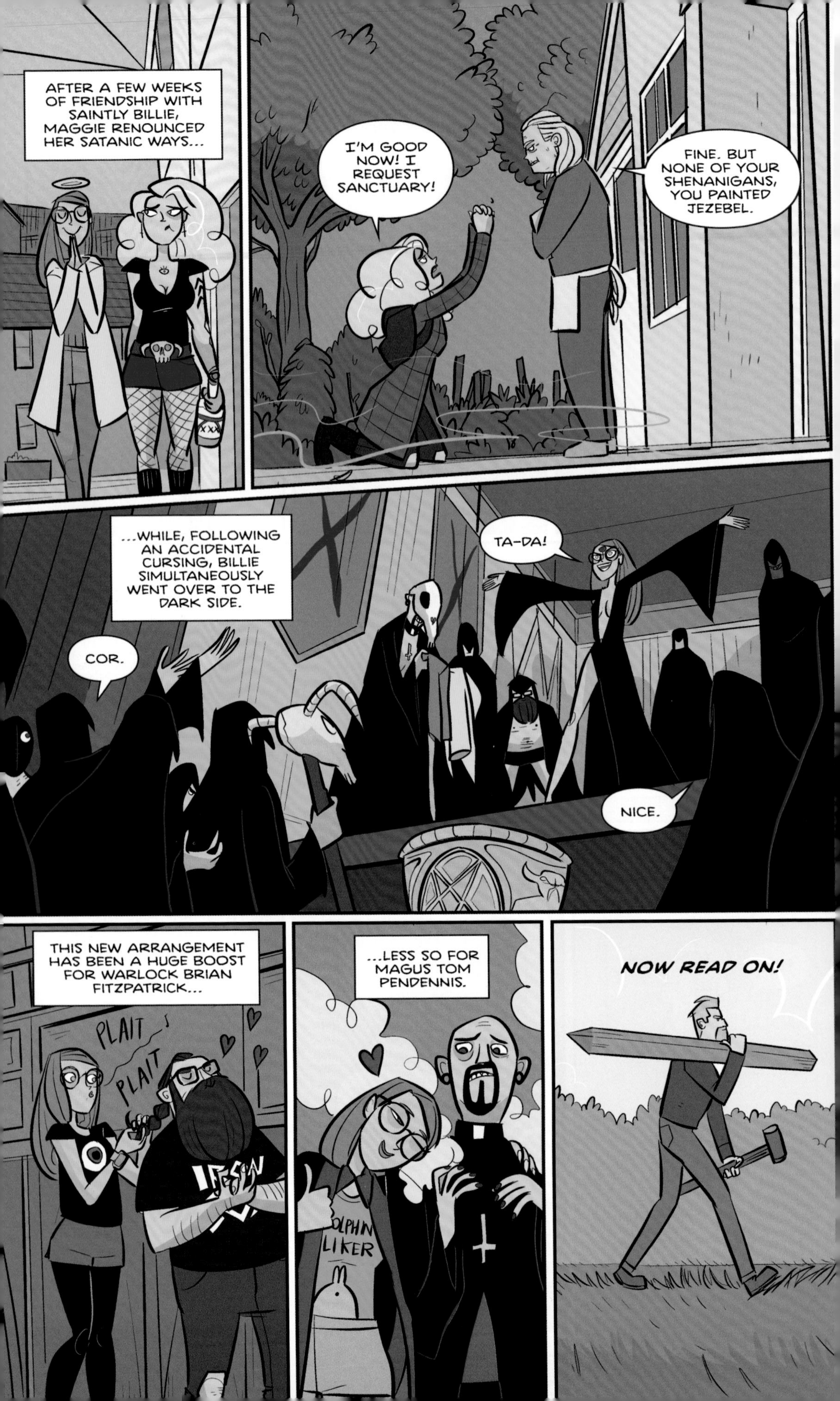
AFTER A FEW WEEKS OF FRIENDSHIP WITH SAINTLY BILLIE, MAGGIE RENOUNCED HER SATANIC WAYS...
I'M GOOD NOW! I REQUEST SANCTUARY!
FINE. BUT NONE OF YOUR SHENANIGANS, YOU PAINTED JEZEBEL.
...WHILE, FOLLOWING AN ACCIDENTAL CURSING, BILLIE SIMULTANEOUSLY WENT OVER TO THE DARK SIDE.
TA-DA!
COR.
NICE.
THIS NEW ARRANGEMENT HAS BEEN A HUGE BOOST FOR WARLOCK BRIAN FITZPATRICK...
PLAIT
PLAIT
...LESS SO FOR MAGUS TOM PENDENNIS.
OLPHIN LIKER
NOW READ ON!

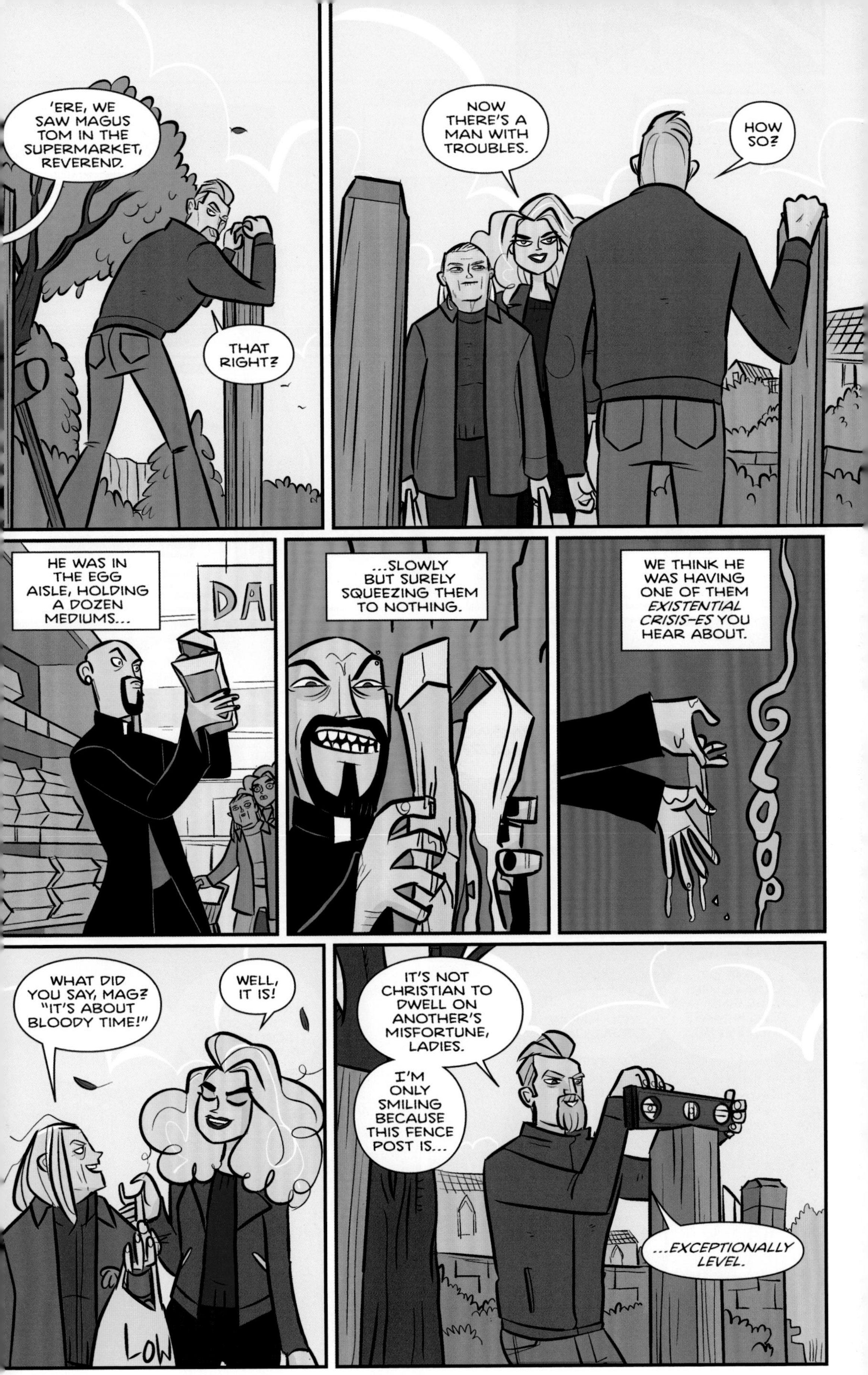

'ERE, WE SAW MAGUS TOM IN THE SUPERMARKET, REVEREND.
THAT RIGHT?
NOW THERE'S A MAN WITH TROUBLES.
HOW SO?
HE WAS IN THE EGG AISLE, HOLDING A DOZEN MEDIUMS...
DA
...SLOWLY BUT SURELY SQUEEZING THEM TO NOTHING.
WE THINK HE WAS HAVING ONE OF THEM *EXISTENTIAL CRISIS-ES* YOU HEAR ABOUT.
GLOOP
WHAT DID YOU SAY, MAG? "IT'S ABOUT BLOODY TIME!"
WELL, IT IS!
LOW
IT'S NOT CHRISTIAN TO DWELL ON ANOTHER'S MISFORTUNE, LADIES.
I'M ONLY SMILING BECAUSE THIS FENCE POST IS...
...EXCEPTIONALLY LEVEL.

O BELIAL! HAVE I NOT SERVED YOU WELL?

TELL ME WHY I MUST SUFFER SO!

LET TODAY BE AN END TO MY TRIALS!

CHVRCH OF SATAN

PARISH NOTICES

BLACK MASS SCHEDULE

Singing Aloud
Tredregyn

New singers always welcome, come and join us!

Singing Aloud
Tredregyn

We're fun, informal and we sing beautiful harmonies for female voices to a wide range of song styles, - all taught in a friendly and relaxed environment. A reasonable singing ability is all you need!

No auditions, no need to read music
Come for a trial session (£4)
Make new friends and experience the joy of singing with others

GRIND

SINGING ALOUD, BILLIE?

SINGING ALOUD?

TOM, YOU'RE BACK! YES! WHAT DO YOU THINK?

WE'VE ALREADY GOT SIX SIGN-UPS!

SOME OF OUR OLDER LADIES FIND THE BLACK MASS ORGIES A BIT...

...YOU KNOW, STRENUOUS.

PLINK PLINK PLINK

SO I THOUGHT, HAVE A BIT OF A SING-SONG FOR THEM! FUN, RIGHT?

AFTER ALL, THEY SAY THE DEVIL HAS ALL THE BEST TUNES!

PLAY THE HITS THE RINGO WAY!

Scouse the Mouse
Don't Pass Me By
Le Jardin de Poulpe
Goldfinger
AND MORE!

RINGO STARR
PLAY IN A DAY

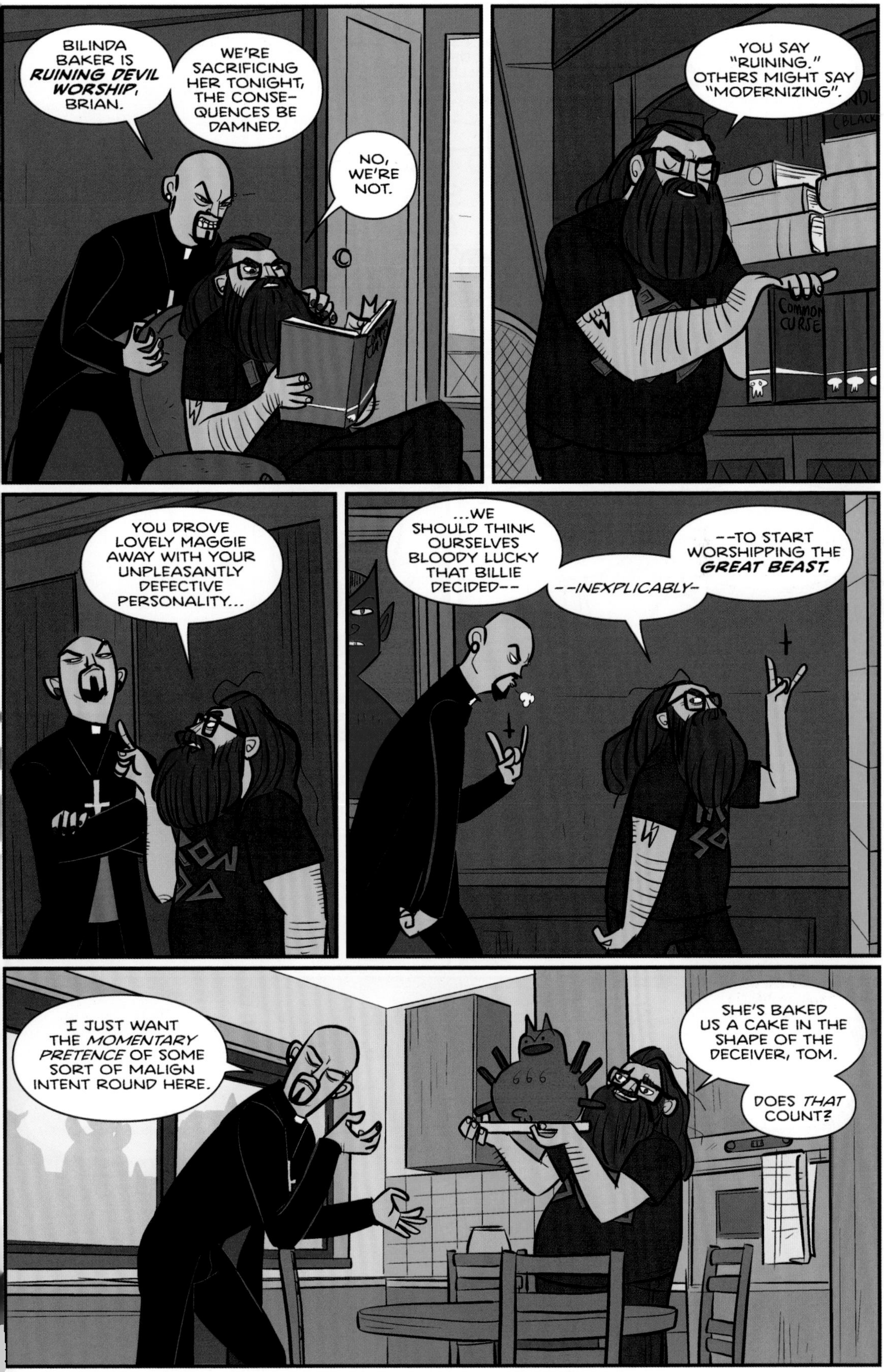
BILINDA BAKER IS ***RUINING DEVIL WORSHIP***, BRIAN.
WE'RE SACRIFICING HER TONIGHT, THE CONSE-QUENCES BE DAMNED.
NO, WE'RE NOT.
YOU SAY "RUINING." OTHERS MIGHT SAY "MODERNIZING".
COMMON CURSE
YOU DROVE LOVELY MAGGIE AWAY WITH YOUR UNPLEASANTLY DEFECTIVE PERSONALITY...
...WE SHOULD THINK OURSELVES BLOODY LUCKY THAT BILLIE DECIDED--
--*INEXPLICABLY*-
--TO START WORSHIPPING THE ***GREAT BEAST.***
I JUST WANT THE *MOMENTARY PRETENCE* OF SOME SORT OF MALIGN INTENT ROUND HERE.
666
SHE'S BAKED US A CAKE IN THE SHAPE OF THE DECEIVER, TOM.
DOES *THAT* COUNT?

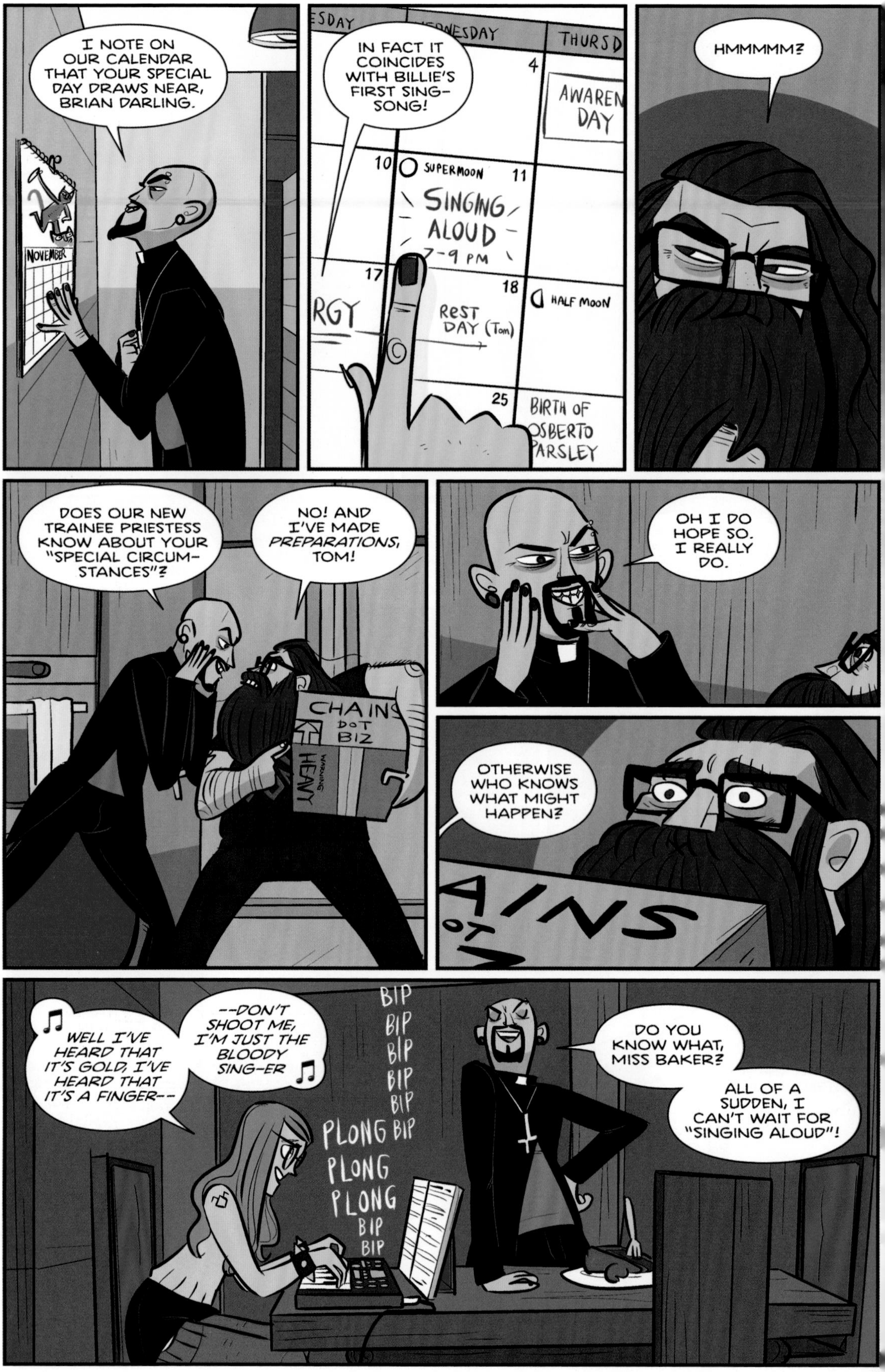
I NOTE ON OUR CALENDAR THAT YOUR SPECIAL DAY DRAWS NEAR, BRIAN DARLING.
NOVEMBER
IN FACT IT COINCIDES WITH BILLIE'S FIRST SING-SONG!
SDAY
WEDNESDAY
THURSD
4
AWAREN DAY
10
SUPERMOON
11
SINGING ALOUD
7-9 PM
17
RGY
18
HALF MOON
REST DAY (Tom)
25
BIRTH OF OSBERTO PARSLEY
HMMMMM?
DOES OUR NEW TRAINEE PRIESTESS KNOW ABOUT YOUR "SPECIAL CIRCUMSTANCES"?
NO! AND I'VE MADE *PREPARATIONS*, TOM!
CHAINS DOT BIZ
HEAVY
OH I DO HOPE SO. I REALLY DO.
OTHERWISE WHO KNOWS WHAT MIGHT HAPPEN?
AINS
♫ *WELL I'VE HEARD THAT IT'S GOLD, I'VE HEARD THAT IT'S A FINGER--*
--DON'T SHOOT ME, I'M JUST THE BLOODY SING-ER ♫
BIP BIP BIP BIP BIP BIP BIP
PLONG PLONG PLONG
BIP BIP
DO YOU KNOW WHAT, MISS BAKER?
ALL OF A SUDDEN, I CAN'T WAIT FOR "SINGING ALOUD"!

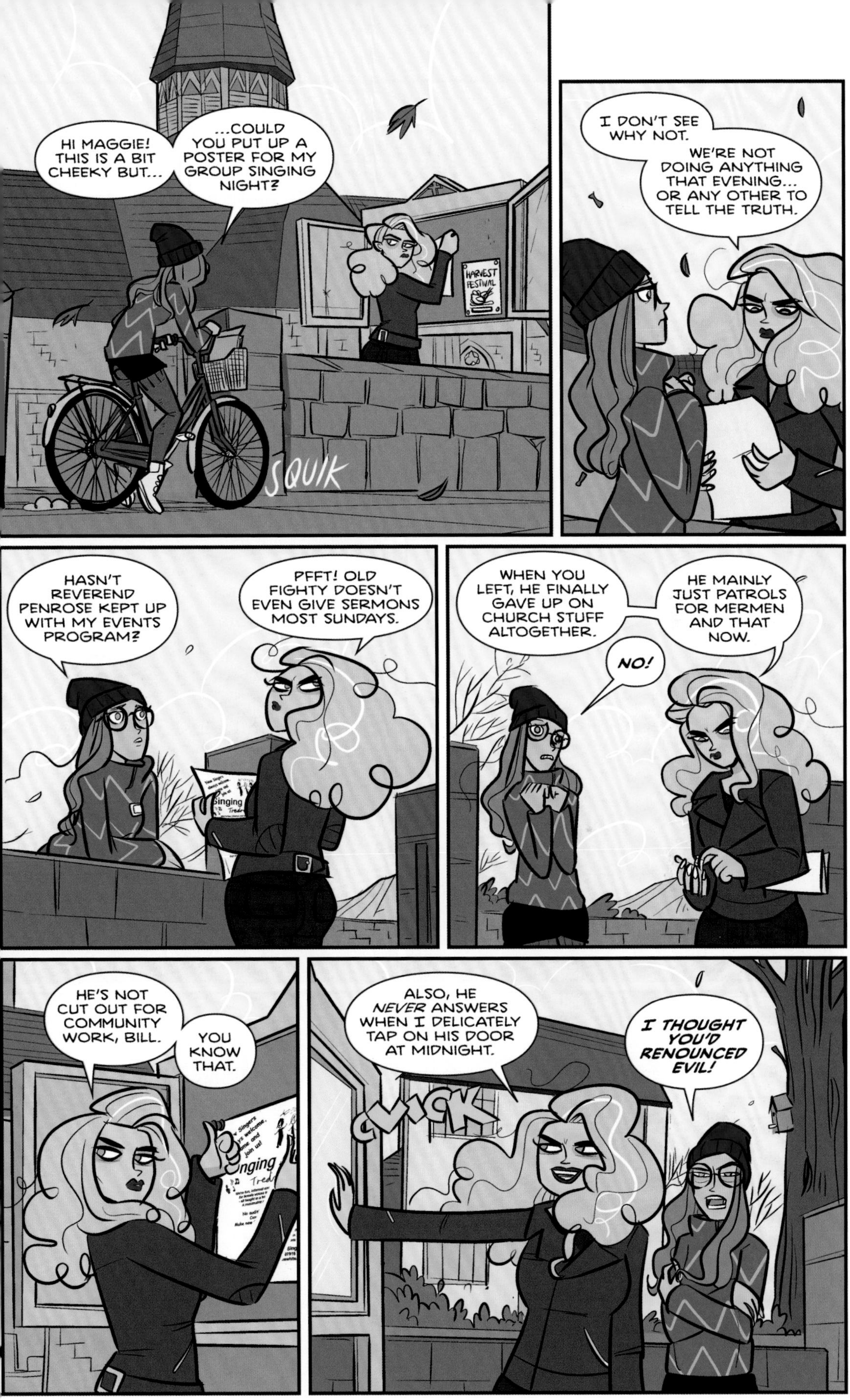
HI MAGGIE! THIS IS A BIT CHEEKY BUT...
...COULD YOU PUT UP A POSTER FOR MY GROUP SINGING NIGHT?
HARVEST FESTIVAL
SQUIK
I DON'T SEE WHY NOT.
WE'RE NOT DOING ANYTHING THAT EVENING... OR ANY OTHER TO TELL THE TRUTH.
HASN'T REVEREND PENROSE KEPT UP WITH MY EVENTS PROGRAM?
PFFT! OLD FIGHTY DOESN'T EVEN GIVE SERMONS MOST SUNDAYS.
WHEN YOU LEFT, HE FINALLY GAVE UP ON CHURCH STUFF ALTOGETHER.
HE MAINLY JUST PATROLS FOR MERMEN AND THAT NOW.
NO!
HE'S NOT CUT OUT FOR COMMUNITY WORK, BILL.
YOU KNOW THAT.
ALSO, HE *NEVER* ANSWERS WHEN I DELICATELY TAP ON HIS DOOR AT MIDNIGHT.
CLICK
I THOUGHT YOU'D RENOUNCED EVIL!

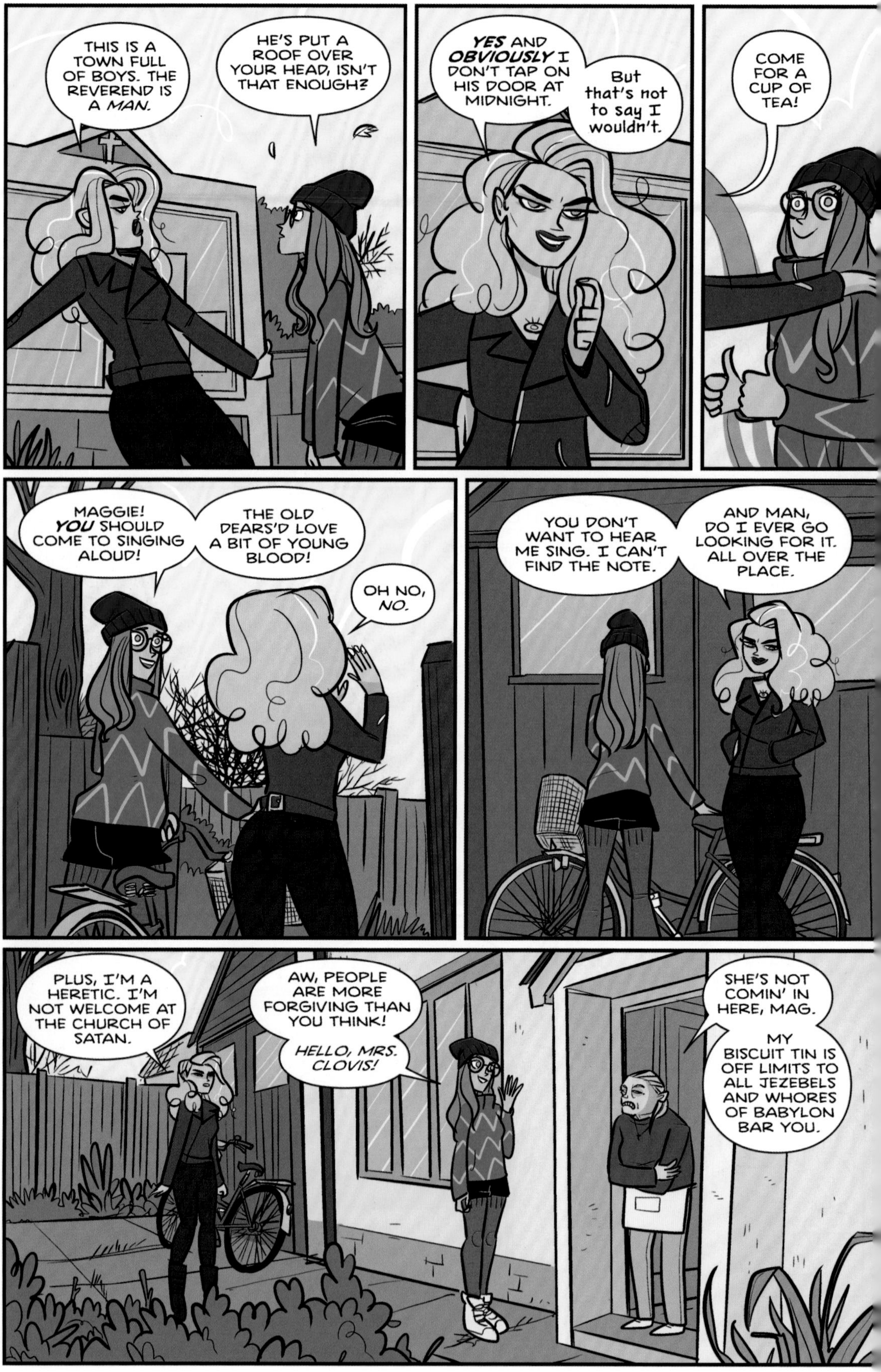
THIS IS A TOWN FULL OF BOYS. THE REVEREND IS A *MAN*.
HE'S PUT A ROOF OVER YOUR HEAD, ISN'T THAT ENOUGH?
YES AND ***OBVIOUSLY*** I DON'T TAP ON HIS DOOR AT MIDNIGHT.
But that's not to say I wouldn't.
COME FOR A CUP OF TEA!
MAGGIE! ***YOU*** SHOULD COME TO SINGING ALOUD!
THE OLD DEARS'D LOVE A BIT OF YOUNG BLOOD!
OH NO, *NO*.
YOU DON'T WANT TO HEAR ME SING. I CAN'T FIND THE NOTE.
AND MAN, DO I EVER GO LOOKING FOR IT. ALL OVER THE PLACE.
PLUS, I'M A HERETIC. I'M NOT WELCOME AT THE CHURCH OF SATAN.
AW, PEOPLE ARE MORE FORGIVING THAN YOU THINK!
HELLO, MRS. CLOVIS!
SHE'S NOT COMIN' IN HERE, MAG.
MY BISCUIT TIN IS OFF LIMITS TO ALL JEZEBELS AND WHORES OF BABYLON BAR YOU.

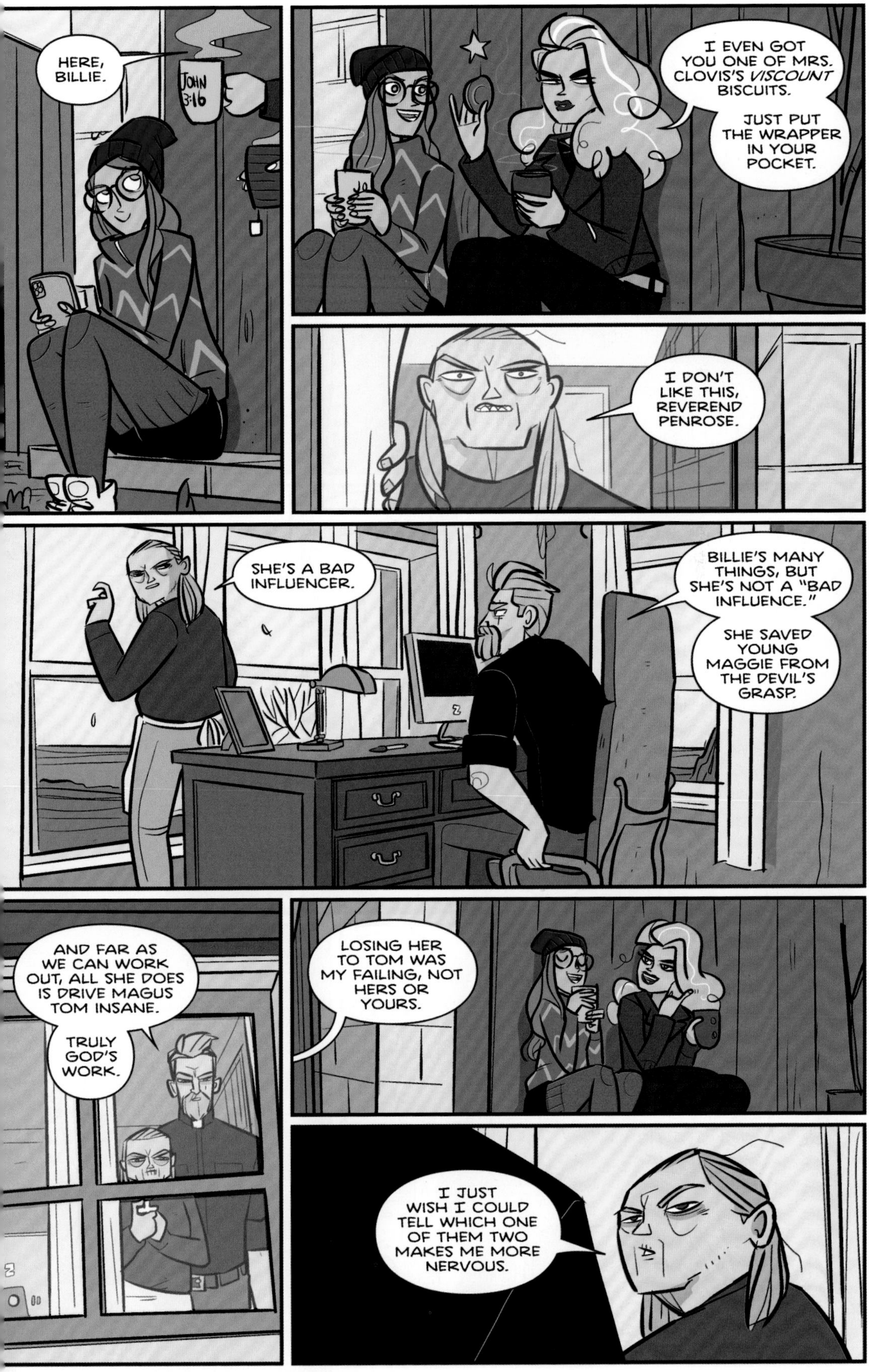
HERE, BILLIE.
JOHN 3:16
I EVEN GOT YOU ONE OF MRS. CLOVIS'S *VISCOUNT* BISCUITS.
JUST PUT THE WRAPPER IN YOUR POCKET.
I DON'T LIKE THIS, REVEREND PENROSE.
SHE'S A BAD INFLUENCER.
BILLIE'S MANY THINGS, BUT SHE'S NOT A "BAD INFLUENCE."
SHE SAVED YOUNG MAGGIE FROM THE DEVIL'S GRASP.
AND FAR AS WE CAN WORK OUT, ALL SHE DOES IS DRIVE MAGUS TOM INSANE.
TRULY GOD'S WORK.
LOSING HER TO TOM WAS MY FAILING, NOT HERS OR YOURS.
I JUST WISH I COULD TELL WHICH ONE OF THEM TWO MAKES ME MORE NERVOUS.

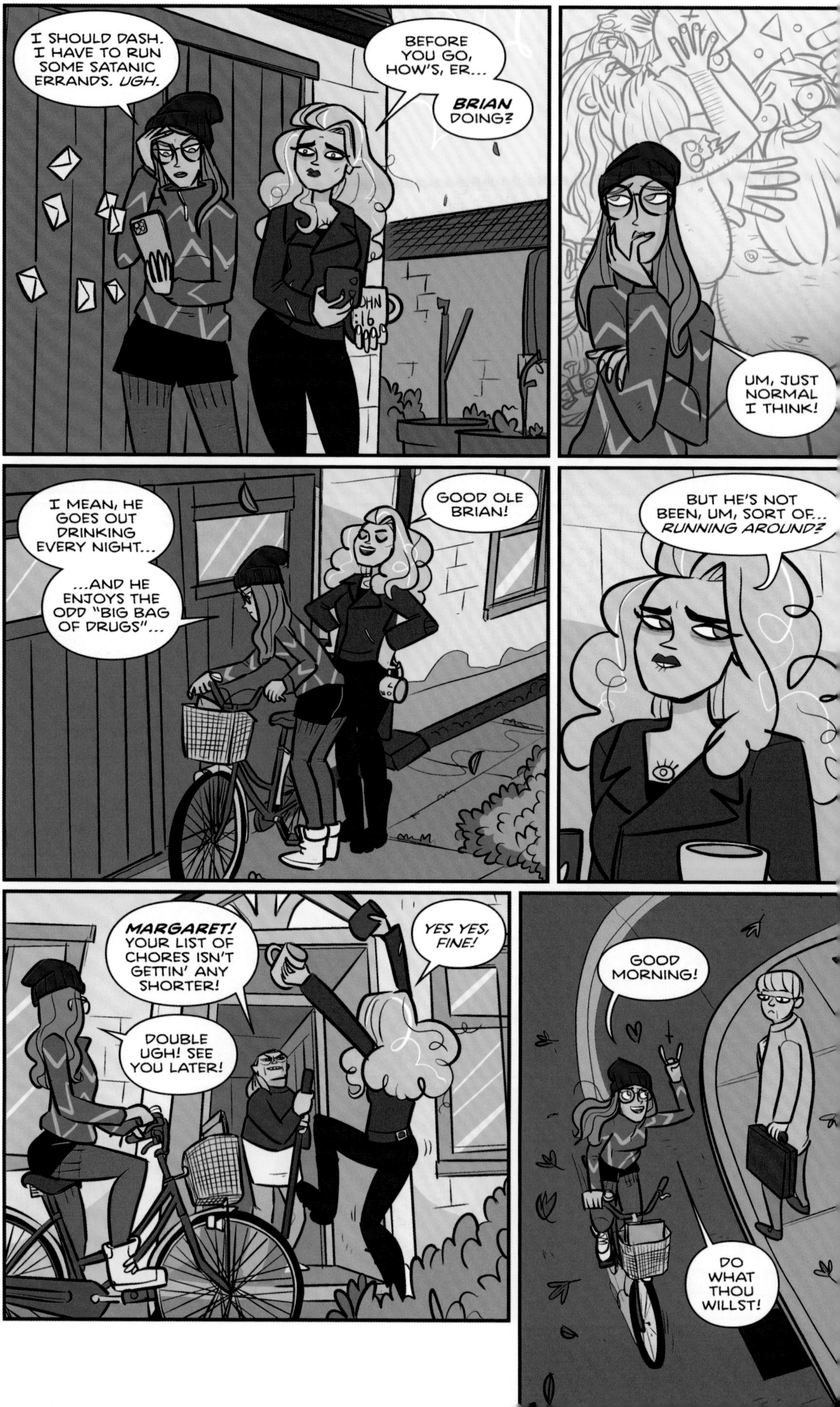
I SHOULD DASH. I HAVE TO RUN SOME SATANIC ERRANDS. *UGH*.
BEFORE YOU GO, HOW'S, ER...
BRIAN DOING?
JOHN 3:16
UM, JUST NORMAL I THINK!
I MEAN, HE GOES OUT DRINKING EVERY NIGHT...
...AND HE ENJOYS THE ODD "BIG BAG OF DRUGS"...
GOOD OLE BRIAN!
BUT HE'S NOT BEEN, UM, SORT OF... *RUNNING AROUND?*
MARGARET! YOUR LIST OF CHORES ISN'T GETTIN' ANY SHORTER!
YES YES, FINE!
DOUBLE UGH! SEE YOU LATER!
GOOD MORNING!
DO WHAT THOU WILLST!

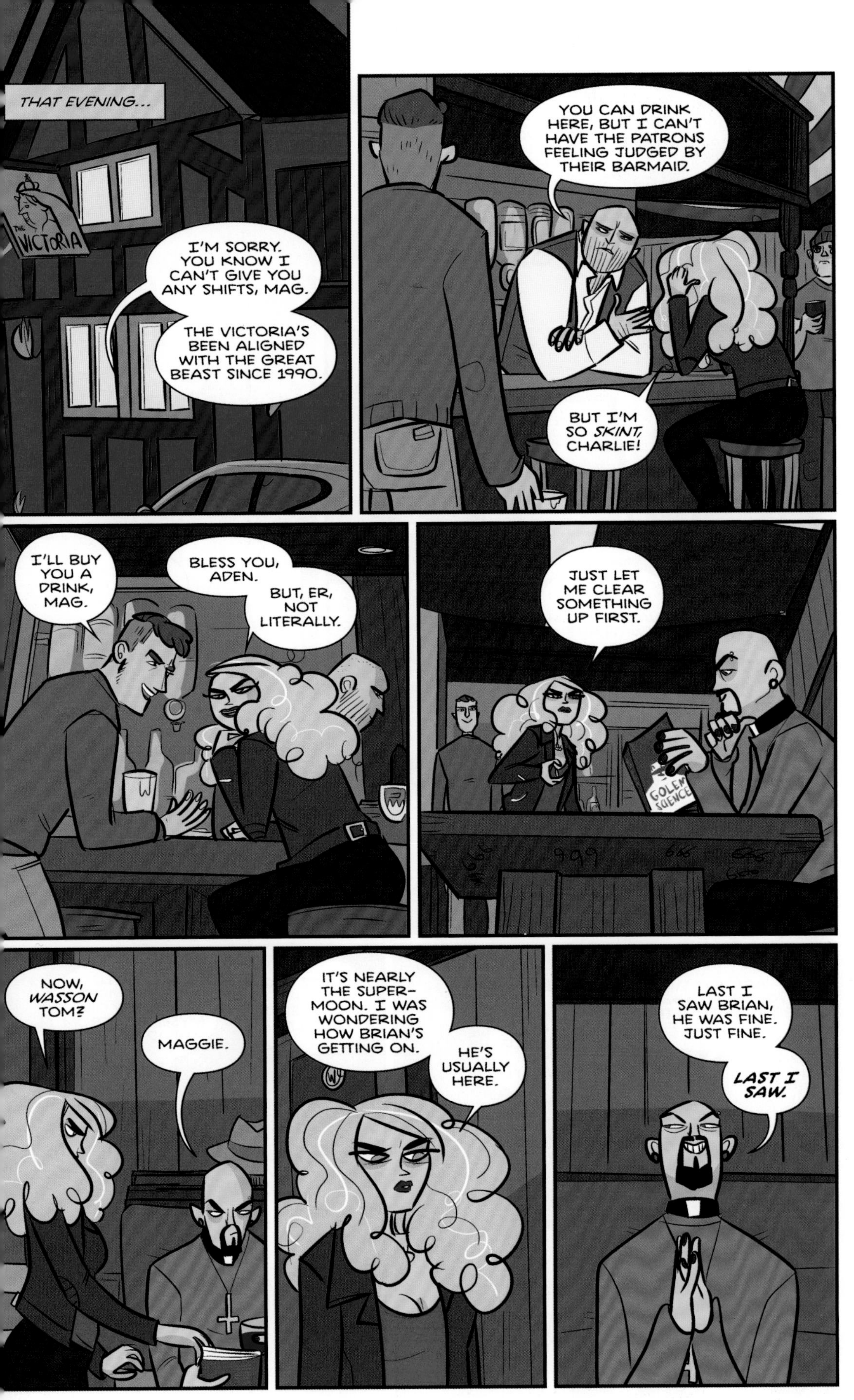
THAT EVENING...
THE VICTORIA
I'M SORRY. YOU KNOW I CAN'T GIVE YOU ANY SHIFTS, MAG.
THE VICTORIA'S BEEN ALIGNED WITH THE GREAT BEAST SINCE 1990.
YOU CAN DRINK HERE, BUT I CAN'T HAVE THE PATRONS FEELING JUDGED BY THEIR BARMAID.
BUT I'M SO *SKINT*, CHARLIE!
I'LL BUY YOU A DRINK, MAG.
BLESS YOU, ADEN.
BUT, ER, NOT LITERALLY.
JUST LET ME CLEAR SOMETHING UP FIRST.
GOLEM SCIENCE
NOW, *WASSON* TOM?
MAGGIE.
IT'S NEARLY THE SUPER-MOON. I WAS WONDERING HOW BRIAN'S GETTING ON.
HE'S USUALLY HERE.
LAST I SAW BRIAN, HE WAS FINE. JUST FINE.
LAST I SAW.

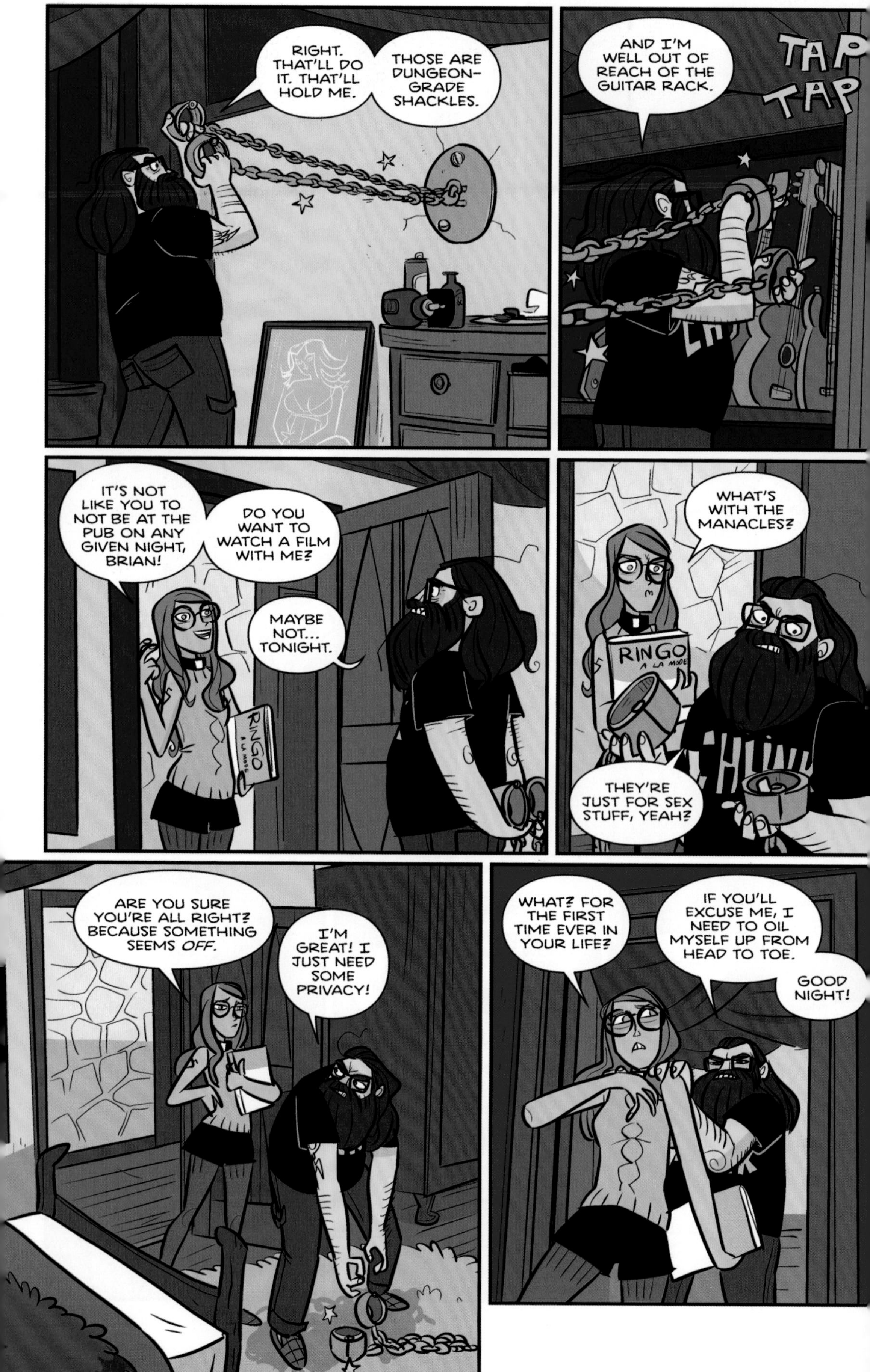
RIGHT. THAT'LL DO IT. THAT'LL HOLD ME.
THOSE ARE DUNGEON-GRADE SHACKLES.
AND I'M WELL OUT OF REACH OF THE GUITAR RACK.
TAP TAP
IT'S NOT LIKE YOU TO NOT BE AT THE PUB ON ANY GIVEN NIGHT, BRIAN!
DO YOU WANT TO WATCH A FILM WITH ME?
MAYBE NOT... TONIGHT.
RINGO A LA MODE
WHAT'S WITH THE MANACLES?
RINGO A LA MODE
THEY'RE JUST FOR SEX STUFF, YEAH?
ARE YOU SURE YOU'RE ALL RIGHT? BECAUSE SOMETHING SEEMS *OFF*.
I'M GREAT! I JUST NEED SOME PRIVACY!
WHAT? FOR THE FIRST TIME EVER IN YOUR LIFE?
IF YOU'LL EXCUSE ME, I NEED TO OIL MYSELF UP FROM HEAD TO TOE.
GOOD NIGHT!

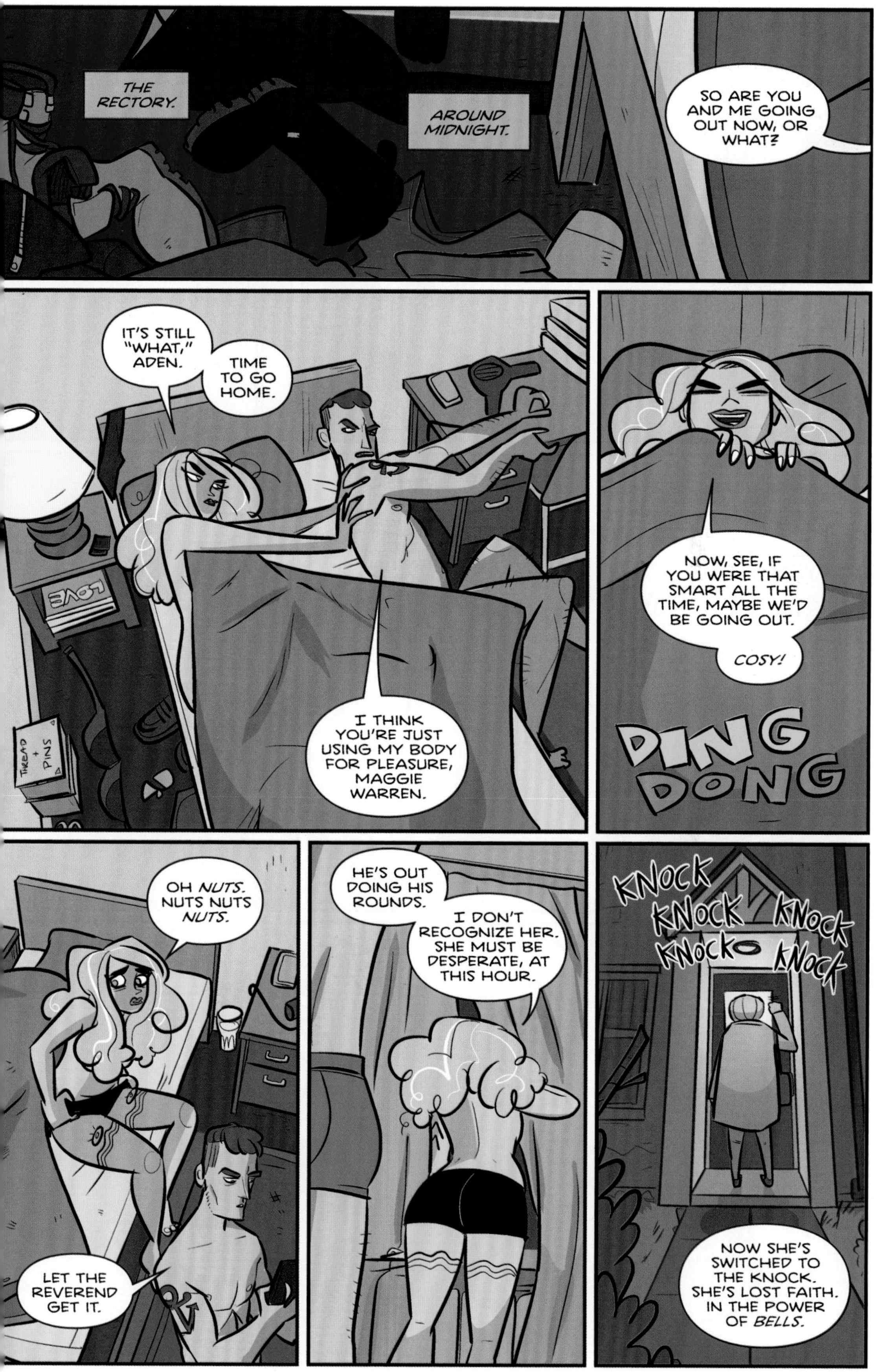
THE RECTORY.
AROUND MIDNIGHT.
SO ARE YOU AND ME GOING OUT NOW, OR WHAT?
IT'S STILL "WHAT," ADEN.
TIME TO GO HOME.
I THINK YOU'RE JUST USING MY BODY FOR PLEASURE, MAGGIE WARREN.
NOW, SEE, IF YOU WERE THAT SMART ALL THE TIME, MAYBE WE'D BE GOING OUT.
COSY!
DING DONG
OH NUTS. NUTS NUTS NUTS.
LET THE REVEREND GET IT.
HE'S OUT DOING HIS ROUNDS.
I DON'T RECOGNIZE HER. SHE MUST BE DESPERATE, AT THIS HOUR.
KNOCK KNOCK KNOCK KNOCK KNOCK KNOCK
NOW SHE'S SWITCHED TO THE KNOCK. SHE'S LOST FAITH. IN THE POWER OF BELLS.

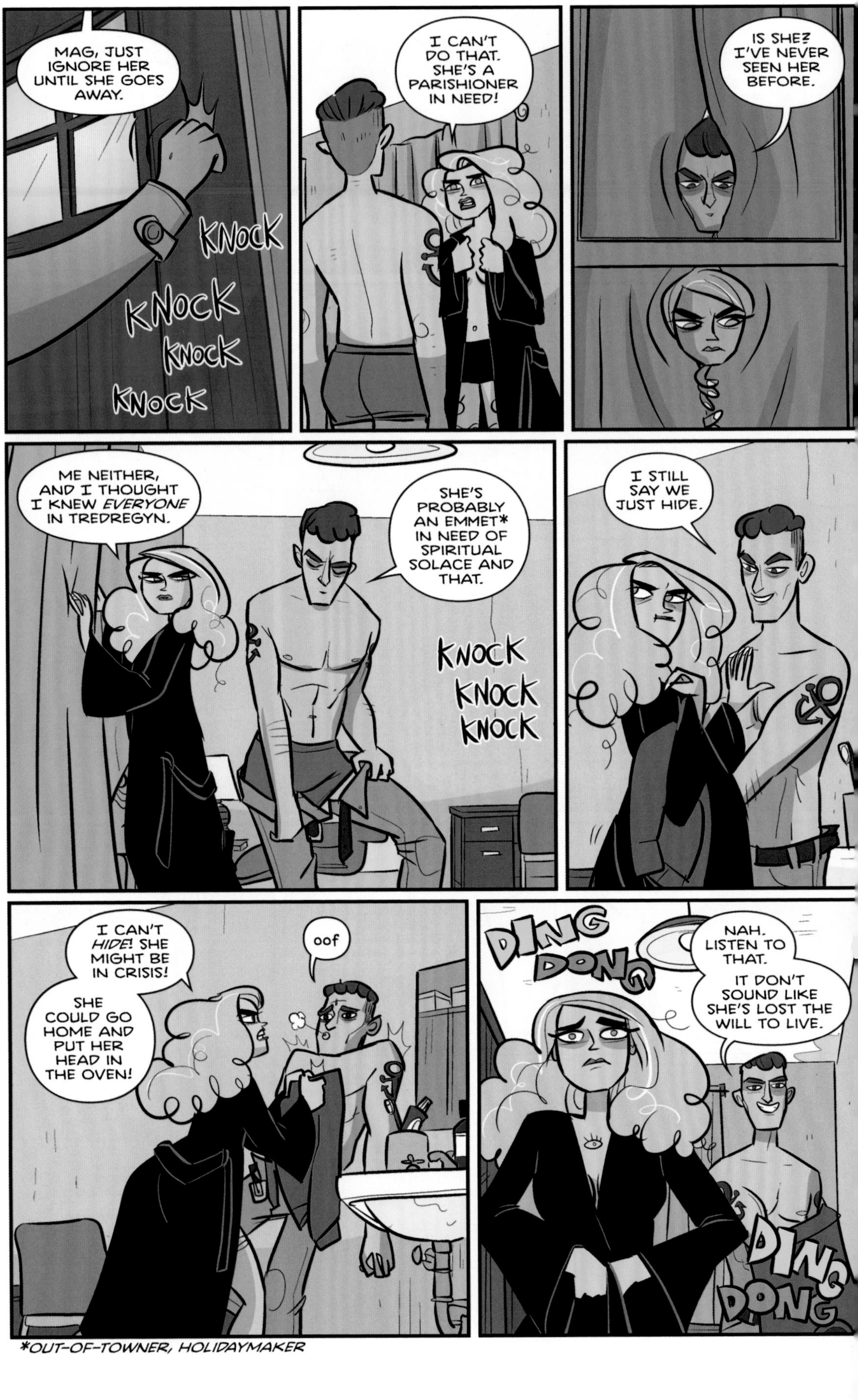
MAG, JUST IGNORE HER UNTIL SHE GOES AWAY.
KNOCK
KNOCK
KNOCK
KNOCK
I CAN'T DO THAT. SHE'S A PARISHIONER IN NEED!
IS SHE? I'VE NEVER SEEN HER BEFORE.
ME NEITHER, AND I THOUGHT I KNEW *EVERYONE* IN TREDREGYN.
SHE'S PROBABLY AN EMMET* IN NEED OF SPIRITUAL SOLACE AND THAT.
KNOCK
KNOCK
KNOCK
I STILL SAY WE JUST HIDE.
I CAN'T *HIDE*! SHE MIGHT BE IN CRISIS!
SHE COULD GO HOME AND PUT HER HEAD IN THE OVEN!
oof
DING DONG
NAH. LISTEN TO THAT.
IT DON'T SOUND LIKE SHE'S LOST THE WILL TO LIVE.
DING DONG

*OUT-OF-TOWNER, HOLIDAYMAKER

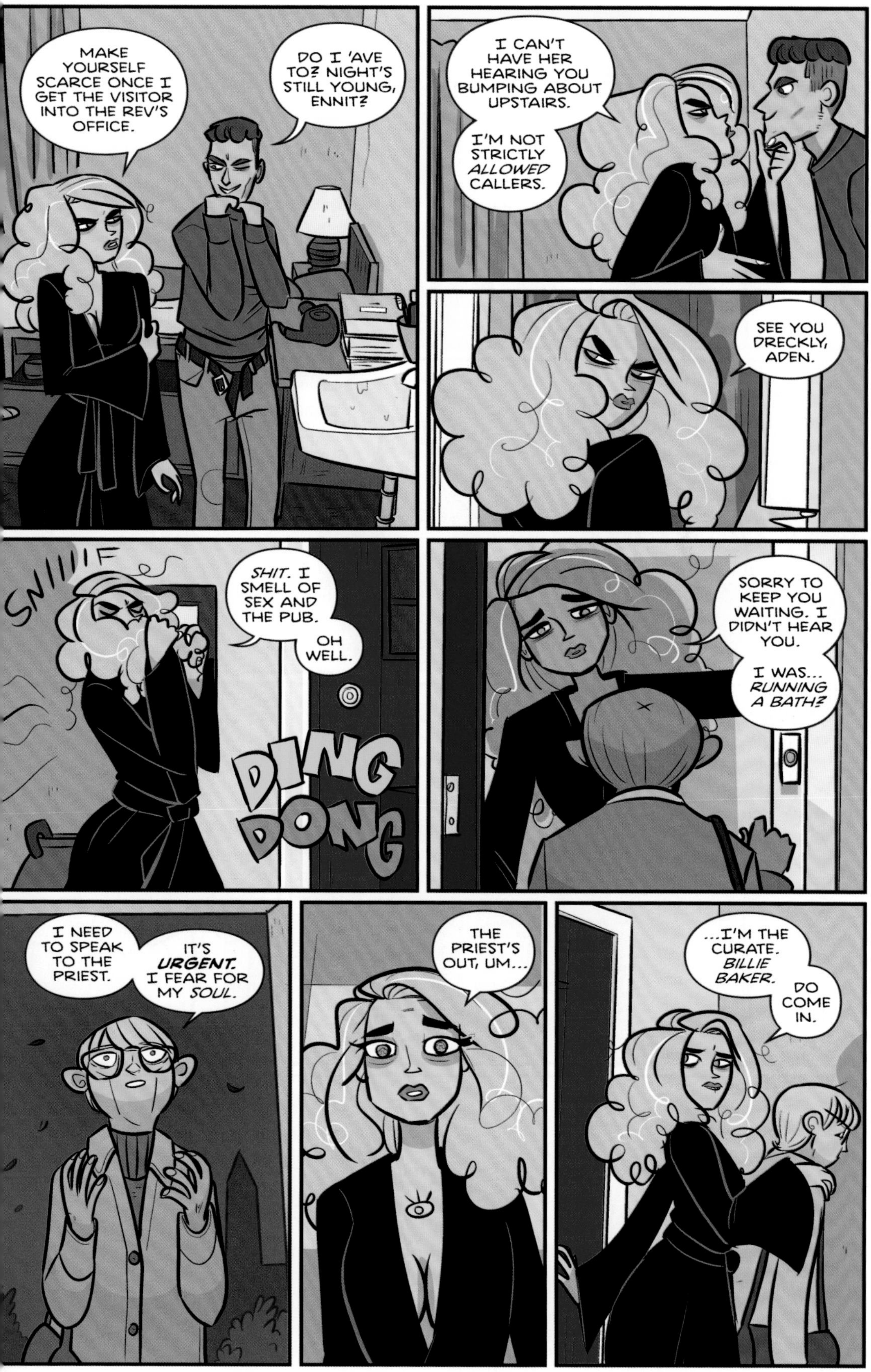
MAKE YOURSELF SCARCE ONCE I GET THE VISITOR INTO THE REV'S OFFICE.
DO I 'AVE TO? NIGHT'S STILL YOUNG, ENNIT?
I CAN'T HAVE HER HEARING YOU BUMPING ABOUT UPSTAIRS.
I'M NOT STRICTLY *ALLOWED* CALLERS.
SEE YOU DRECKLY, ADEN.
SNIIIIIF
SHIT. I SMELL OF SEX AND THE PUB.
OH WELL.
DING DONG
SORRY TO KEEP YOU WAITING. I DIDN'T HEAR YOU.
I WAS... *RUNNING A BATH?*
I NEED TO SPEAK TO THE PRIEST.
IT'S ***URGENT.*** I FEAR FOR MY *SOUL.*
THE PRIEST'S OUT, UM...
...I'M THE CURATE. *BILLIE BAKER.*
DO COME IN.

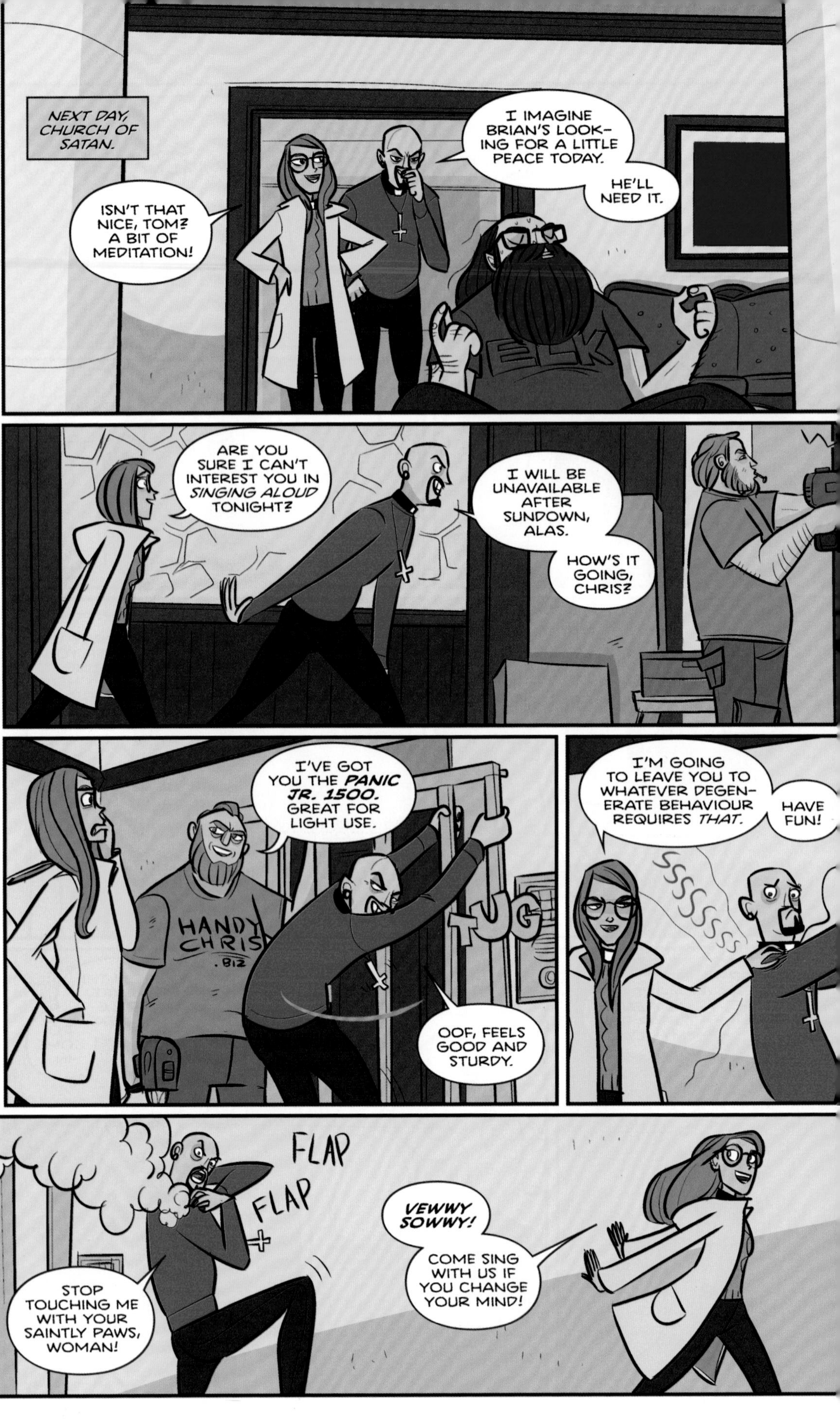
NEXT DAY, CHURCH OF SATAN.
ISN'T THAT NICE, TOM? A BIT OF MEDITATION!
I IMAGINE BRIAN'S LOOK-ING FOR A LITTLE PEACE TODAY.
HE'LL NEED IT.
ELK
ARE YOU SURE I CAN'T INTEREST YOU IN *SINGING ALOUD* TONIGHT?
I WILL BE UNAVAILABLE AFTER SUNDOWN, ALAS.
HOW'S IT GOING, CHRIS?
I'VE GOT YOU THE ***PANIC JR. 1500.*** GREAT FOR LIGHT USE.
HANDY CHRIS .BIZ
TUG
OOF, FEELS GOOD AND STURDY.
I'M GOING TO LEAVE YOU TO WHATEVER DEGEN-ERATE BEHAVIOUR REQUIRES *THAT*.
HAVE FUN!
SSSSSSS
FLAP
FLAP
VEWWY SOWWY!
COME SING WITH US IF YOU CHANGE YOUR MIND!
STOP TOUCHING ME WITH YOUR SAINTLY PAWS, WOMAN!

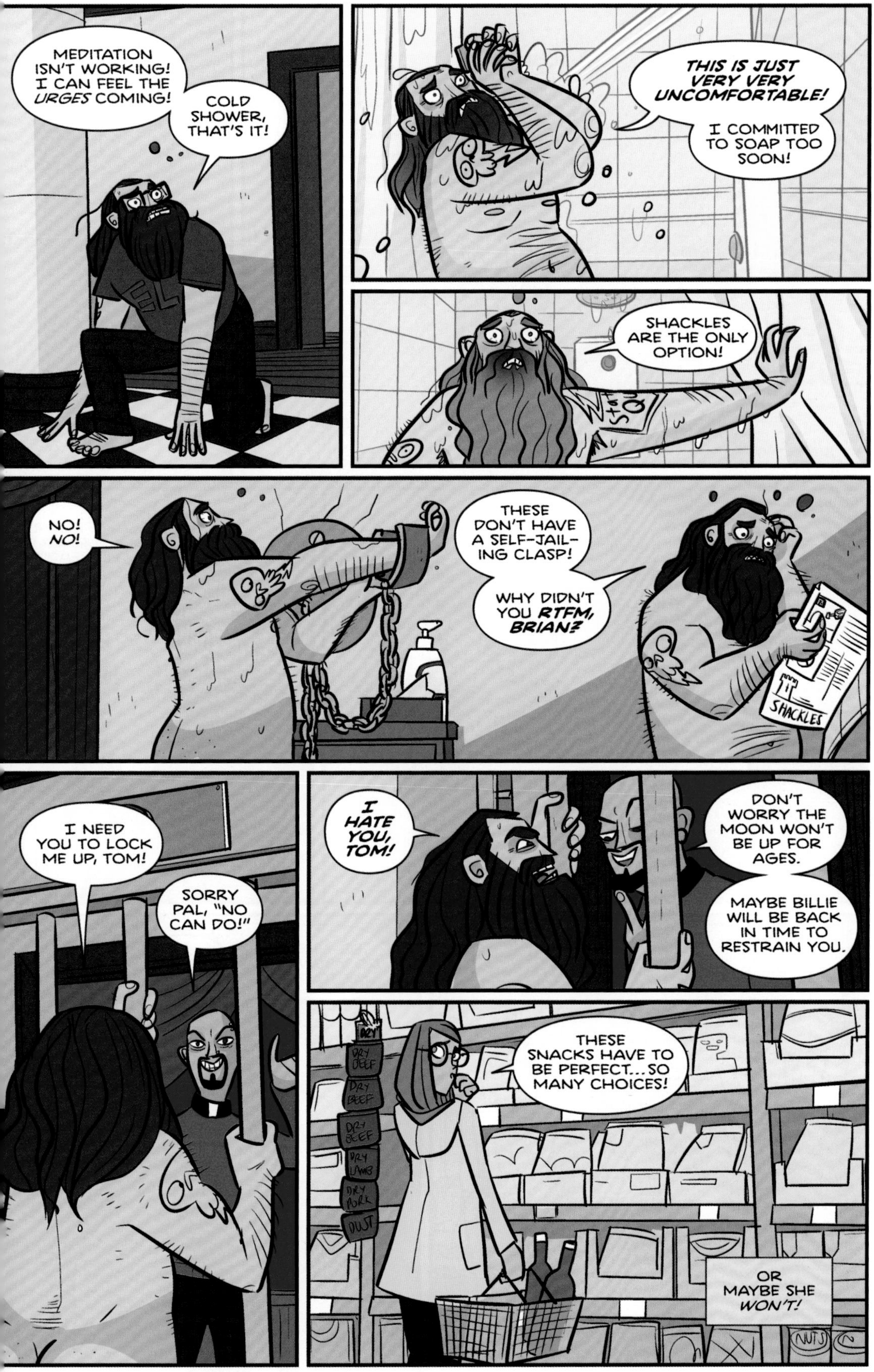
MEDITATION ISN'T WORKING! I CAN FEEL THE *URGES* COMING!
COLD SHOWER, THAT'S IT!
THIS IS JUST VERY VERY UNCOMFORTABLE!
I COMMITTED TO SOAP TOO SOON!
SHACKLES ARE THE ONLY OPTION!
NO! *NO!*
THESE DON'T HAVE A SELF-JAILING CLASP!
WHY DIDN'T YOU ***RTFM, BRIAN?***
SHACKLES
I NEED YOU TO LOCK ME UP, TOM!
SORRY PAL, "NO CAN DO!"
I HATE YOU, TOM!
DON'T WORRY THE MOON WON'T BE UP FOR AGES.
MAYBE BILLIE WILL BE BACK IN TIME TO RESTRAIN YOU.
THESE SNACKS HAVE TO BE PERFECT... SO MANY CHOICES!
DRY BEEF
DRY BEEF
DRY BEEF
DRY LAMB
DRY PORK
DUST
OR MAYBE SHE *WON'T!*
NUTS

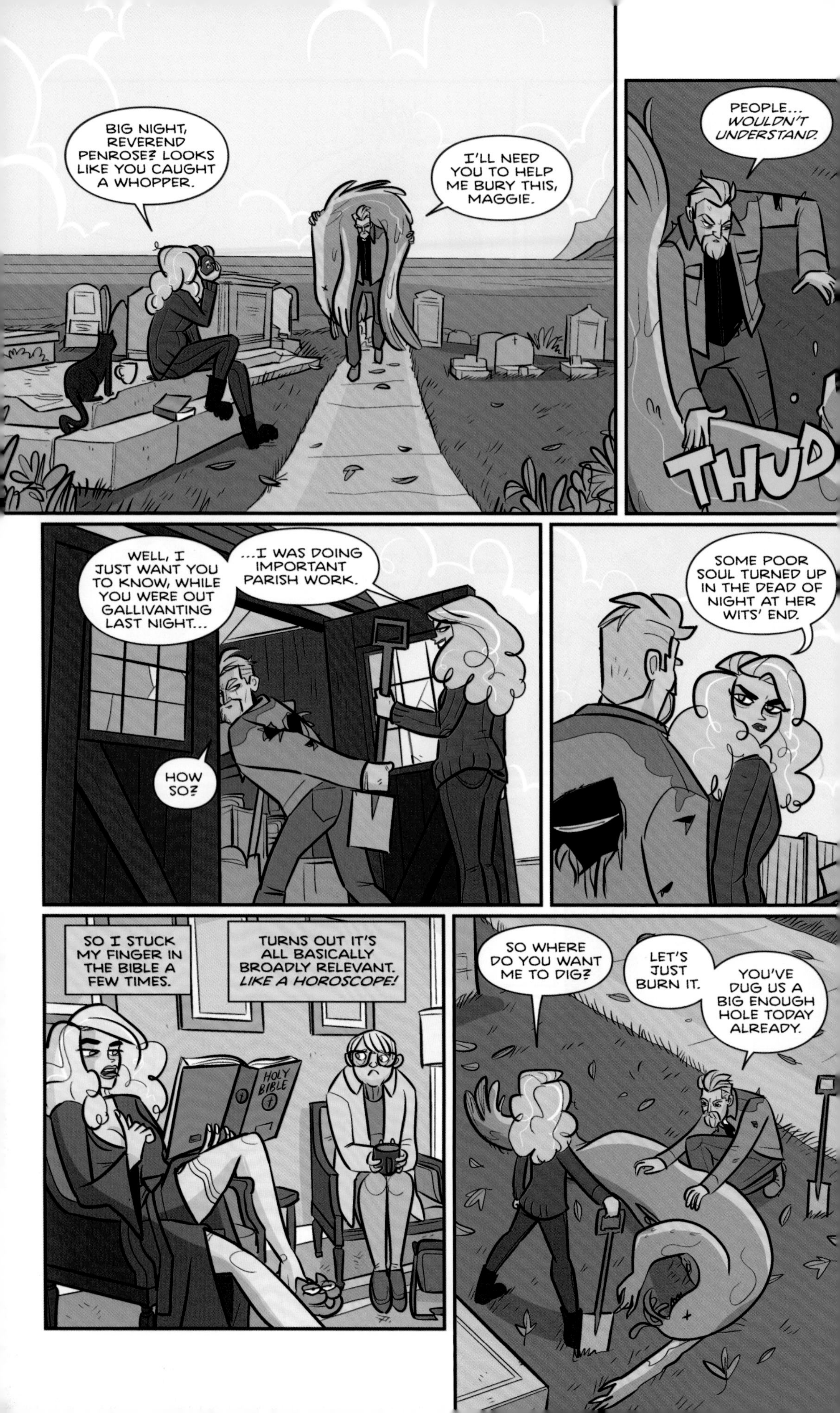
BIG NIGHT, REVEREND PENROSE? LOOKS LIKE YOU CAUGHT A WHOPPER.
I'LL NEED YOU TO HELP ME BURY THIS, MAGGIE.
PEOPLE... WOULDN'T UNDERSTAND.
THUD
WELL, I JUST WANT YOU TO KNOW, WHILE YOU WERE OUT GALLIVANTING LAST NIGHT...
...I WAS DOING IMPORTANT PARISH WORK.
HOW SO?
SOME POOR SOUL TURNED UP IN THE DEAD OF NIGHT AT HER WITS' END.
SO I STUCK MY FINGER IN THE BIBLE A FEW TIMES.
TURNS OUT IT'S ALL BASICALLY BROADLY RELEVANT. LIKE A HOROSCOPE!
HOLY BIBLE
SO WHERE DO YOU WANT ME TO DIG?
LET'S JUST BURN IT.
YOU'VE DUG US A BIG ENOUGH HOLE TODAY ALREADY.

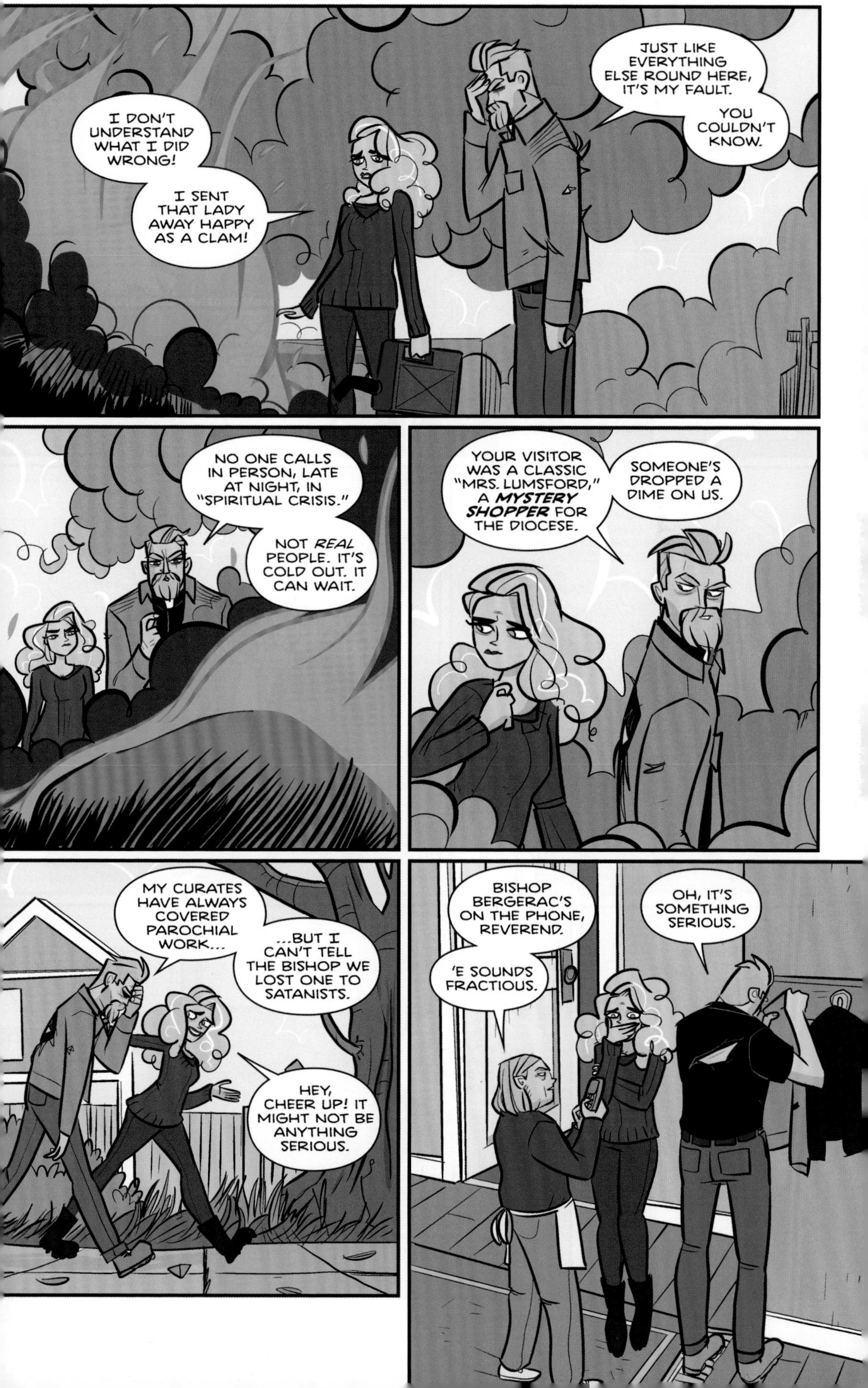
I DON'T UNDERSTAND WHAT I DID WRONG!
I SENT THAT LADY AWAY HAPPY AS A CLAM!
JUST LIKE EVERYTHING ELSE ROUND HERE, IT'S MY FAULT.
YOU COULDN'T KNOW.
NO ONE CALLS IN PERSON, LATE AT NIGHT, IN "SPIRITUAL CRISIS."
NOT *REAL* PEOPLE. IT'S COLD OUT. IT CAN WAIT.
YOUR VISITOR WAS A CLASSIC "MRS. LUMSFORD," A ***MYSTERY SHOPPER*** FOR THE DIOCESE.
SOMEONE'S DROPPED A DIME ON US.
MY CURATES HAVE ALWAYS COVERED PAROCHIAL WORK...
...BUT I CAN'T TELL THE BISHOP WE LOST ONE TO SATANISTS.
HEY, CHEER UP! IT MIGHT NOT BE ANYTHING SERIOUS.
BISHOP BERGERAC'S ON THE PHONE, REVEREND.
'E SOUNDS FRACTIOUS.
OH, IT'S SOMETHING SERIOUS.

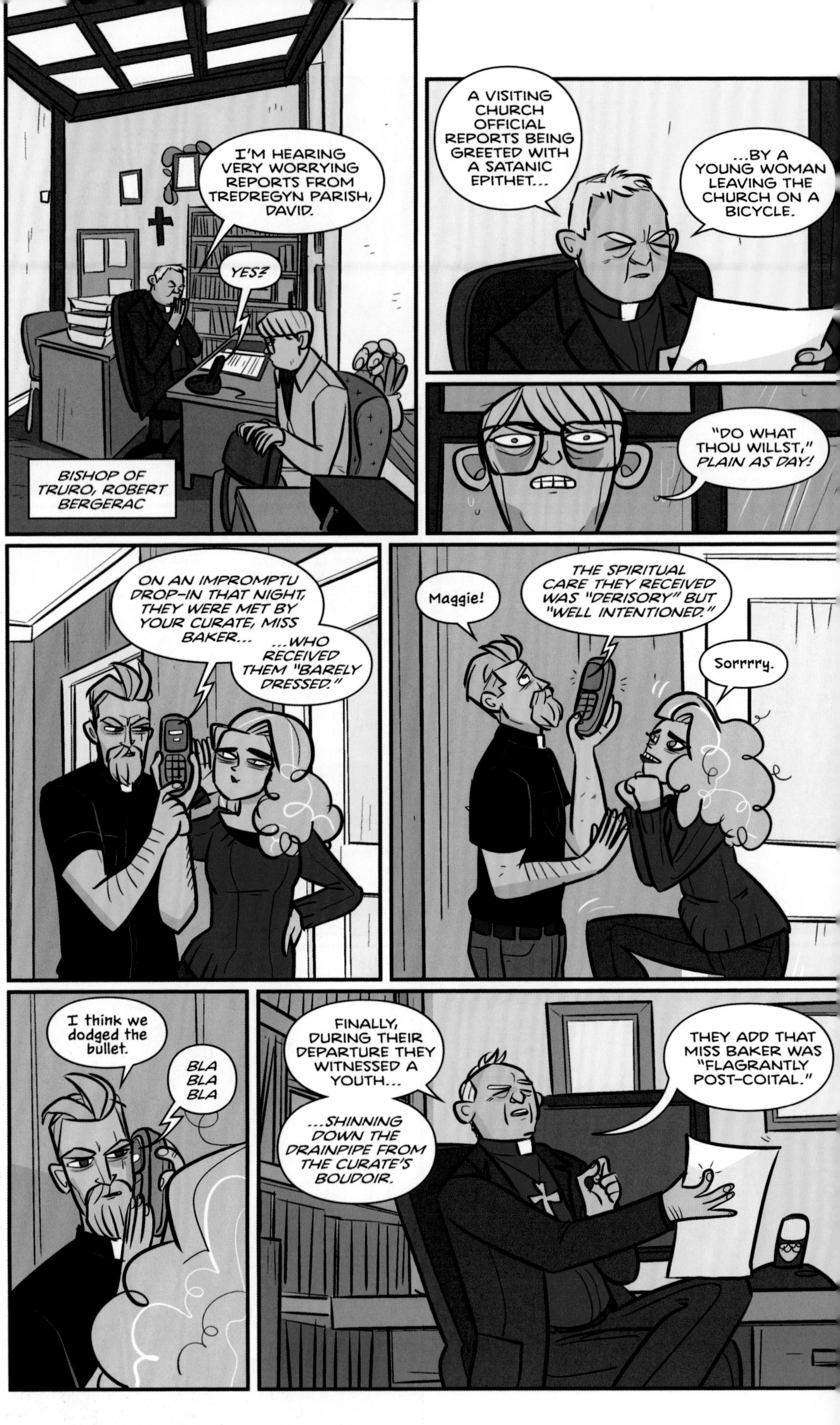
I'M HEARING VERY WORRYING REPORTS FROM TREDREGYN PARISH, DAVID.
YES?
BISHOP OF TRURO, ROBERT BERGERAC
A VISITING CHURCH OFFICIAL REPORTS BEING GREETED WITH A SATANIC EPITHET...
...BY A YOUNG WOMAN LEAVING THE CHURCH ON A BICYCLE.
"DO WHAT THOU WILLST," PLAIN AS DAY!
ON AN IMPROMPTU DROP-IN THAT NIGHT, THEY WERE MET BY YOUR CURATE, MISS BAKER...
...WHO RECEIVED THEM "BARELY DRESSED."
Maggie!
THE SPIRITUAL CARE THEY RECEIVED WAS "DERISORY" BUT "WELL INTENTIONED."
Sorrrry.
I think we dodged the bullet.
BLA BLA BLA
FINALLY, DURING THEIR DEPARTURE THEY WITNESSED A YOUTH...
...SHINNING DOWN THE DRAINPIPE FROM THE CURATE'S BOUDOIR.
THEY ADD THAT MISS BAKER WAS "FLAGRANTLY POST-COITAL."

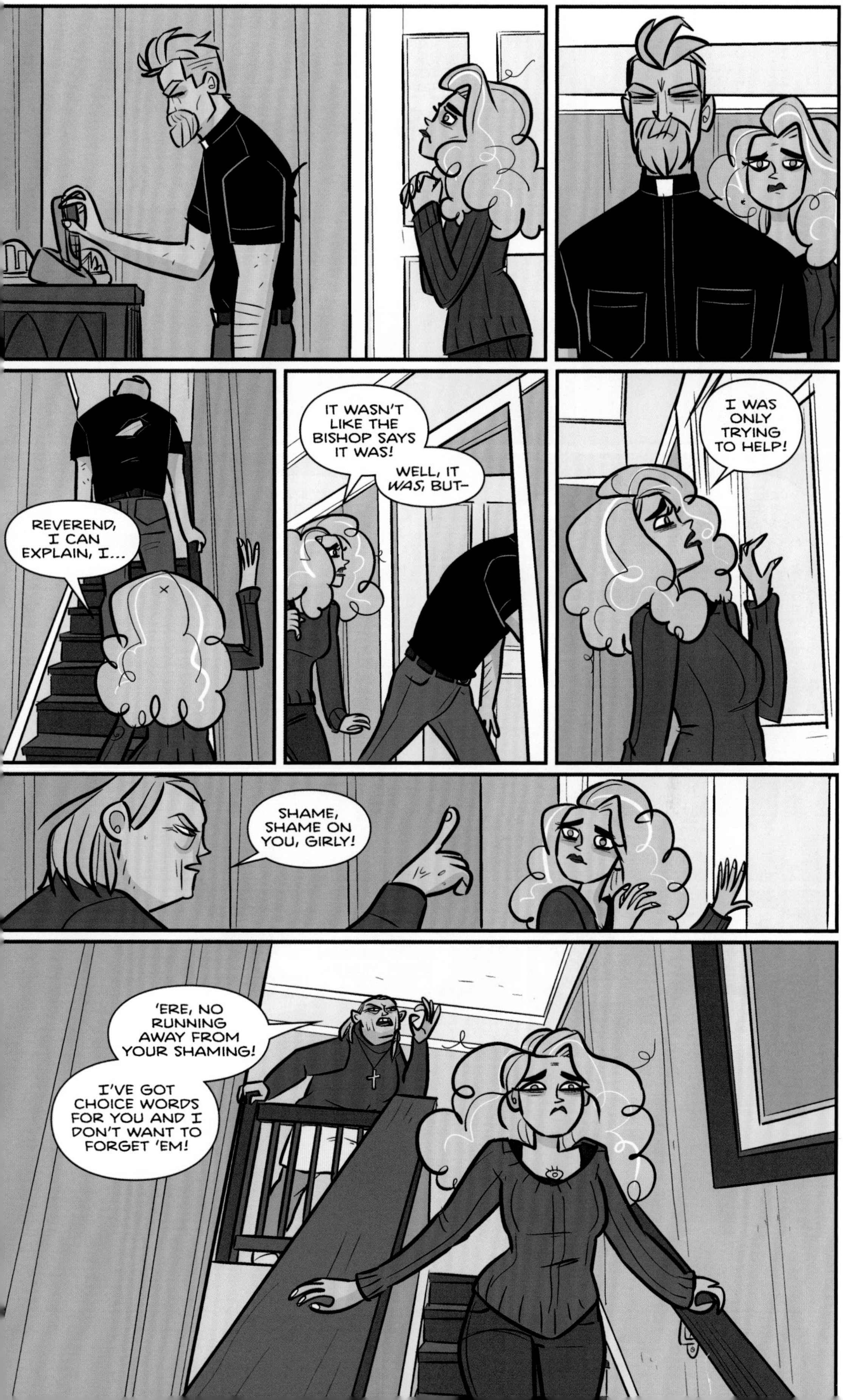
REVEREND, I CAN EXPLAIN, I...
IT WASN'T LIKE THE BISHOP SAYS IT WAS!
WELL, IT *WAS*, BUT-
I WAS ONLY TRYING TO HELP!
SHAME, SHAME ON YOU, GIRLY!
'ERE, NO RUNNING AWAY FROM YOUR SHAMING!
I'VE GOT CHOICE WORDS FOR YOU AND I DON'T WANT TO FORGET 'EM!

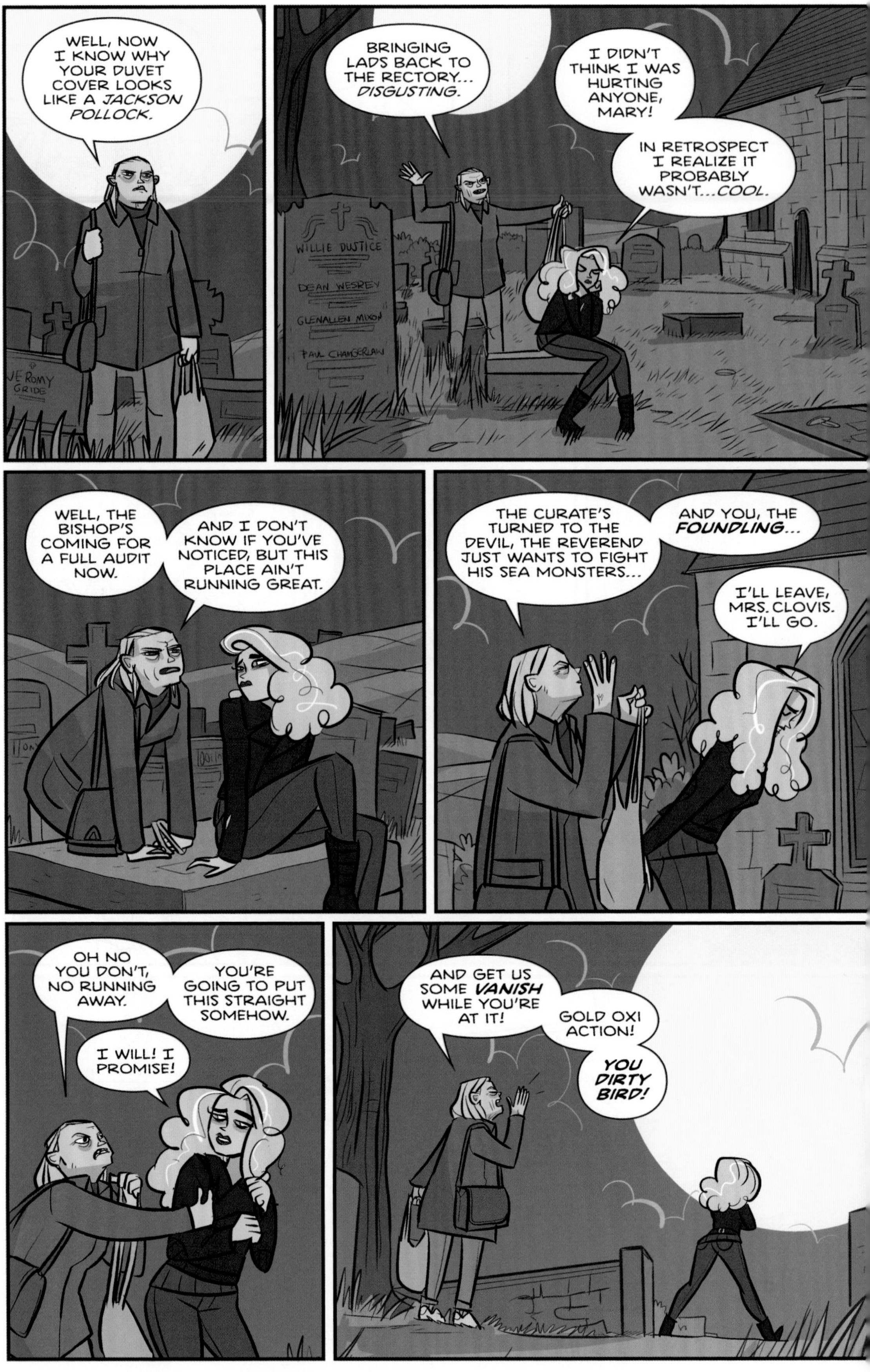
WELL, NOW I KNOW WHY YOUR DUVET COVER LOOKS LIKE A *JACKSON POLLOCK.*
BRINGING LADS BACK TO THE RECTORY... *DISGUSTING.*
I DIDN'T THINK I WAS HURTING ANYONE, MARY!
IN RETROSPECT I REALIZE IT PROBABLY WASN'T... *COOL.*
WILLIE DUSTICE
DEAN WESREY
GLENALLEN MIXON
PAUL CHAMBERLAIN
WELL, THE BISHOP'S COMING FOR A FULL AUDIT NOW.
AND I DON'T KNOW IF YOU'VE NOTICED, BUT THIS PLACE AIN'T RUNNING GREAT.
THE CURATE'S TURNED TO THE DEVIL, THE REVEREND JUST WANTS TO FIGHT HIS SEA MONSTERS...
AND YOU, THE ***FOUNDLING***...
I'LL LEAVE, MRS. CLOVIS. I'LL GO.
OH NO YOU DON'T, NO RUNNING AWAY.
YOU'RE GOING TO PUT THIS STRAIGHT SOMEHOW.
I WILL! I PROMISE!
AND GET US SOME ***VANISH*** WHILE YOU'RE AT IT!
GOLD OXI ACTION!
YOU DIRTY BIRD!

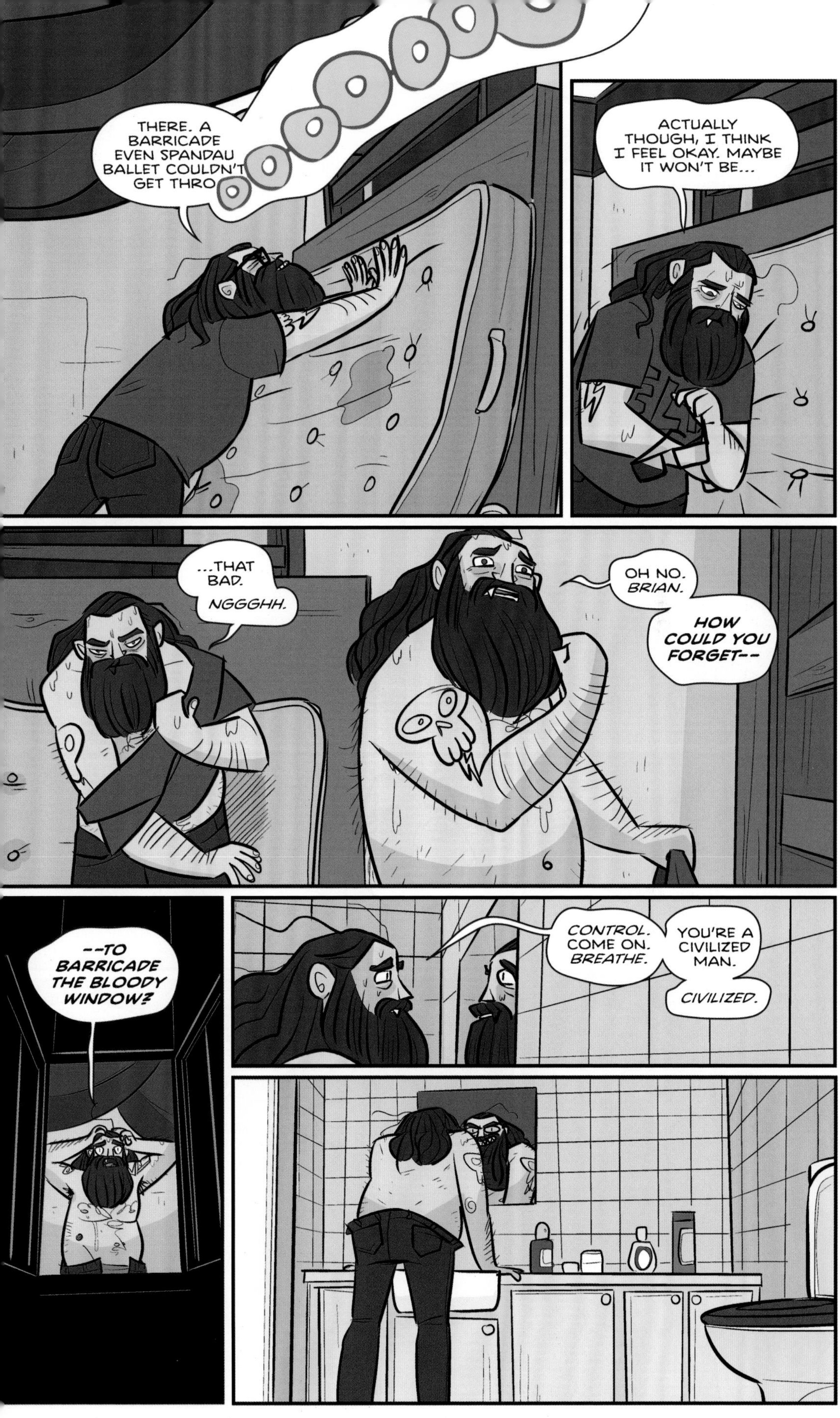
THERE. A BARRICADE EVEN SPANDAU BALLET COULDN'T GET THRO
OOOOOOOO
ACTUALLY THOUGH, I THINK I FEEL OKAY. MAYBE IT WON'T BE...
...THAT BAD.
NGGGHH.
OH NO. BRIAN.
HOW COULD YOU FORGET--
--TO BARRICADE THE BLOODY WINDOW?
CONTROL. COME ON. BREATHE.
YOU'RE A CIVILIZED MAN.
CIVILIZED.

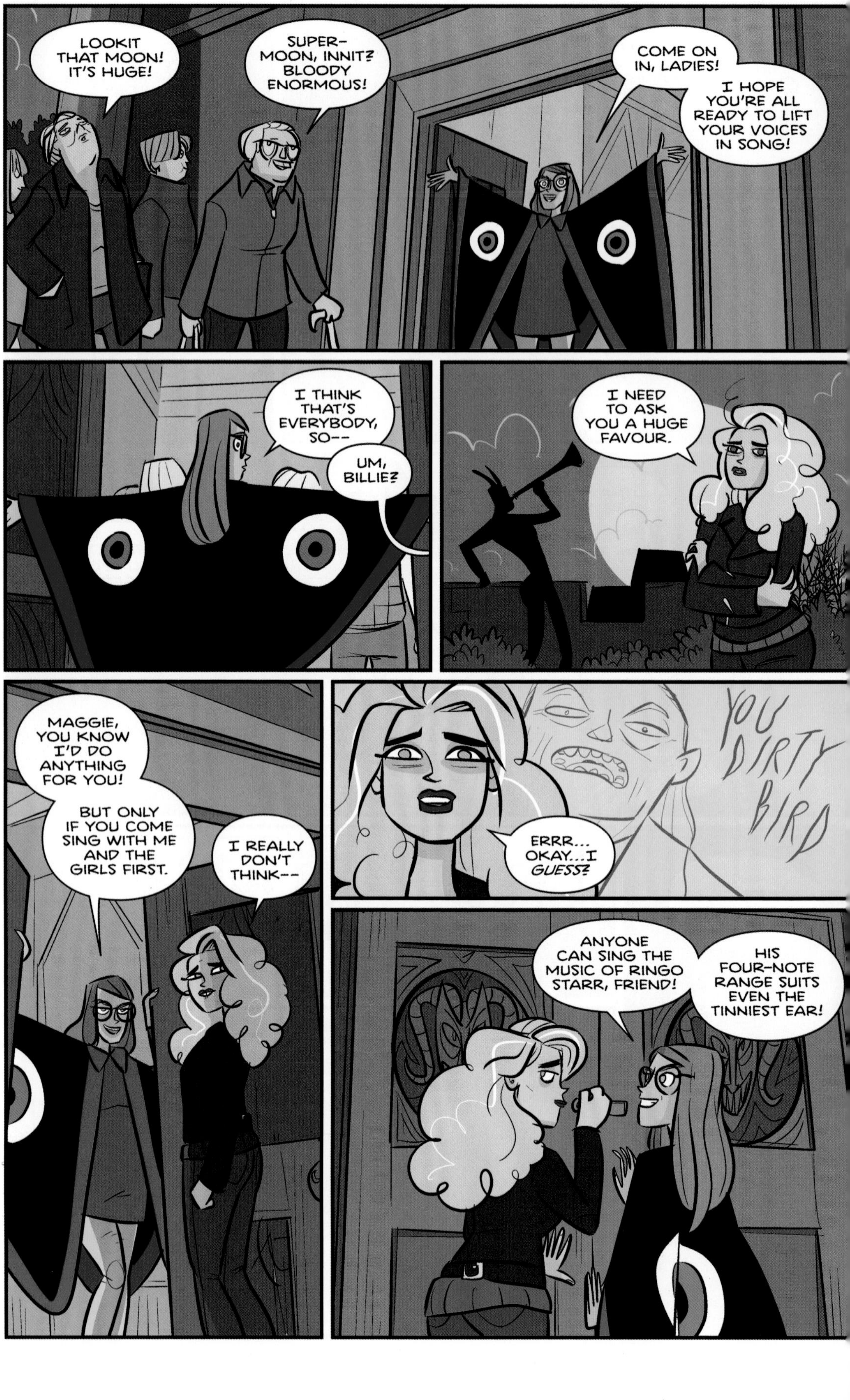
LOOKIT THAT MOON! IT'S HUGE!
SUPER-MOON, INNIT? BLOODY ENORMOUS!
COME ON IN, LADIES!
I HOPE YOU'RE ALL READY TO LIFT YOUR VOICES IN SONG!
I THINK THAT'S EVERYBODY, SO--
UM, BILLIE?
I NEED TO ASK YOU A HUGE FAVOUR.
MAGGIE, YOU KNOW I'D DO ANYTHING FOR YOU!
BUT ONLY IF YOU COME SING WITH ME AND THE GIRLS FIRST.
I REALLY DON'T THINK--
YOU DIRTY BIRD
ERRR... OKAY...I *GUESS?*
ANYONE CAN SING THE MUSIC OF RINGO STARR, FRIEND!
HIS FOUR-NOTE RANGE SUITS EVEN THE TINNIEST EAR!

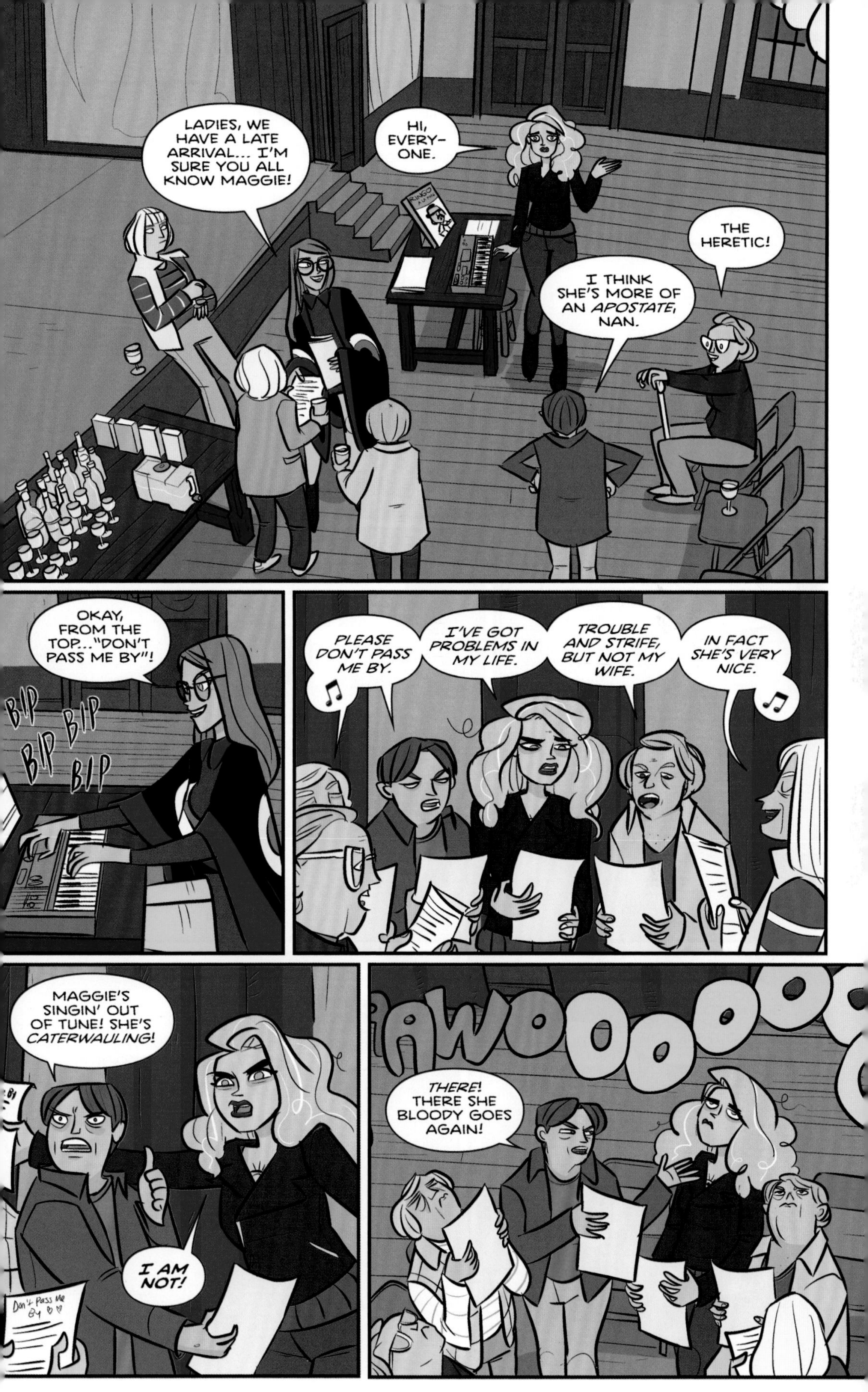
LADIES, WE HAVE A LATE ARRIVAL... I'M SURE YOU ALL KNOW MAGGIE!
HI, EVERY-ONE.
THE HERETIC!
I THINK SHE'S MORE OF AN *APOSTATE*, NAN.
OKAY, FROM THE TOP..."DON'T PASS ME BY"!
BIP BIP BIP BIP BIP
PLEASE DON'T PASS ME BY.
I'VE GOT PROBLEMS IN MY LIFE.
TROUBLE AND STRIFE, BUT NOT MY WIFE.
IN FACT SHE'S VERY NICE.
MAGGIE'S SINGIN' OUT OF TUNE! SHE'S *CATERWAULING!*
I AM NOT!
Don't Pass Me By
AWOOOOOO
THERE! THERE SHE BLOODY GOES AGAIN!

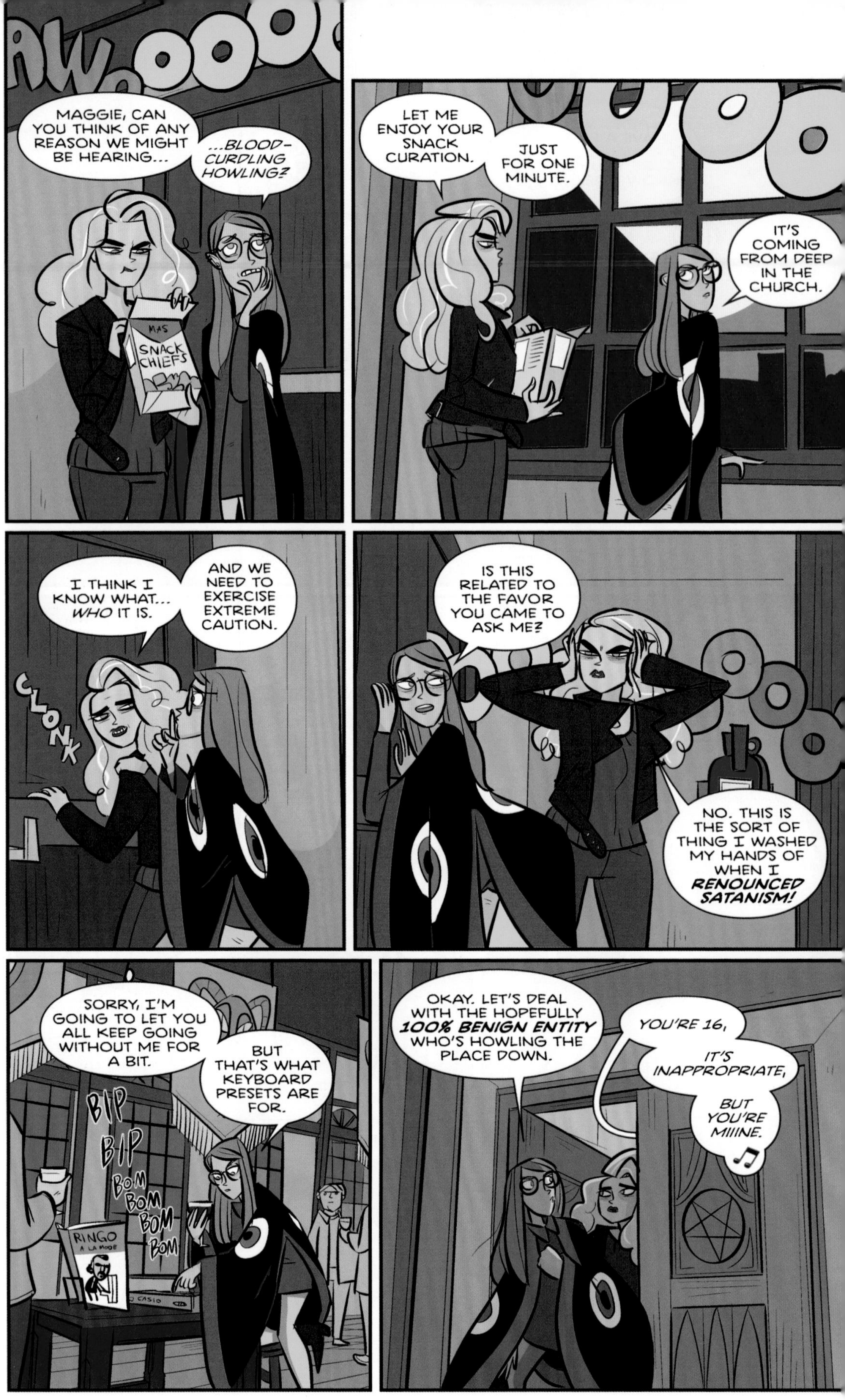
AWOOOOO
MAGGIE, CAN YOU THINK OF ANY REASON WE MIGHT BE HEARING...
...BLOOD-CURDLING HOWLING?
SNACK CHIEFS
OOOOO
LET ME ENJOY YOUR SNACK CURATION.
JUST FOR ONE MINUTE.
IT'S COMING FROM DEEP IN THE CHURCH.
I THINK I KNOW WHAT... *WHO* IT IS.
AND WE NEED TO EXERCISE EXTREME CAUTION.
CLONK
IS THIS RELATED TO THE FAVOR YOU CAME TO ASK ME?
NO. THIS IS THE SORT OF THING I WASHED MY HANDS OF WHEN I ***RENOUNCED SATANISM!***
SORRY, I'M GOING TO LET YOU ALL KEEP GOING WITHOUT ME FOR A BIT.
BUT THAT'S WHAT KEYBOARD PRESETS ARE FOR.
BIP
BIP
BOM BOM BOM BOM
RINGO
A LA MODE
CASIO
OKAY. LET'S DEAL WITH THE HOPEFULLY ***100% BENIGN ENTITY*** WHO'S HOWLING THE PLACE DOWN.
YOU'RE 16,
IT'S INAPPROPRIATE,
BUT YOU'RE MIIINE. ♫

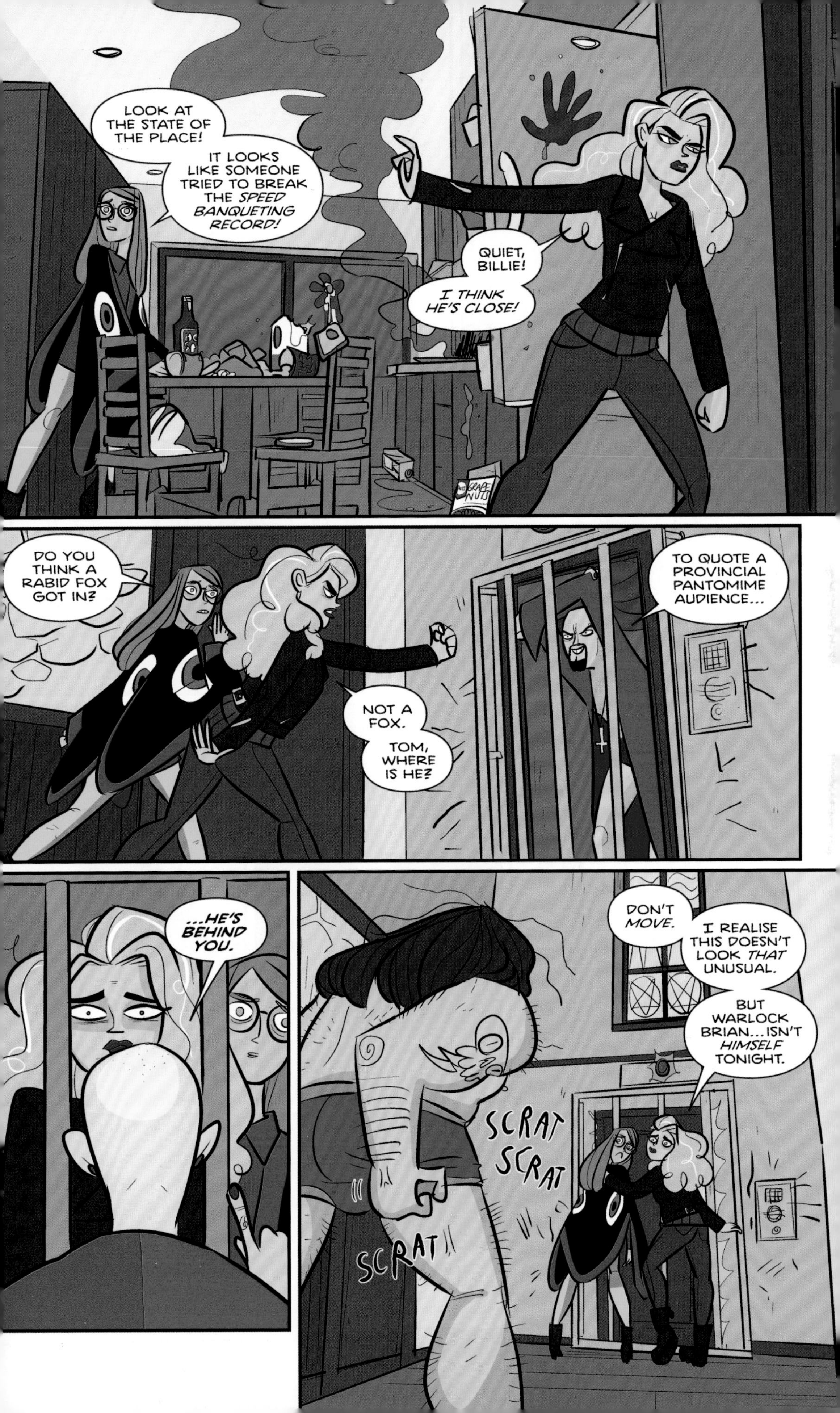
LOOK AT THE STATE OF THE PLACE!
IT LOOKS LIKE SOMEONE TRIED TO BREAK THE *SPEED BANQUETING RECORD!*
QUIET, BILLIE!
I THINK HE'S CLOSE!
GRAPE NUTS
DO YOU THINK A RABID FOX GOT IN?
NOT A FOX.
TOM, WHERE IS HE?
TO QUOTE A PROVINCIAL PANTOMIME AUDIENCE...
...HE'S BEHIND YOU.
DON'T *MOVE.*
I REALISE THIS DOESN'T LOOK *THAT* UNUSUAL.
BUT WARLOCK BRIAN...ISN'T *HIMSELF* TONIGHT.
SCRAT
SCRAT
SCRAT

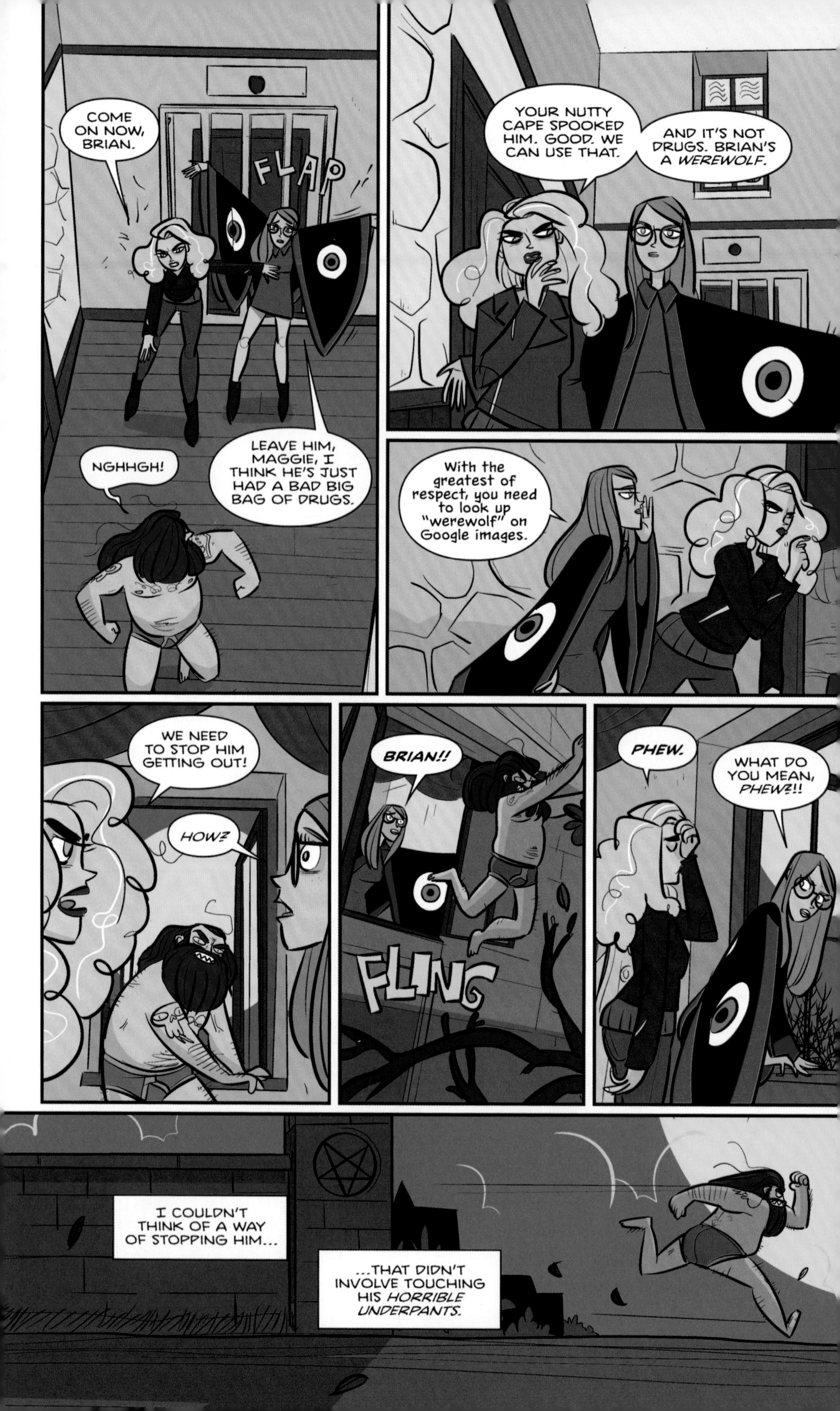
COME ON NOW, BRIAN.
FLAP
NGHHGH!
LEAVE HIM, MAGGIE, I THINK HE'S JUST HAD A BAD BIG BAG OF DRUGS.
YOUR NUTTY CAPE SPOOKED HIM. GOOD. WE CAN USE THAT.
AND IT'S NOT DRUGS. BRIAN'S A *WEREWOLF.*
With the greatest of respect, you need to look up "werewolf" on Google images.
WE NEED TO STOP HIM GETTING OUT!
HOW?
BRIAN!!
FLING
PHEW.
WHAT DO YOU MEAN, *PHEW?!!*
I COULDN'T THINK OF A WAY OF STOPPING HIM...
...THAT DIDN'T INVOLVE TOUCHING HIS *HORRIBLE UNDERPANTS.*

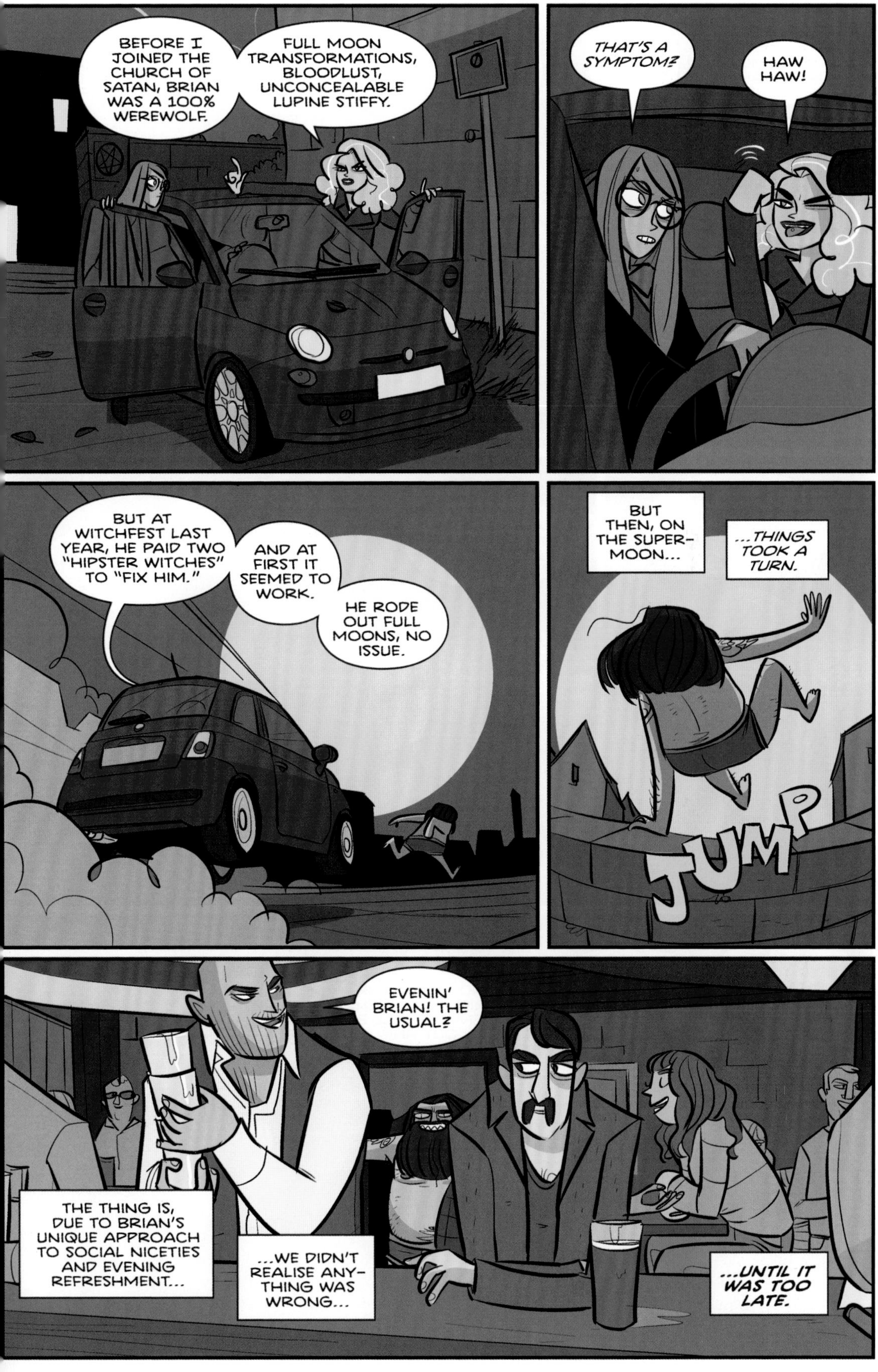

BEFORE I JOINED THE CHURCH OF SATAN, BRIAN WAS A 100% WEREWOLF.
FULL MOON TRANSFORMATIONS, BLOODLUST, UNCONCEALABLE LUPINE STIFFY.
THAT'S A SYMPTOM?
HAW HAW!
BUT AT WITCHFEST LAST YEAR, HE PAID TWO "HIPSTER WITCHES" TO "FIX HIM."
AND AT FIRST IT SEEMED TO WORK.
HE RODE OUT FULL MOONS, NO ISSUE.
BUT THEN, ON THE SUPER-MOON...
...THINGS TOOK A TURN.
JUMP
EVENIN' BRIAN! THE USUAL?
THE THING IS, DUE TO BRIAN'S UNIQUE APPROACH TO SOCIAL NICETIES AND EVENING REFRESHMENT...
...WE DIDN'T REALISE ANY-THING WAS WRONG...
...UNTIL IT WAS TOO LATE.

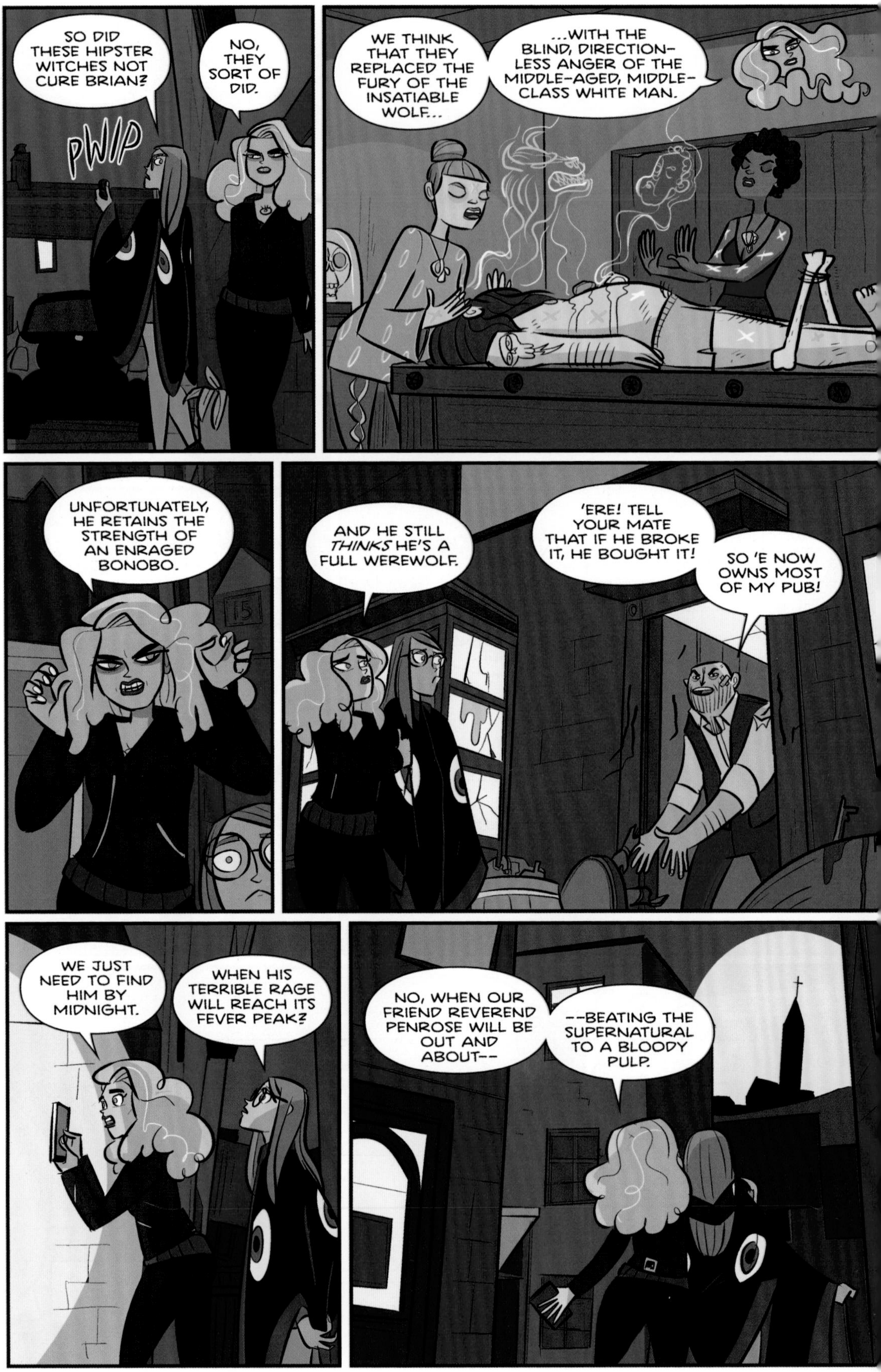
SO DID THESE HIPSTER WITCHES NOT CURE BRIAN?
NO, THEY SORT OF DID.
PWIP
WE THINK THAT THEY REPLACED THE FURY OF THE INSATIABLE WOLF...
...WITH THE BLIND, DIRECTION-LESS ANGER OF THE MIDDLE-AGED, MIDDLE-CLASS WHITE MAN.
UNFORTUNATELY, HE RETAINS THE STRENGTH OF AN ENRAGED BONOBO.
15
AND HE STILL *THINKS* HE'S A FULL WEREWOLF.
'ERE! TELL YOUR MATE THAT IF HE BROKE IT, HE BOUGHT IT!
SO 'E NOW OWNS MOST OF MY PUB!
WE JUST NEED TO FIND HIM BY MIDNIGHT.
WHEN HIS TERRIBLE RAGE WILL REACH ITS FEVER PEAK?
NO, WHEN OUR FRIEND REVEREND PENROSE WILL BE OUT AND ABOUT--
--BEATING THE SUPERNATURAL TO A BLOODY PULP.

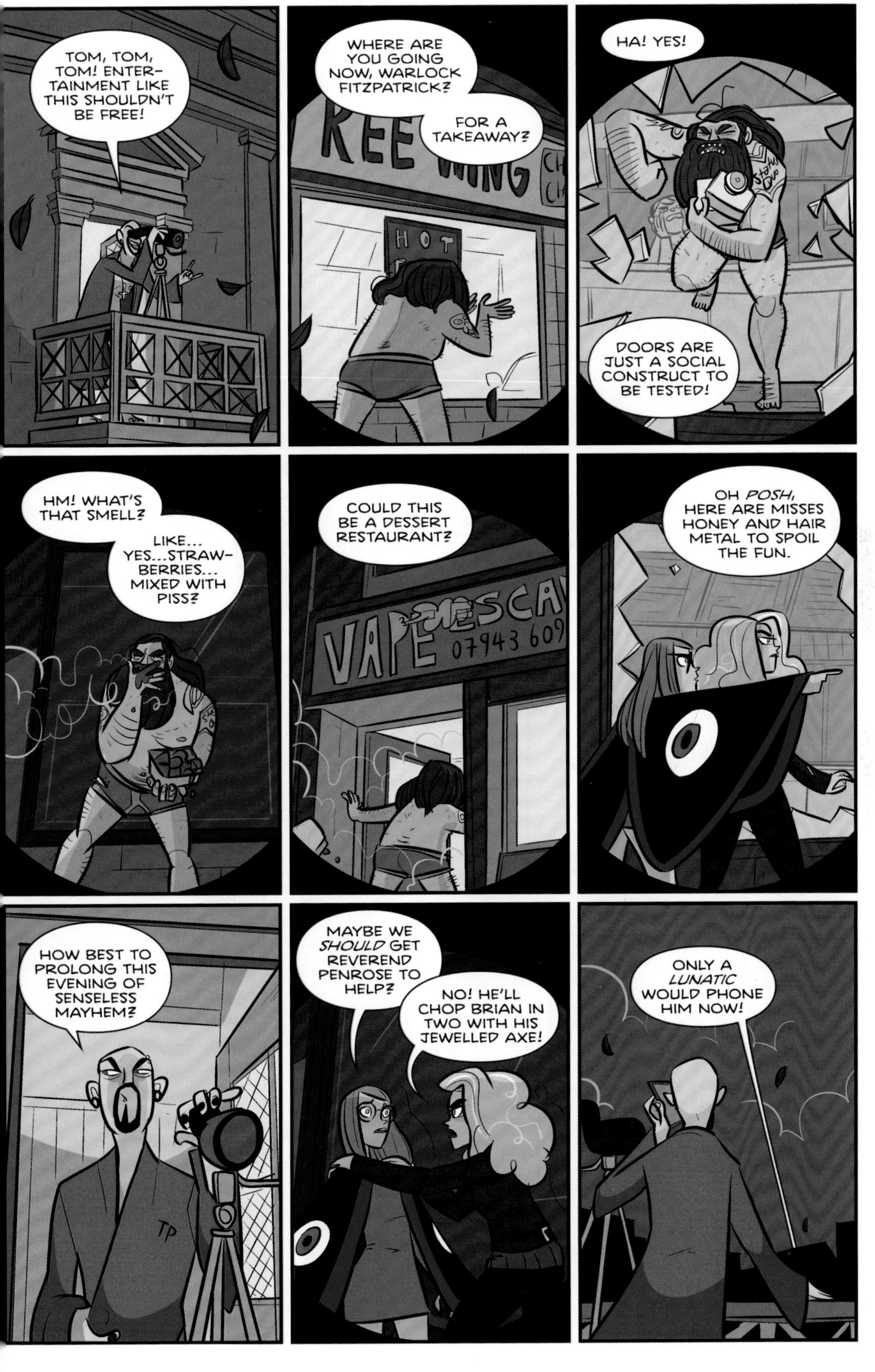

TOM, TOM, TOM! ENTER-TAINMENT LIKE THIS SHOULDN'T BE FREE!
WHERE ARE YOU GOING NOW, WARLOCK FITZPATRICK?
FOR A TAKEAWAY?
KEE WONG
HOT
HA! YES!
Status Quo
DOORS ARE JUST A SOCIAL CONSTRUCT TO BE TESTED!
HM! WHAT'S THAT SMELL?
LIKE... YES...STRAW-BERRIES... MIXED WITH PISS?
COULD THIS BE A DESSERT RESTAURANT?
VAPE
07943 609
OH *POSH*, HERE ARE MISSES HONEY AND HAIR METAL TO SPOIL THE FUN.
HOW BEST TO PROLONG THIS EVENING OF SENSELESS MAYHEM?
TP
MAYBE WE *SHOULD* GET REVEREND PENROSE TO HELP?
NO! HE'LL CHOP BRIAN IN TWO WITH HIS JEWELLED AXE!
ONLY A *LUNATIC* WOULD PHONE HIM NOW!

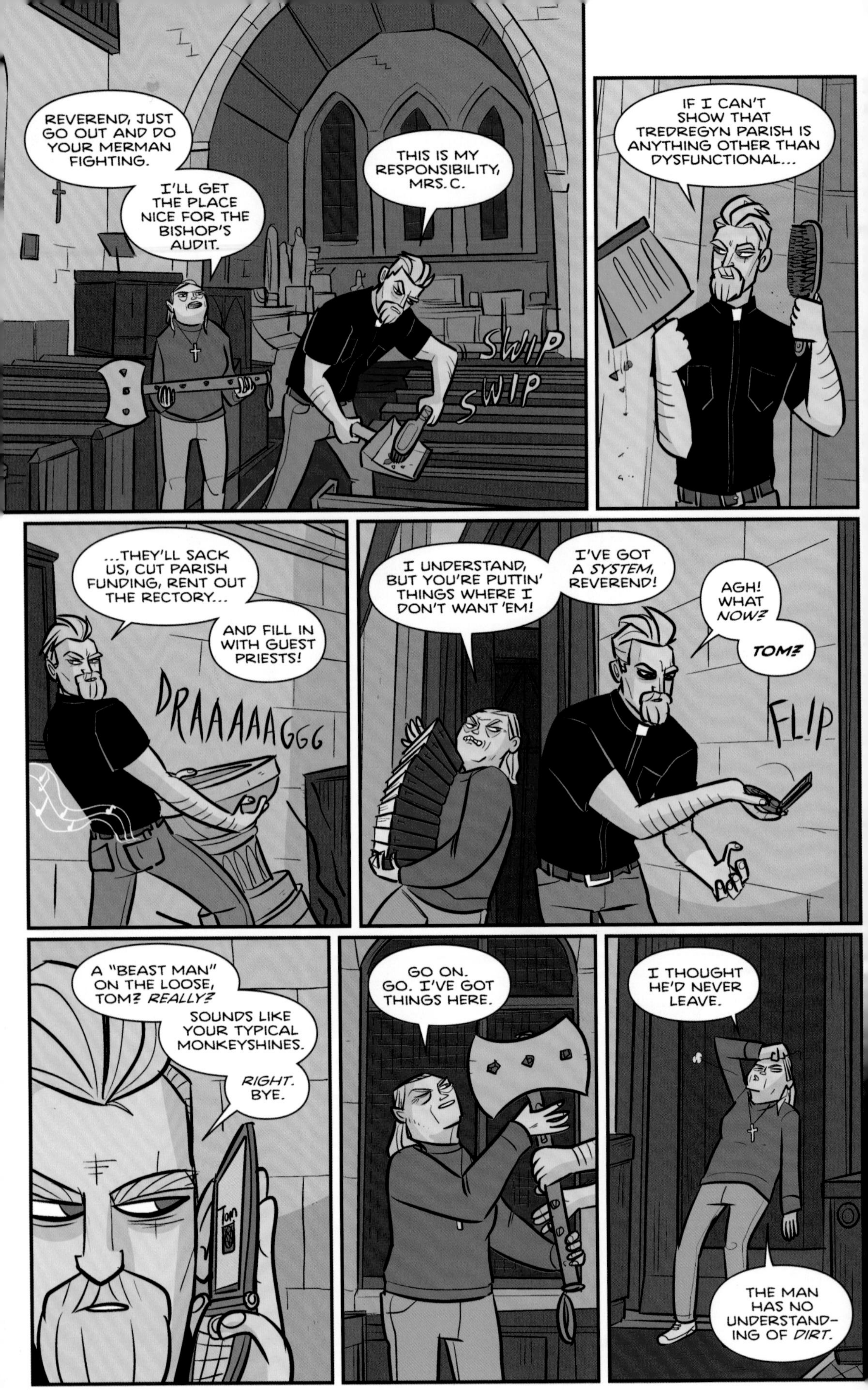

REVEREND, JUST GO OUT AND DO YOUR MERMAN FIGHTING.
I'LL GET THE PLACE NICE FOR THE BISHOP'S AUDIT.
THIS IS MY RESPONSIBILITY, MRS. C.
SWIP
SWIP
IF I CAN'T SHOW THAT TREDREGYN PARISH IS ANYTHING OTHER THAN DYSFUNCTIONAL...
...THEY'LL SACK US, CUT PARISH FUNDING, RENT OUT THE RECTORY...
AND FILL IN WITH GUEST PRIESTS!
DRAAAAAGGG
I UNDERSTAND, BUT YOU'RE PUTTIN' THINGS WHERE I DON'T WANT 'EM!
I'VE GOT A *SYSTEM*, REVEREND!
AGH! WHAT *NOW?*
TOM?
FLIP
A "BEAST MAN" ON THE LOOSE, TOM? *REALLY?*
SOUNDS LIKE YOUR TYPICAL MONKEYSHINES.
RIGHT. BYE.
TOM
GO ON. GO. I'VE GOT THINGS HERE.
I THOUGHT HE'D NEVER LEAVE.
THE MAN HAS NO UNDERSTAND-ING OF *DIRT*.

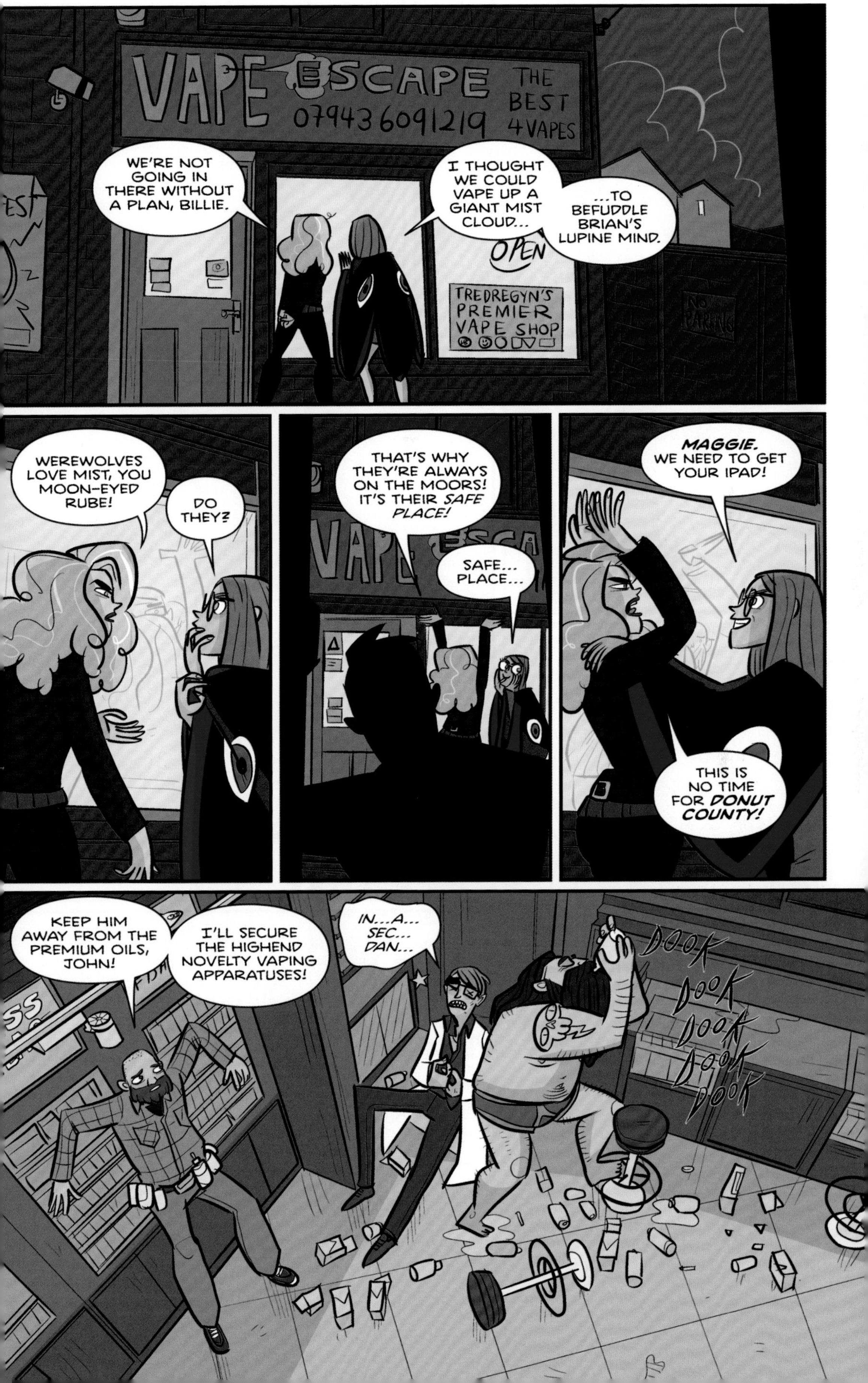
VAPE ESCAPE
07943 6091219
THE BEST 4 VAPES
WE'RE NOT GOING IN THERE WITHOUT A PLAN, BILLIE.
I THOUGHT WE COULD VAPE UP A GIANT MIST CLOUD...
...TO BEFUDDLE BRIAN'S LUPINE MIND.
OPEN
TREDREGYN'S PREMIER VAPE SHOP
NO PARKING
WEREWOLVES LOVE MIST, YOU MOON-EYED RUBE!
DO THEY?
THAT'S WHY THEY'RE ALWAYS ON THE MOORS! IT'S THEIR *SAFE PLACE!*
SAFE... PLACE...
MAGGIE. WE NEED TO GET YOUR IPAD!
THIS IS NO TIME FOR ***DONUT COUNTY!***
KEEP HIM AWAY FROM THE PREMIUM OILS, JOHN!
I'LL SECURE THE HIGHEND NOVELTY VAPING APPARATUSES!
IN...A... SEC... DAN...
DOOK DOOK DOOK DOOK DOOK

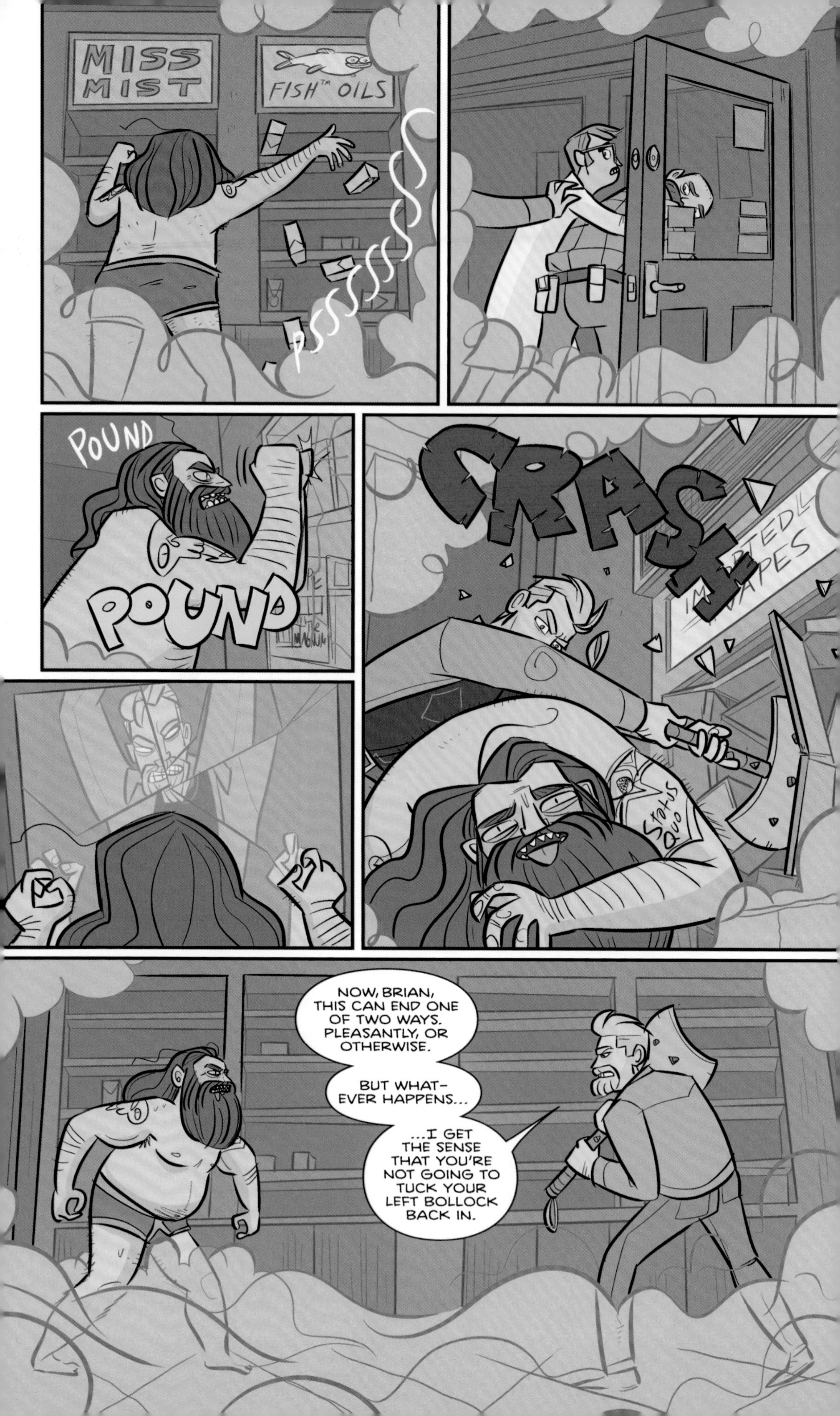
MISS MIST
FISH™ OILS
PSSSSSSSSS
POUND
POUND
CRASH
IMPORTEDLY VAPES
STATUS QUO
NOW, BRIAN, THIS CAN END ONE OF TWO WAYS. PLEASANTLY, OR OTHERWISE.
BUT WHAT-EVER HAPPENS...
...I GET THE SENSE THAT YOU'RE NOT GOING TO TUCK YOUR LEFT BOLLOCK BACK IN.

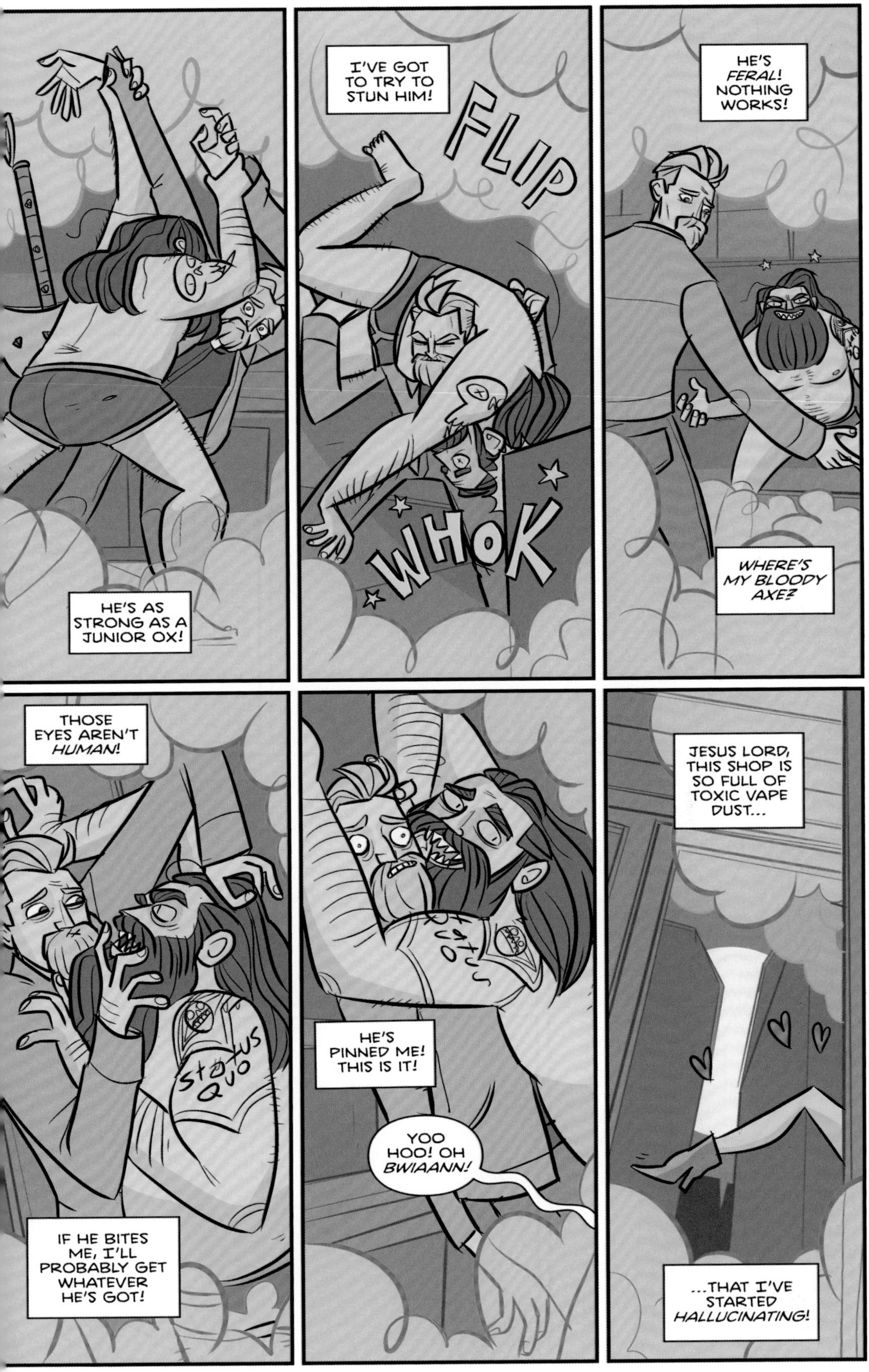
HE'S AS STRONG AS A JUNIOR OX!
I'VE GOT TO TRY TO STUN HIM!
FLIP
WHOK
HE'S *FERAL*! NOTHING WORKS!
WHERE'S MY BLOODY AXE?
THOSE EYES AREN'T *HUMAN*!
STATUS QUO
IF HE BITES ME, I'LL PROBABLY GET WHATEVER HE'S GOT!
HE'S PINNED ME! THIS IS IT!
YOO HOO! OH *BWIAANN!*
JESUS LORD, THIS SHOP IS SO FULL OF TOXIC VAPE DUST...
...THAT I'VE STARTED *HALLUCINATING*!

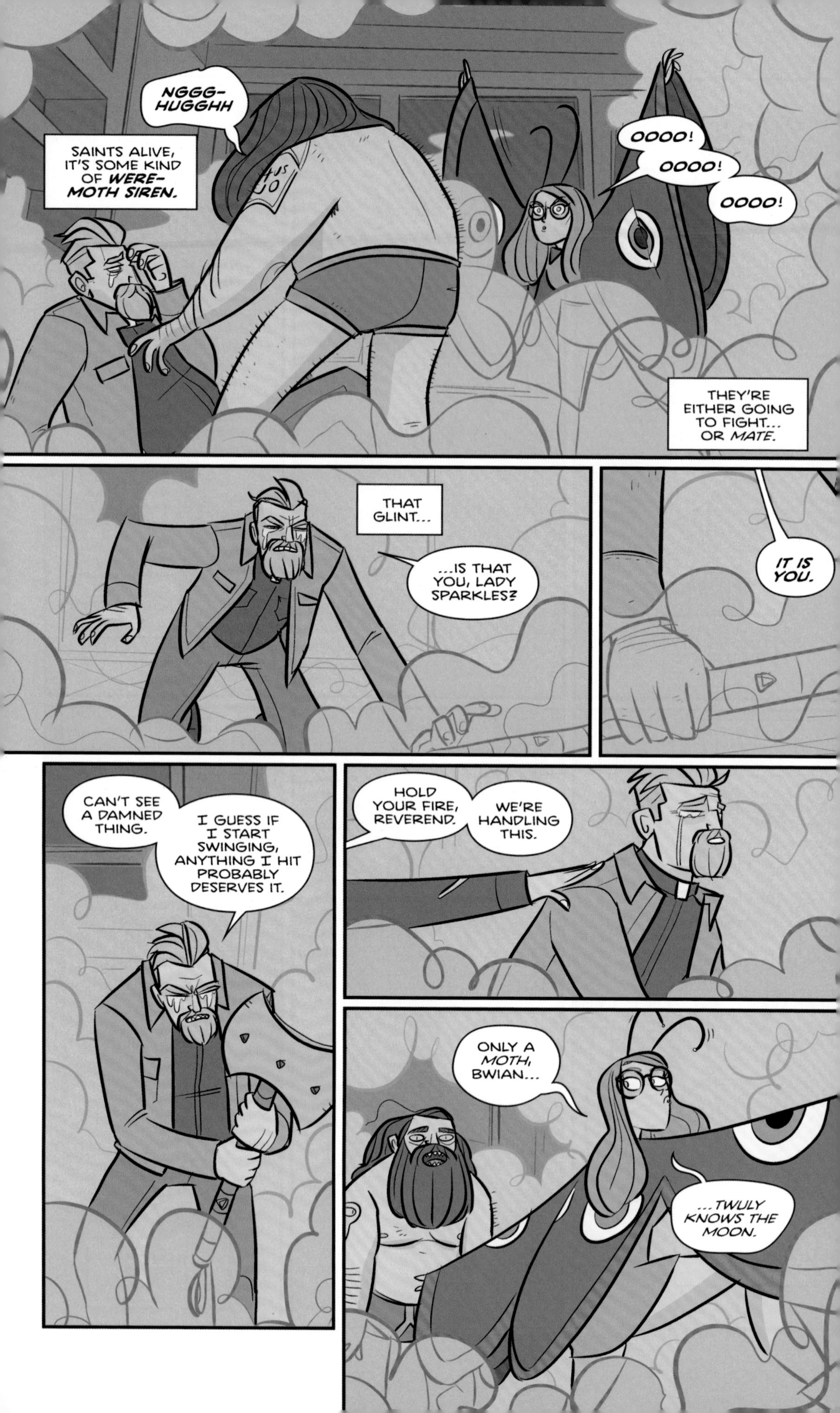
NGGG-HUGGHH
SAINTS ALIVE, IT'S SOME KIND OF WERE-MOTH SIREN.
OOOO!
OOOO!
OOOO!
THEY'RE EITHER GOING TO FIGHT... OR MATE.
THAT GLINT...
...IS THAT YOU, LADY SPARKLES?
IT IS YOU.
CAN'T SEE A DAMNED THING.
I GUESS IF I START SWINGING, ANYTHING I HIT PROBABLY DESERVES IT.
HOLD YOUR FIRE, REVEREND.
WE'RE HANDLING THIS.
ONLY A MOTH, BWIAN...
...TWULY KNOWS THE MOON.

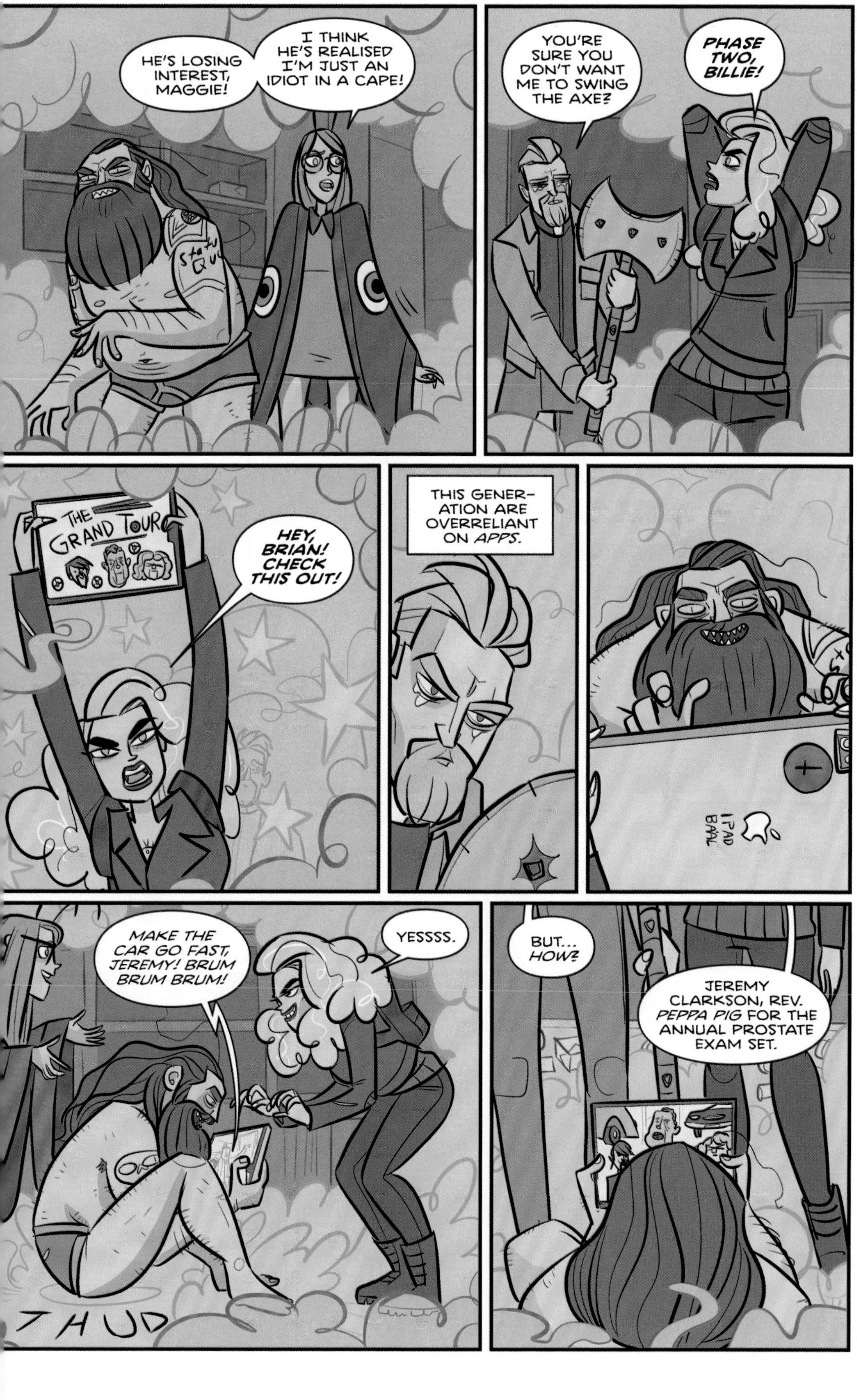

HE'S LOSING INTEREST, MAGGIE!
I THINK HE'S REALISED I'M JUST AN IDIOT IN A CAPE!
YOU'RE SURE YOU DON'T WANT ME TO SWING THE AXE?
PHASE TWO, BILLIE!
THE GRAND TOUR
HEY, BRIAN! CHECK THIS OUT!
THIS GENERATION ARE OVERRELIANT ON *APPS*.
MAKE THE CAR GO FAST, JEREMY! BRUM BRUM BRUM!
YESSSS.
THUD
BUT... *HOW?*
JEREMY CLARKSON, REV. *PEPPA PIG* FOR THE ANNUAL PROSTATE EXAM SET.

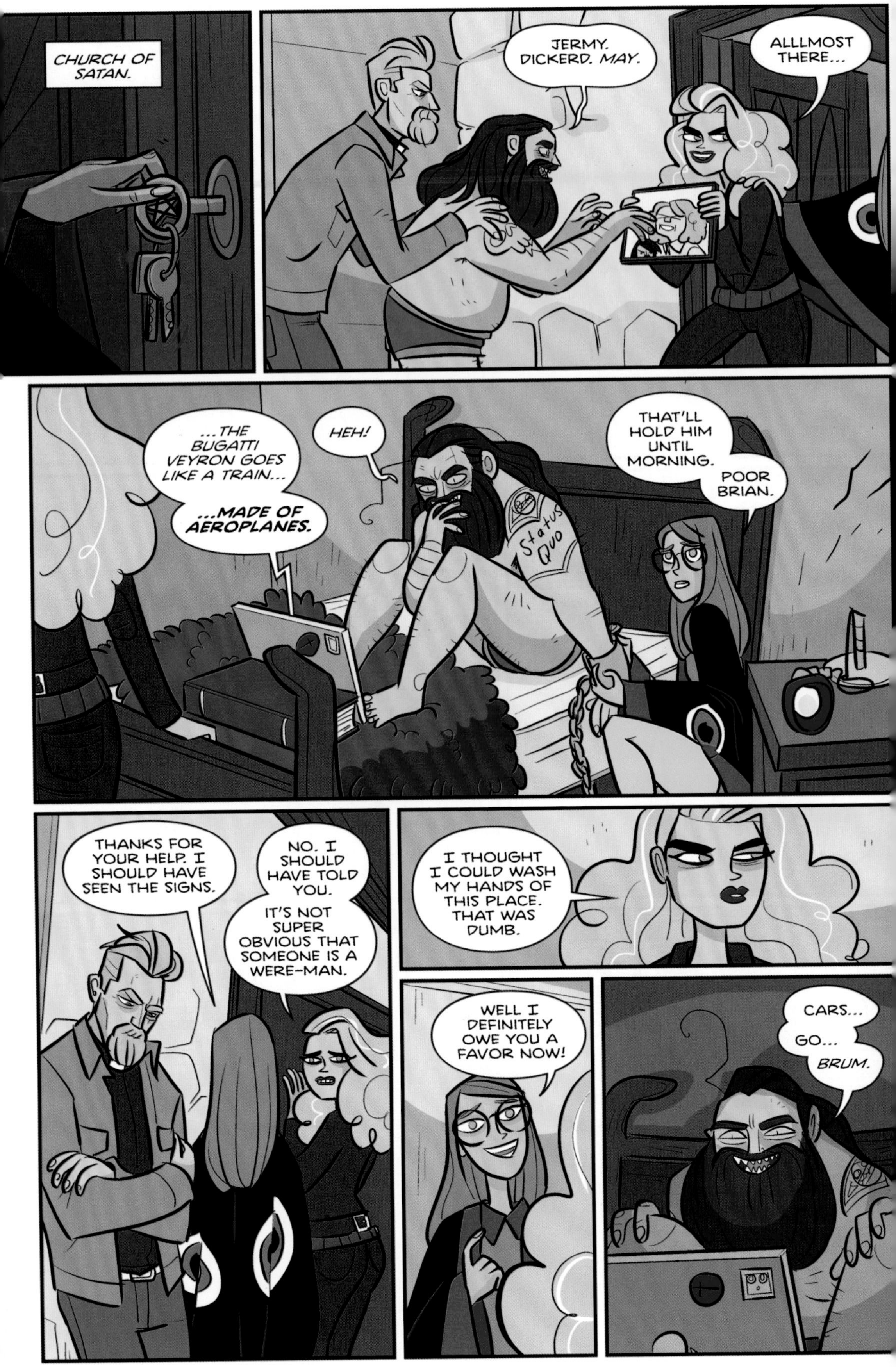
CHURCH OF SATAN.
JERMY. DICKERD. MAY.
ALLLMOST THERE...
...THE BUGATTI VEYRON GOES LIKE A TRAIN...
...MADE OF AEROPLANES.
HEH!
THAT'LL HOLD HIM UNTIL MORNING.
POOR BRIAN.
Status Quo
THANKS FOR YOUR HELP. I SHOULD HAVE SEEN THE SIGNS.
NO. I SHOULD HAVE TOLD YOU.
IT'S NOT SUPER OBVIOUS THAT SOMEONE IS A WERE-MAN.
I THOUGHT I COULD WASH MY HANDS OF THIS PLACE. THAT WAS DUMB.
WELL I DEFINITELY OWE YOU A FAVOR NOW!
CARS...
GO...
BRUM.

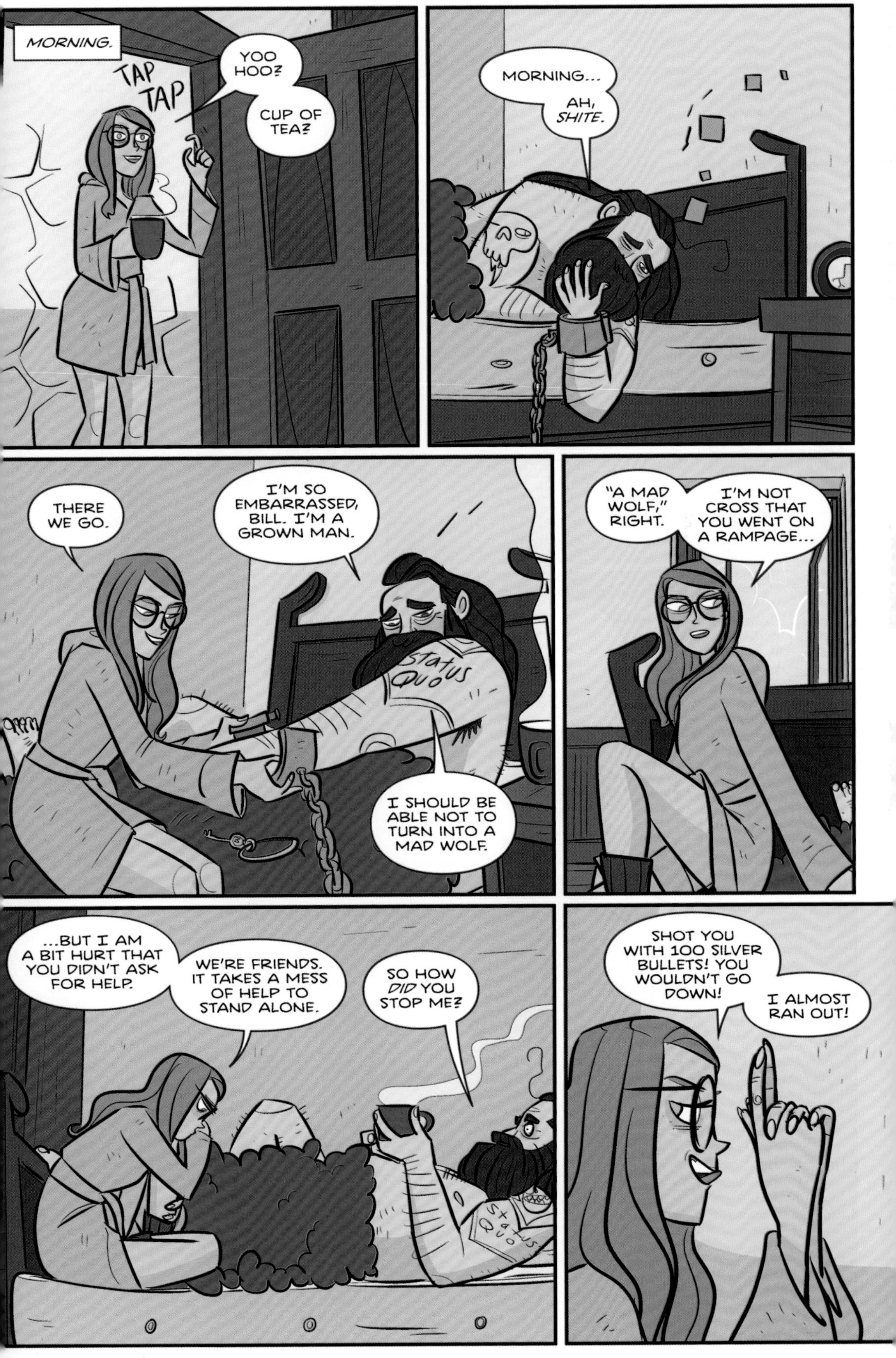
MORNING.
TAP TAP
YOO HOO?
CUP OF TEA?
MORNING...
AH, *SHITE*.
THERE WE GO.
I'M SO EMBARRASSED, BILL. I'M A GROWN MAN.
I SHOULD BE ABLE NOT TO TURN INTO A MAD WOLF.
Status Quo
"A MAD WOLF," RIGHT.
I'M NOT CROSS THAT YOU WENT ON A RAMPAGE...
...BUT I AM A BIT HURT THAT YOU DIDN'T ASK FOR HELP.
WE'RE FRIENDS. IT TAKES A MESS OF HELP TO STAND ALONE.
SO HOW *DID* YOU STOP ME?
Status Quo
SHOT YOU WITH 100 SILVER BULLETS! YOU WOULDN'T GO DOWN!
I ALMOST RAN OUT!

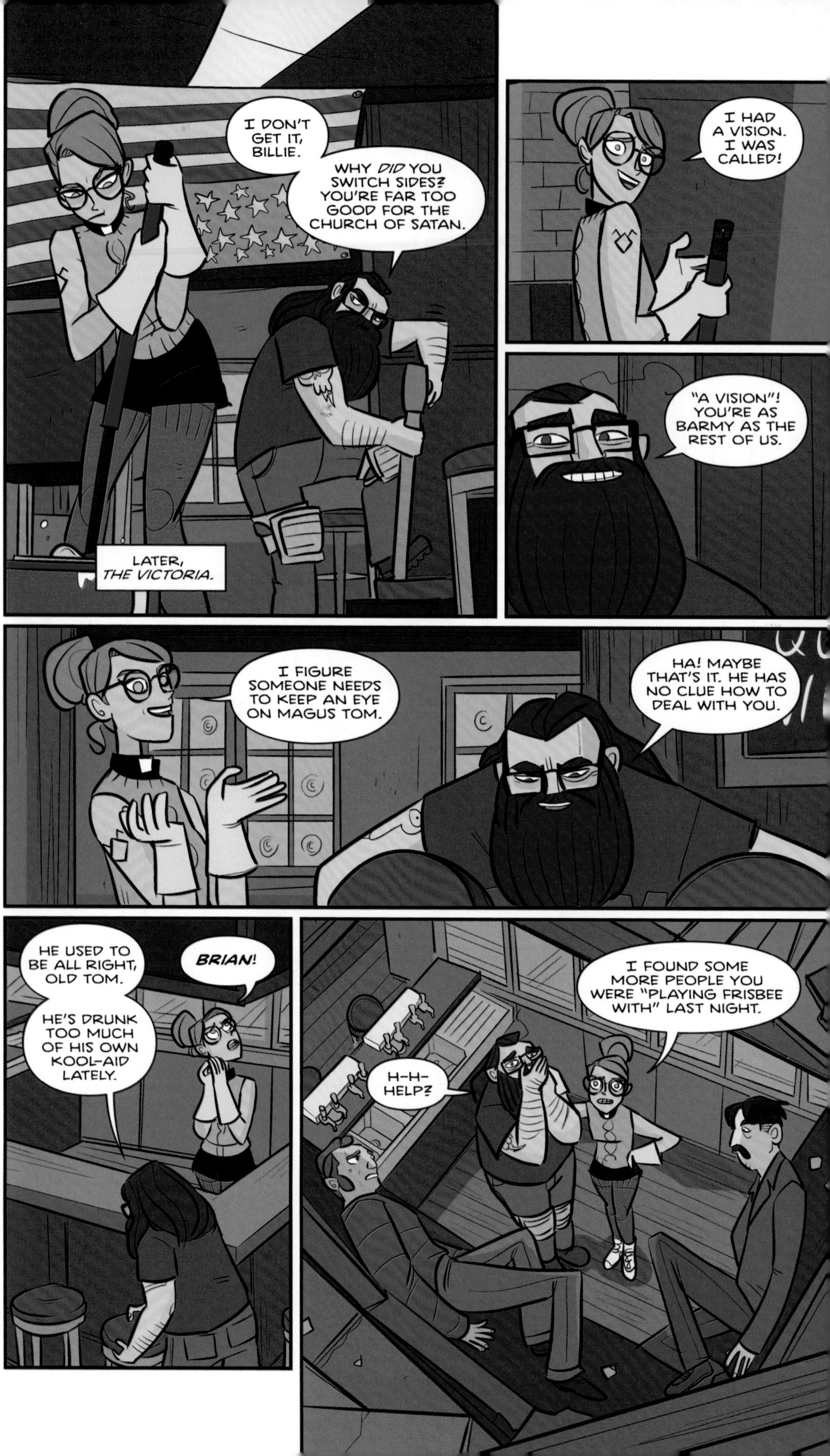
I DON'T GET IT, BILLIE.
WHY *DID* YOU SWITCH SIDES? YOU'RE FAR TOO GOOD FOR THE CHURCH OF SATAN.
LATER, *THE VICTORIA.*
I HAD A VISION. I WAS CALLED!
"A VISION"! YOU'RE AS BARMY AS THE REST OF US.
I FIGURE SOMEONE NEEDS TO KEEP AN EYE ON MAGUS TOM.
HA! MAYBE THAT'S IT. HE HAS NO CLUE HOW TO DEAL WITH YOU.
HE USED TO BE ALL RIGHT, OLD TOM.
HE'S DRUNK TOO MUCH OF HIS OWN KOOL-AID LATELY.
BRIAN!
I FOUND SOME MORE PEOPLE YOU WERE "PLAYING FRISBEE WITH" LAST NIGHT.
H-H-HELP?

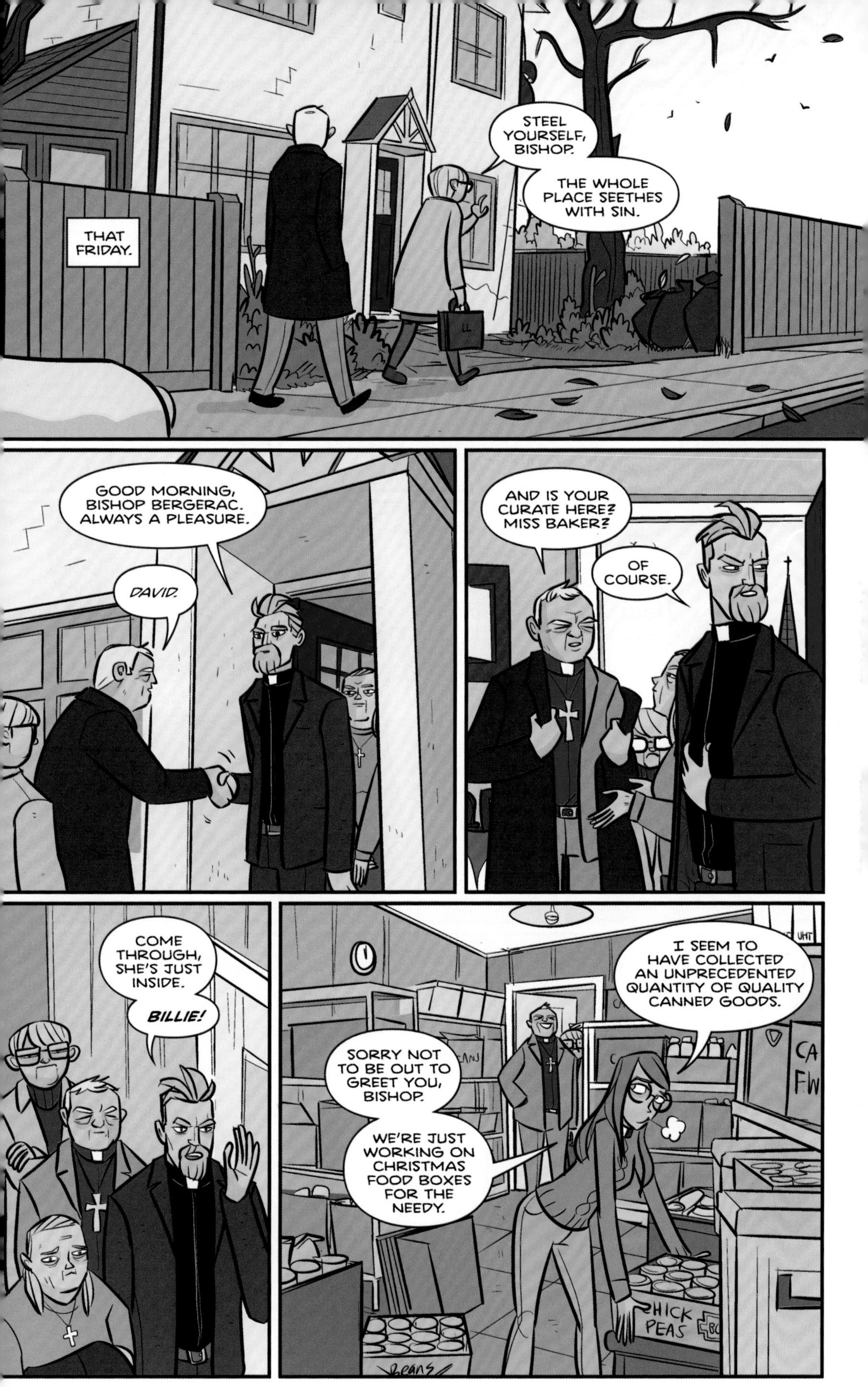
THAT FRIDAY.
STEEL YOURSELF, BISHOP.
THE WHOLE PLACE SEETHES WITH SIN.
GOOD MORNING, BISHOP BERGERAC. ALWAYS A PLEASURE.
DAVID.
AND IS YOUR CURATE HERE? MISS BAKER?
OF COURSE.
COME THROUGH, SHE'S JUST INSIDE.
BILLIE!
SORRY NOT TO BE OUT TO GREET YOU, BISHOP.
WE'RE JUST WORKING ON CHRISTMAS FOOD BOXES FOR THE NEEDY.
I SEEM TO HAVE COLLECTED AN UNPRECEDENTED QUANTITY OF QUALITY CANNED GOODS.
CHICK PEAS
BEANS

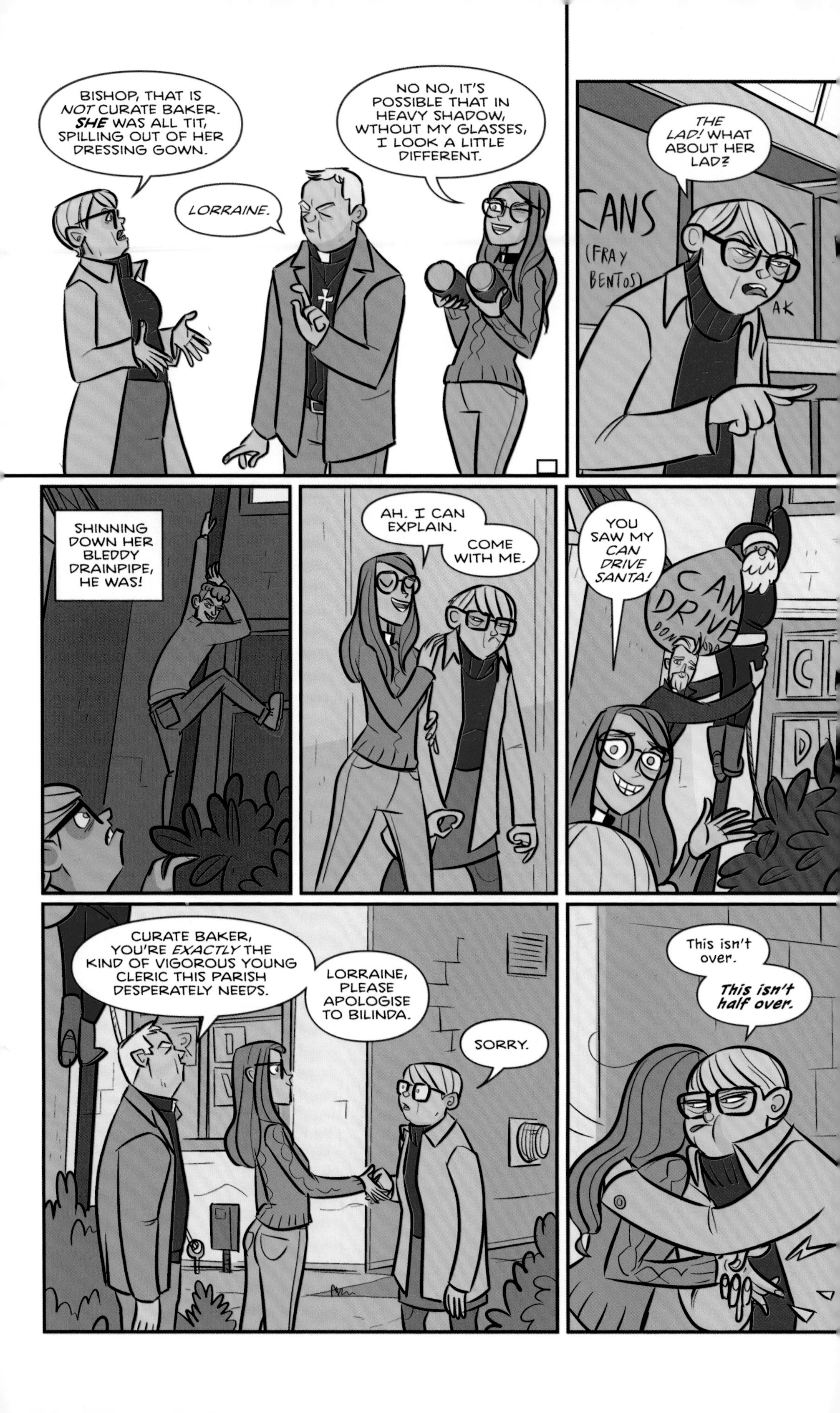
BISHOP, THAT IS *NOT* CURATE BAKER. ***SHE*** WAS ALL TIT, SPILLING OUT OF HER DRESSING GOWN.
LORRAINE.
NO NO, IT'S POSSIBLE THAT IN HEAVY SHADOW, WTHOUT MY GLASSES, I LOOK A LITTLE DIFFERENT.
THE LAD! WHAT ABOUT HER LAD?
CANS (FRAY BENTOS)
SHINNING DOWN HER BLEDDY DRAINPIPE, HE WAS!
AH. I CAN EXPLAIN.
COME WITH ME.
YOU SAW MY *CAN DRIVE SANTA!*
CAN DRIVE
CURATE BAKER, YOU'RE *EXACTLY* THE KIND OF VIGOROUS YOUNG CLERIC THIS PARISH DESPERATELY NEEDS.
LORRAINE, PLEASE APOLOGISE TO BILINDA.
SORRY.
This isn't over.
This isn't half over.

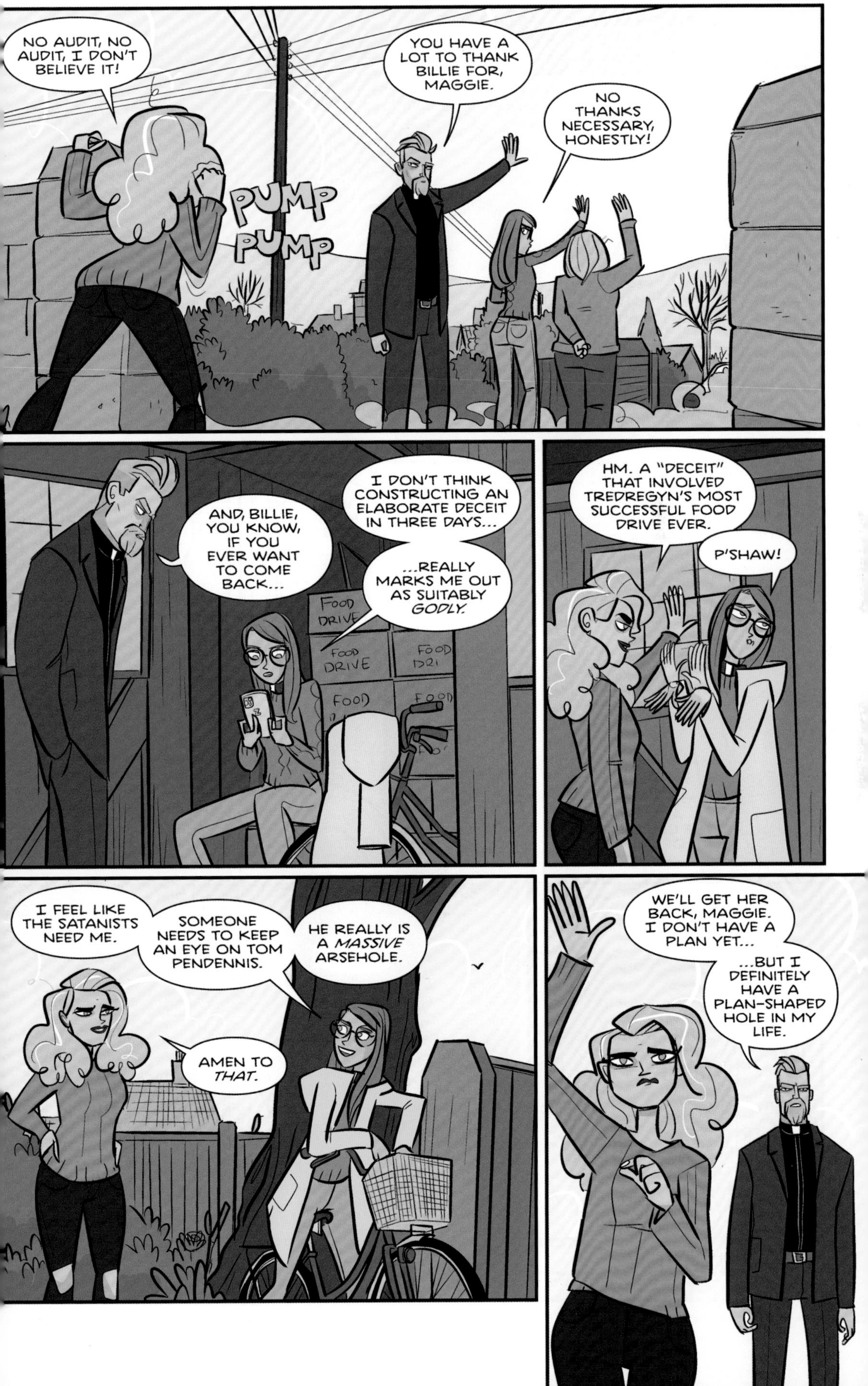
NO AUDIT, NO AUDIT, I DON'T BELIEVE IT!
PUMP PUMP
YOU HAVE A LOT TO THANK BILLIE FOR, MAGGIE.
NO THANKS NECESSARY, HONESTLY!
AND, BILLIE, YOU KNOW, IF YOU EVER WANT TO COME BACK...
I DON'T THINK CONSTRUCTING AN ELABORATE DECEIT IN THREE DAYS...
...REALLY MARKS ME OUT AS SUITABLY *GODLY.*
FOOD DRIVE
HM. A "DECEIT" THAT INVOLVED TREDREGYN'S MOST SUCCESSFUL FOOD DRIVE EVER.
P'SHAW!
I FEEL LIKE THE SATANISTS NEED ME.
SOMEONE NEEDS TO KEEP AN EYE ON TOM PENDENNIS.
HE REALLY IS A *MASSIVE* ARSEHOLE.
AMEN TO *THAT.*
WE'LL GET HER BACK, MAGGIE. I DON'T HAVE A PLAN YET...
...BUT I DEFINITELY HAVE A PLAN-SHAPED HOLE IN MY LIFE.

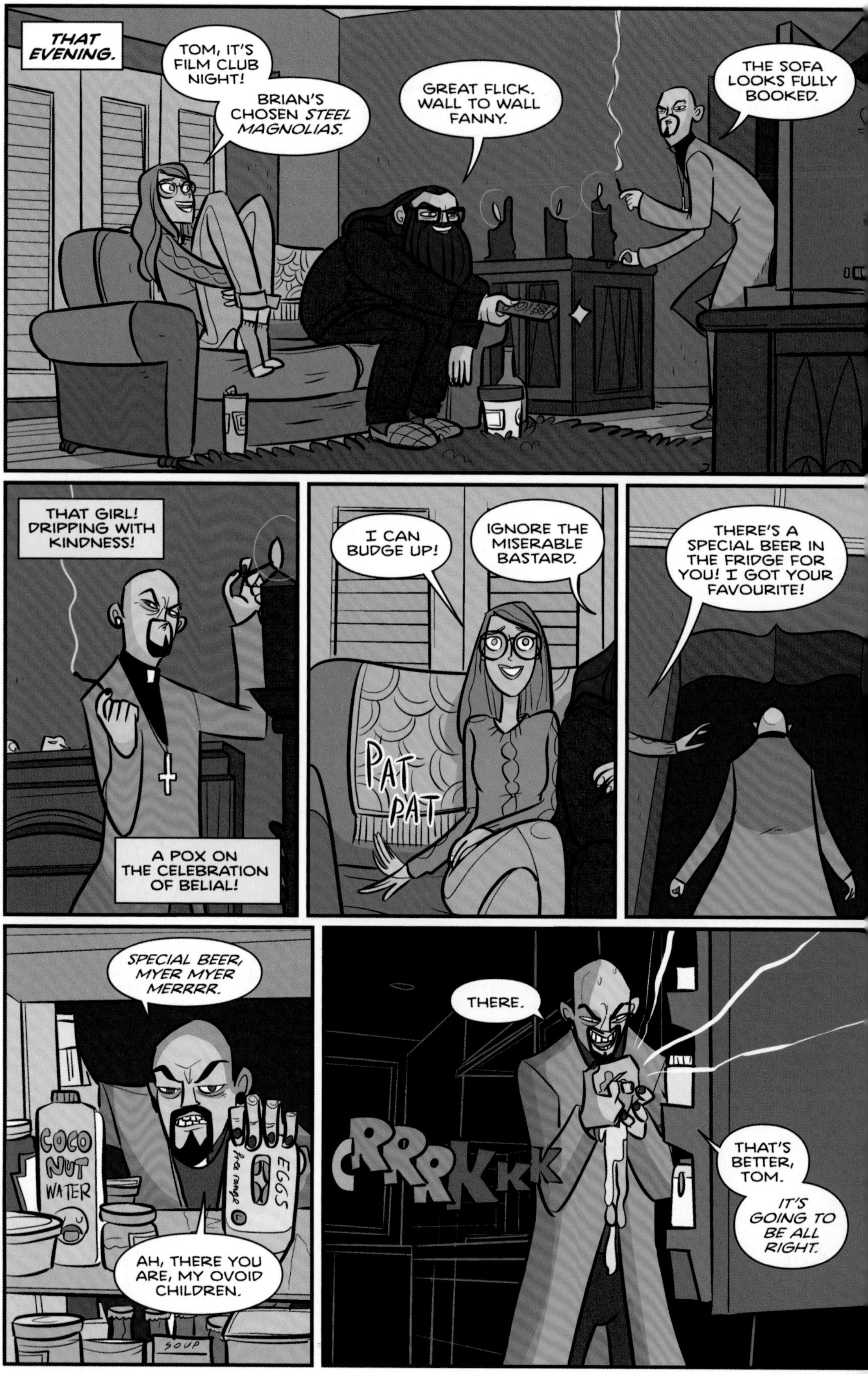
THAT EVENING.
TOM, IT'S FILM CLUB NIGHT!
BRIAN'S CHOSEN *STEEL MAGNOLIAS.*
GREAT FLICK. WALL TO WALL FANNY.
THE SOFA LOOKS FULLY BOOKED.
THAT GIRL! DRIPPING WITH KINDNESS!
A POX ON THE CELEBRATION OF BELIAL!
I CAN BUDGE UP!
IGNORE THE MISERABLE BASTARD.
PAT PAT
THERE'S A SPECIAL BEER IN THE FRIDGE FOR YOU! I GOT YOUR FAVOURITE!
SPECIAL BEER, MYER MYER MERRRR.
COCO NUT WATER
EGGS
free range
AH, THERE YOU ARE, MY OVOID CHILDREN.
SOUP
THERE.
CRRRKKK
THAT'S BETTER, TOM.
IT'S GOING TO BE ALL RIGHT.

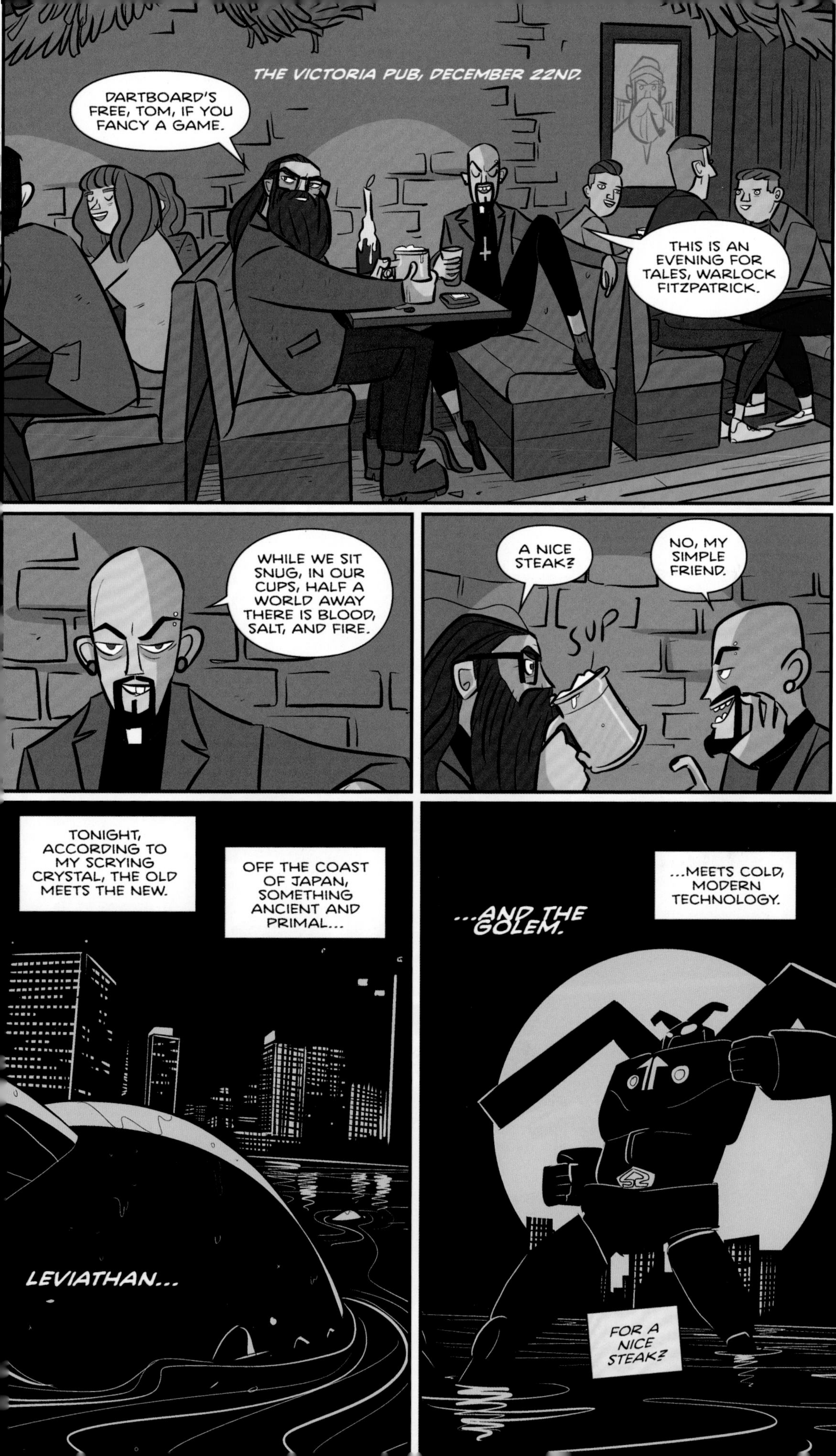
THE VICTORIA PUB, DECEMBER 22ND.
DARTBOARD'S FREE, TOM, IF YOU FANCY A GAME.
THIS IS AN EVENING FOR TALES, WARLOCK FITZPATRICK.
WHILE WE SIT SNUG, IN OUR CUPS, HALF A WORLD AWAY THERE IS BLOOD, SALT, AND FIRE.
A NICE STEAK?
SUP
NO, MY SIMPLE FRIEND.
TONIGHT, ACCORDING TO MY SCRYING CRYSTAL, THE OLD MEETS THE NEW.
OFF THE COAST OF JAPAN, SOMETHING ANCIENT AND PRIMAL...
LEVIATHAN...
...MEETS COLD, MODERN TECHNOLOGY.
...AND THE GOLEM.
FOR A NICE STEAK?

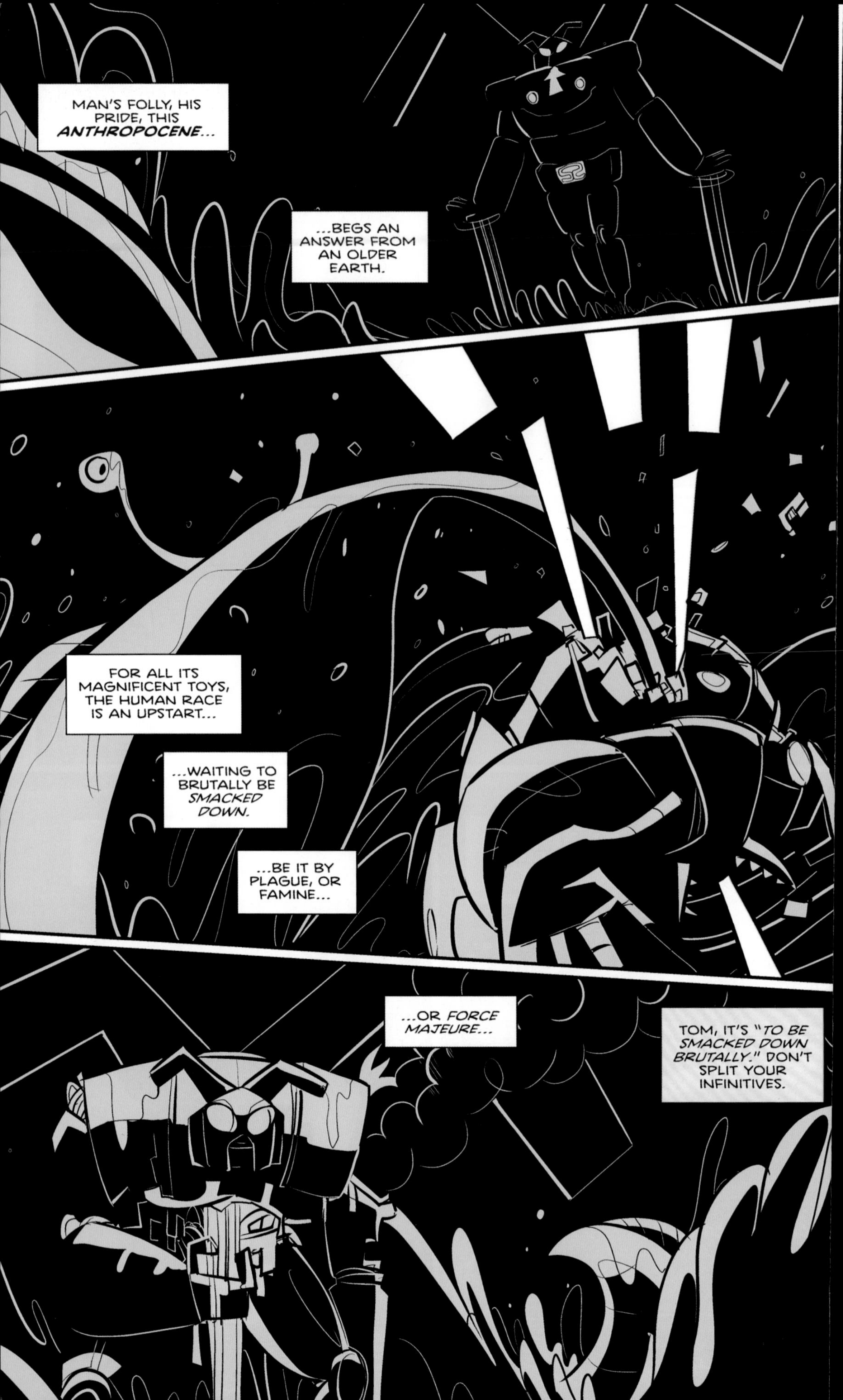
MAN'S FOLLY, HIS PRIDE, THIS *ANTHROPOCENE...*
...BEGS AN ANSWER FROM AN OLDER EARTH.
FOR ALL ITS MAGNIFICENT TOYS, THE HUMAN RACE IS AN UPSTART...
...WAITING TO BRUTALLY BE *SMACKED DOWN.*
...BE IT BY PLAGUE, OR FAMINE...
...OR *FORCE MAJEURE...*
TOM, IT'S "*TO BE SMACKED DOWN BRUTALLY.*" DON'T SPLIT YOUR INFINITIVES.

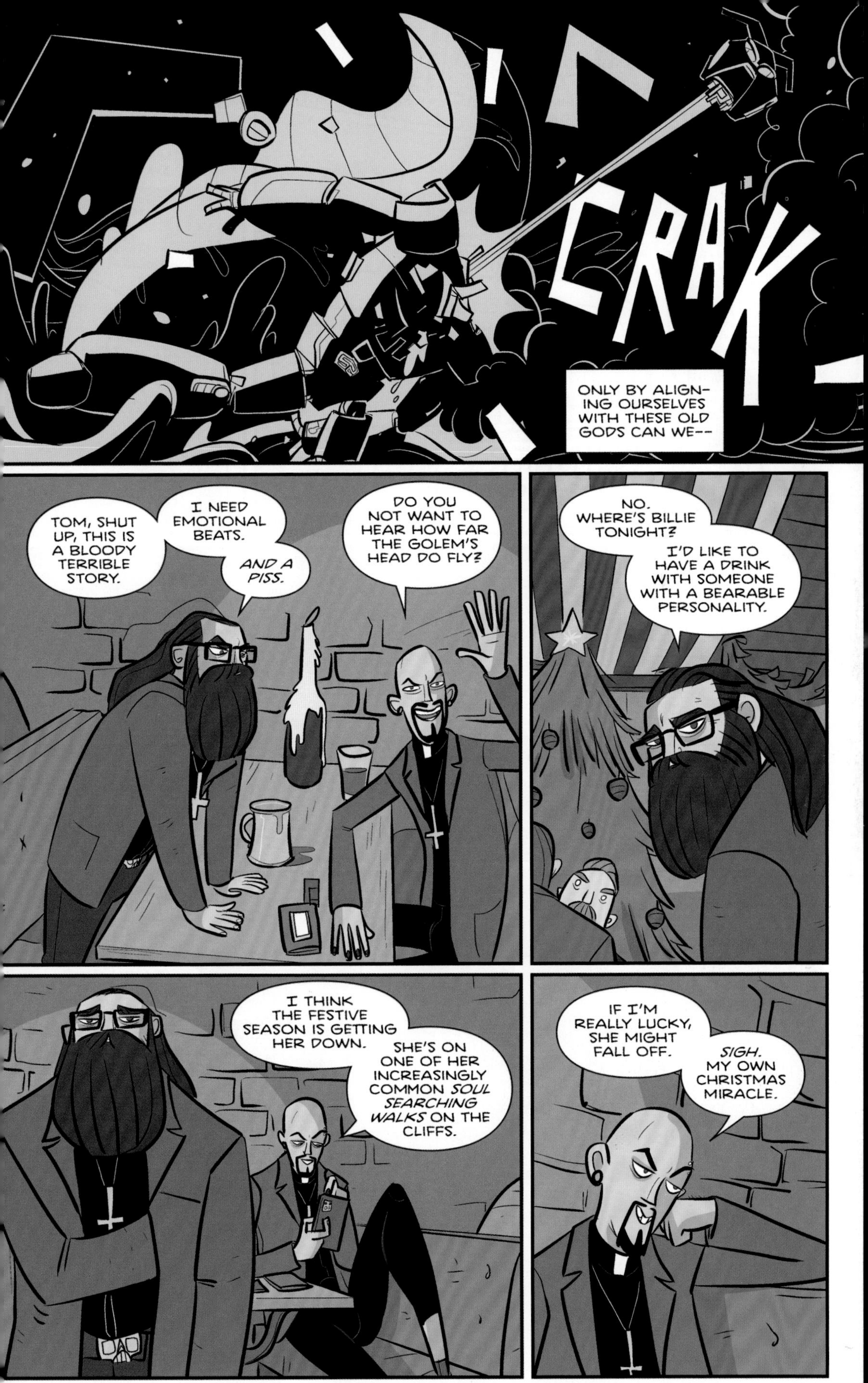

CRAK
ONLY BY ALIGNING OURSELVES WITH THESE OLD GODS CAN WE--
TOM, SHUT UP, THIS IS A BLOODY TERRIBLE STORY.
I NEED EMOTIONAL BEATS.
AND A PISS.
DO YOU NOT WANT TO HEAR HOW FAR THE GOLEM'S HEAD DO FLY?
NO. WHERE'S BILLIE TONIGHT?
I'D LIKE TO HAVE A DRINK WITH SOMEONE WITH A BEARABLE PERSONALITY.
I THINK THE FESTIVE SEASON IS GETTING HER DOWN.
SHE'S ON ONE OF HER INCREASINGLY COMMON SOUL SEARCHING WALKS ON THE CLIFFS.
IF I'M REALLY LUCKY, SHE MIGHT FALL OFF.
SIGH. MY OWN CHRISTMAS MIRACLE.

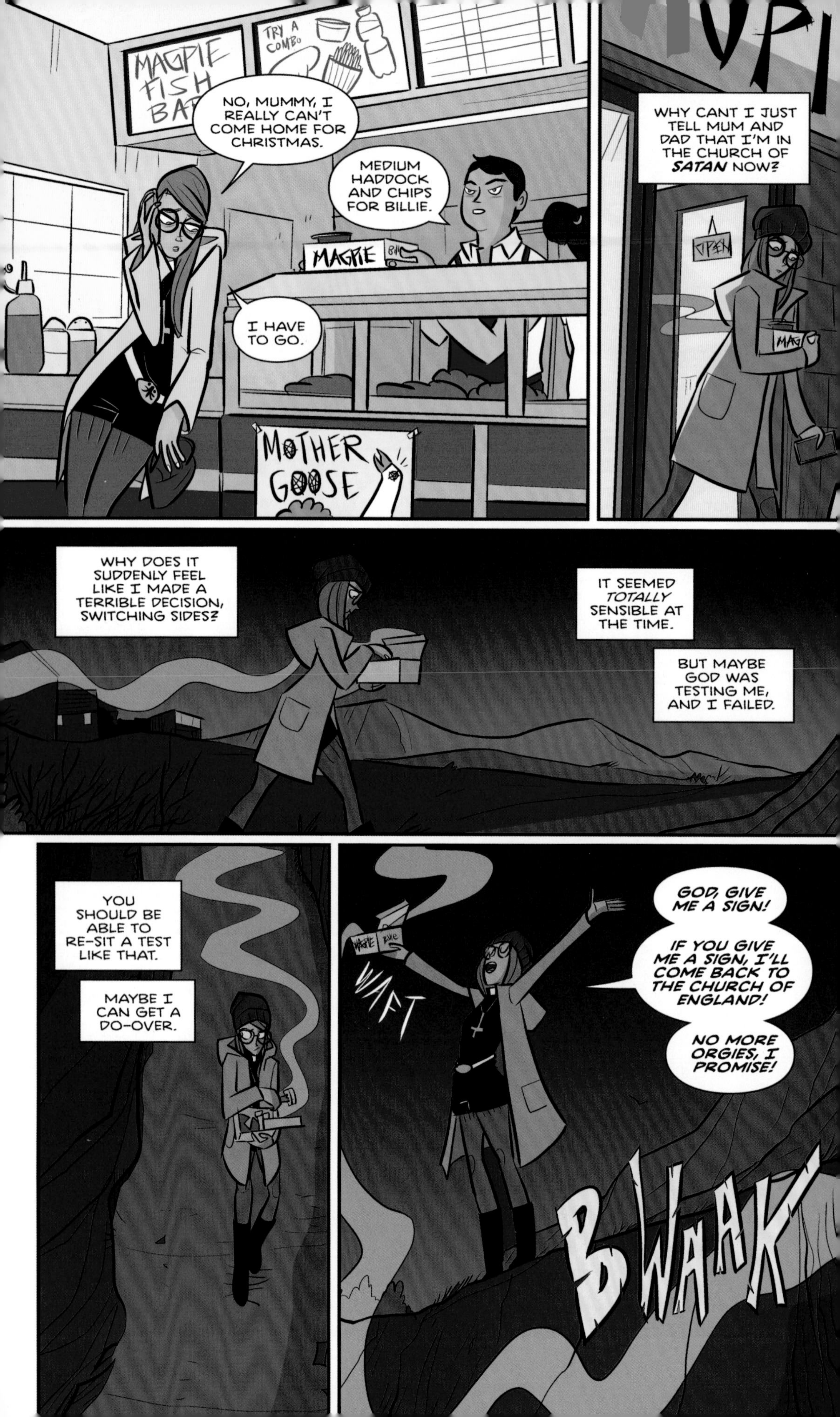
MAGPIE FISH BAR
TRY A COMBO
NO, MUMMY, I REALLY CAN'T COME HOME FOR CHRISTMAS.
MEDIUM HADDOCK AND CHIPS FOR BILLIE.
MAGPIE
I HAVE TO GO.
MOTHER GOOSE
WHY CANT I JUST TELL MUM AND DAD THAT I'M IN THE CHURCH OF SATAN NOW?
WHY DOES IT SUDDENLY FEEL LIKE I MADE A TERRIBLE DECISION, SWITCHING SIDES?
IT SEEMED TOTALLY SENSIBLE AT THE TIME.
BUT MAYBE GOD WAS TESTING ME, AND I FAILED.
YOU SHOULD BE ABLE TO RE-SIT A TEST LIKE THAT.
MAYBE I CAN GET A DO-OVER.
MAGPIE BILLIE
WAFT
GOD, GIVE ME A SIGN!
IF YOU GIVE ME A SIGN, I'LL COME BACK TO THE CHURCH OF ENGLAND!
NO MORE ORGIES, I PROMISE!
BWAAK

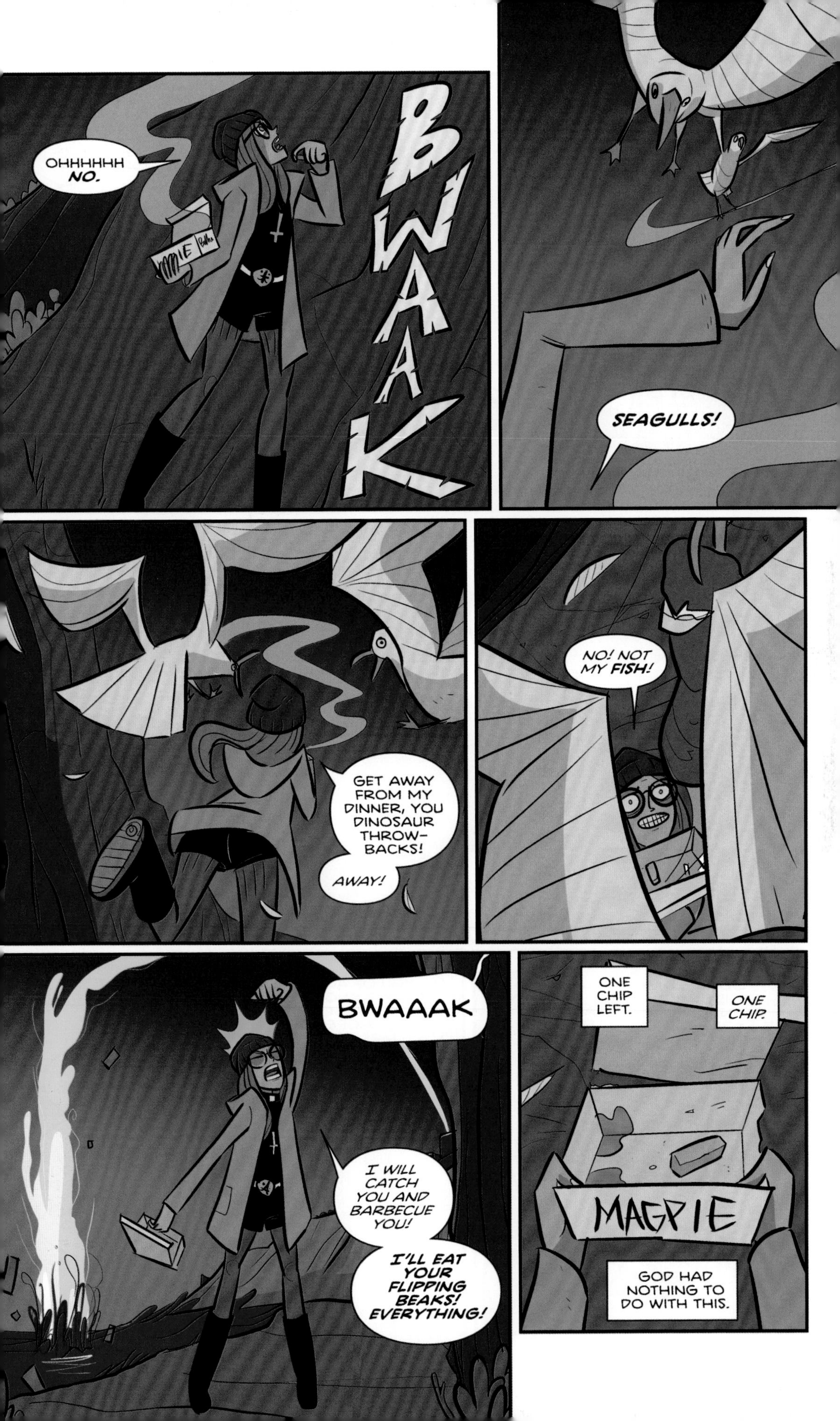
OHHHHHH NO.
BWAAK
SEAGULLS!
GET AWAY FROM MY DINNER, YOU DINOSAUR THROW-BACKS!
AWAY!
NO! NOT MY FISH!
BWAAAK
I WILL CATCH YOU AND BARBECUE YOU!
I'LL EAT YOUR FLIPPING BEAKS! EVERYTHING!
ONE CHIP LEFT.
ONE CHIP.
MAGPIE
GOD HAD NOTHING TO DO WITH THIS.

THE NEXT DAY.

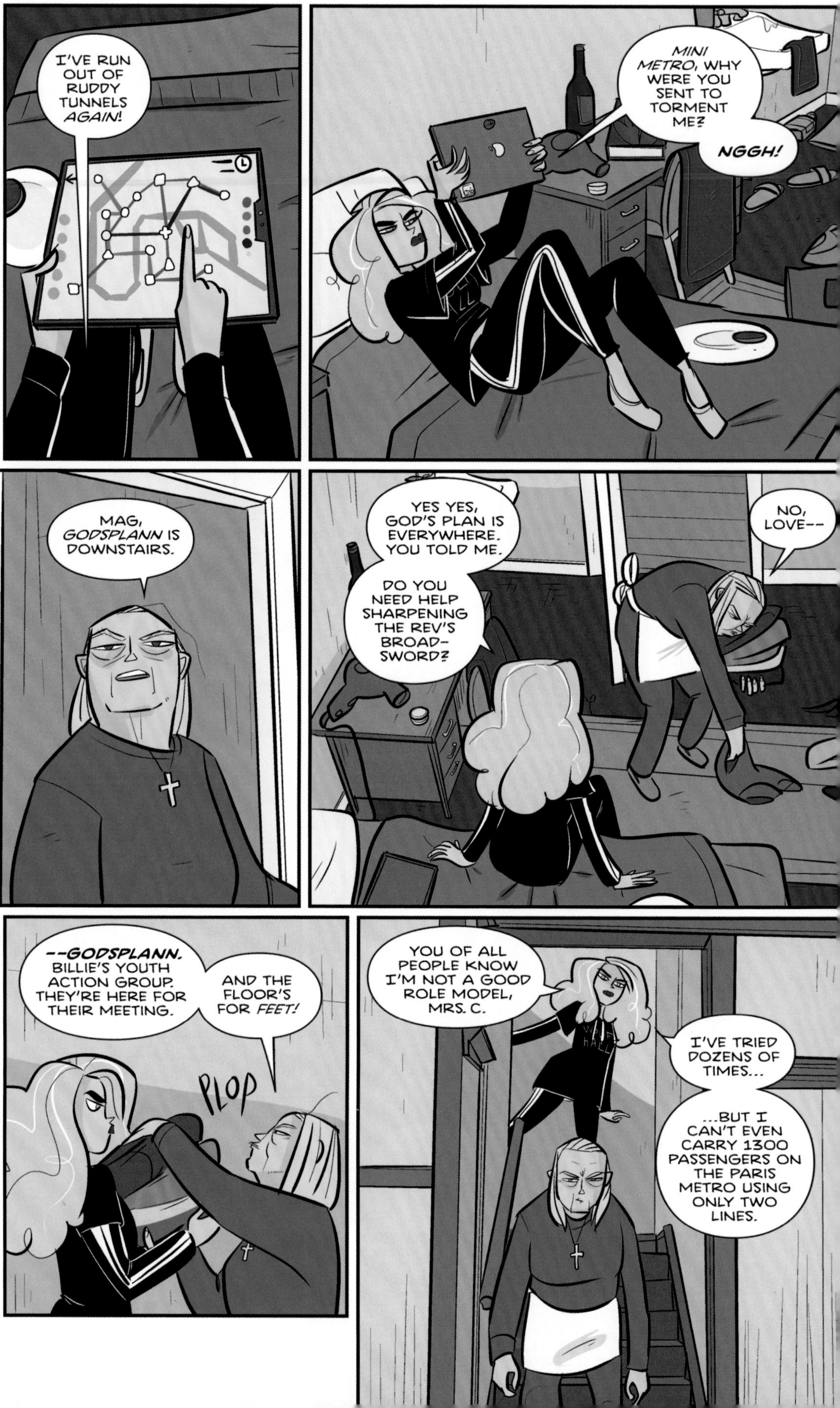

I'VE RUN OUT OF RUDDY TUNNELS *AGAIN!*
MINI METRO, WHY WERE YOU SENT TO TORMENT ME?
NGGH!
MAG, *GODSPLANN* IS DOWNSTAIRS.
YES YES, GOD'S PLAN IS EVERYWHERE. YOU TOLD ME.
DO YOU NEED HELP SHARPENING THE REV'S BROAD-SWORD?
NO, LOVE--
--GODSPLANN. BILLIE'S YOUTH ACTION GROUP. THEY'RE HERE FOR THEIR MEETING.
AND THE FLOOR'S FOR *FEET!*
PLOP
YOU OF ALL PEOPLE KNOW I'M NOT A GOOD ROLE MODEL, MRS. C.
I'VE TRIED DOZENS OF TIMES...
...BUT I CAN'T EVEN CARRY 1300 PASSENGERS ON THE PARIS METRO USING ONLY TWO LINES.

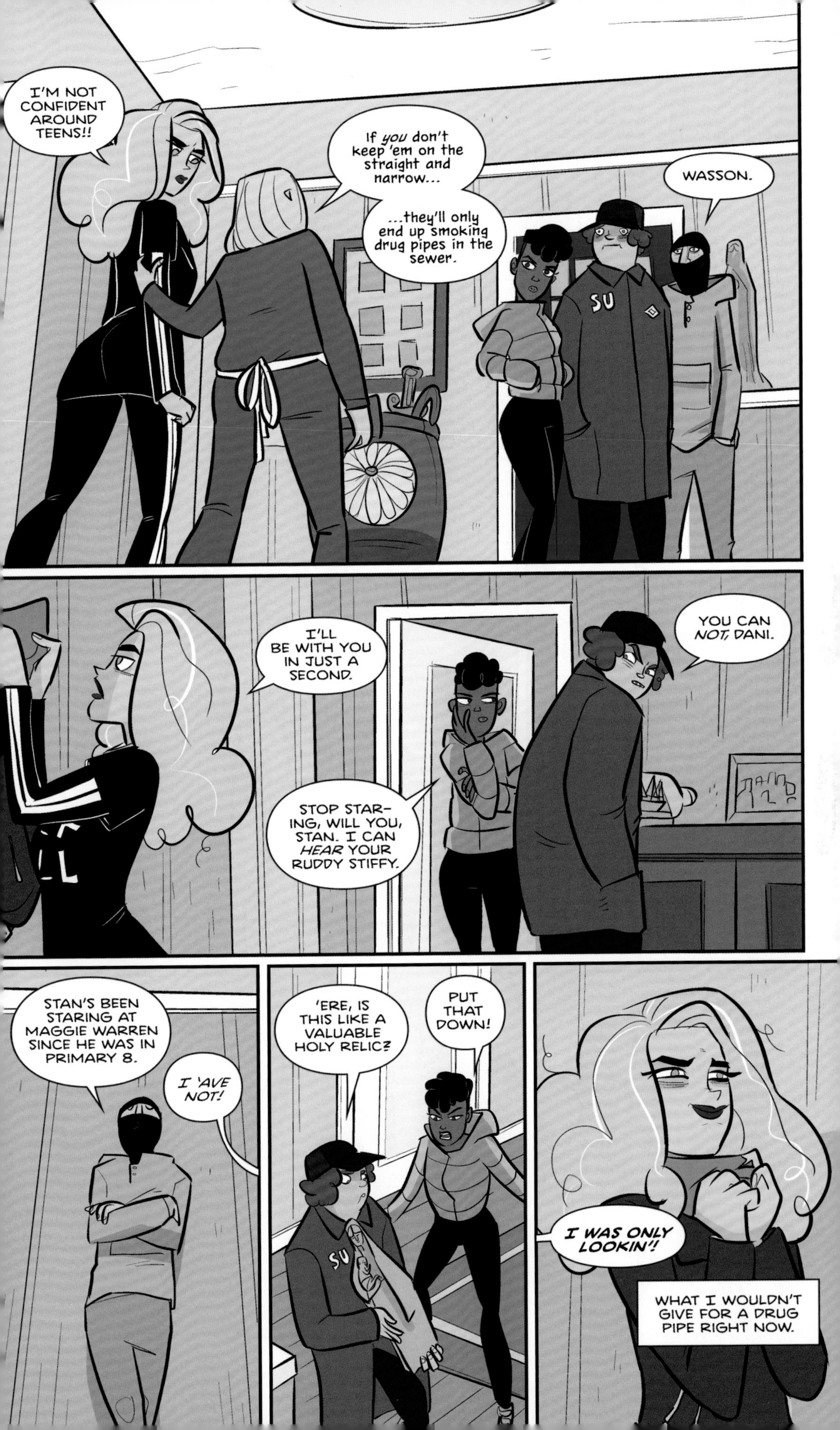
I'M NOT CONFIDENT AROUND TEENS!!
If *you* don't keep 'em on the straight and narrow...
...they'll only end up smoking drug pipes in the sewer.
WASSON.
SU
I'LL BE WITH YOU IN JUST A SECOND.
YOU CAN *NOT,* DANI.
STOP STARING, WILL YOU, STAN. I CAN *HEAR* YOUR RUDDY STIFFY.
STAN'S BEEN STARING AT MAGGIE WARREN SINCE HE WAS IN PRIMARY 8.
I 'AVE NOT!
'ERE, IS THIS LIKE A VALUABLE HOLY RELIC?
PUT THAT DOWN!
SU
I WAS ONLY LOOKIN'!
WHAT I WOULDN'T GIVE FOR A DRUG PIPE RIGHT NOW.

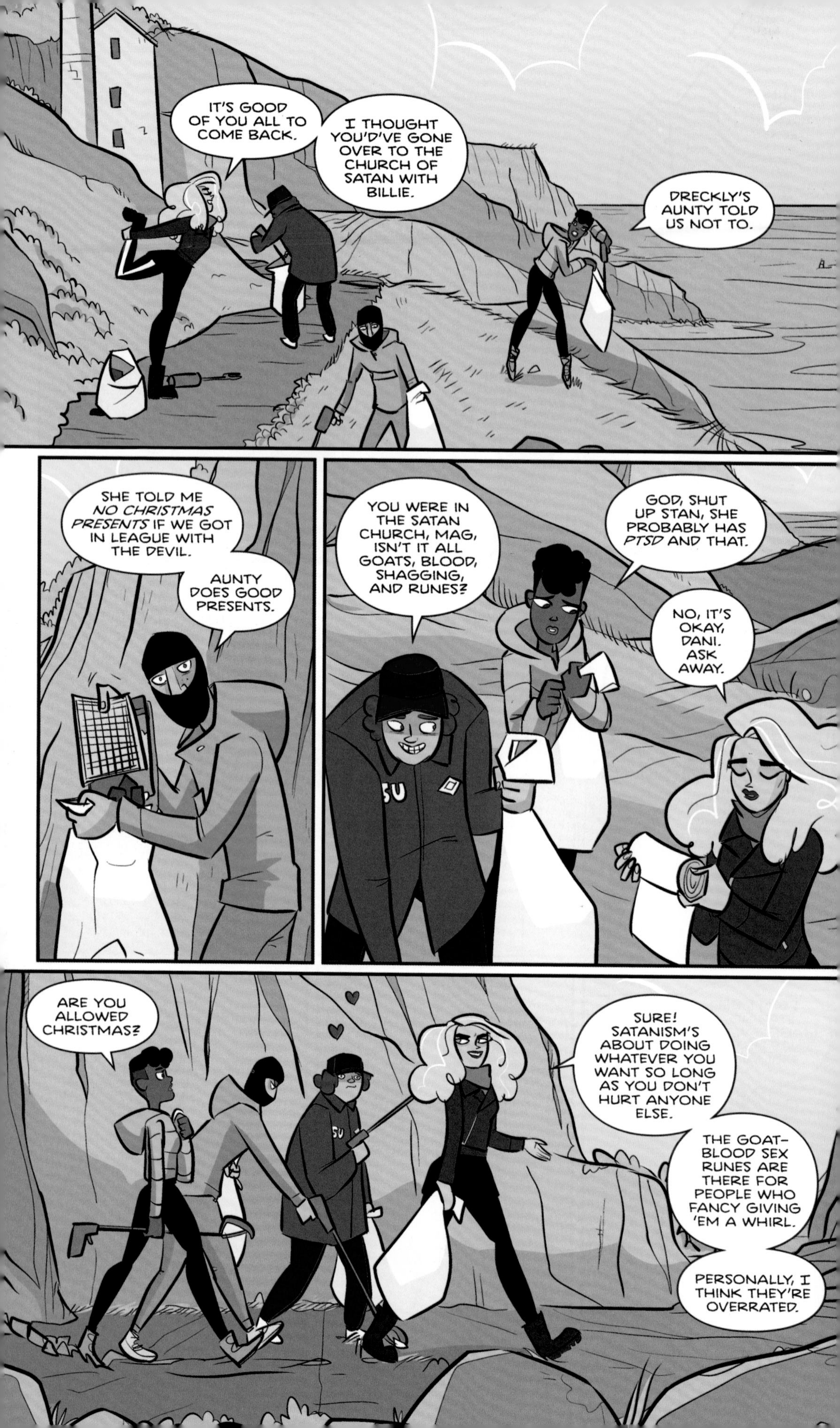
IT'S GOOD OF YOU ALL TO COME BACK.
I THOUGHT YOU'D'VE GONE OVER TO THE CHURCH OF SATAN WITH BILLIE.
DRECKLY'S AUNTY TOLD US NOT TO.
SHE TOLD ME *NO CHRISTMAS PRESENTS* IF WE GOT IN LEAGUE WITH THE DEVIL.
AUNTY DOES GOOD PRESENTS.
YOU WERE IN THE SATAN CHURCH, MAG, ISN'T IT ALL GOATS, BLOOD, SHAGGING, AND RUNES?
GOD, SHUT UP STAN, SHE PROBABLY HAS *PTSD* AND THAT.
NO, IT'S OKAY, DANI. ASK AWAY.
ARE YOU ALLOWED CHRISTMAS?
SURE! SATANISM'S ABOUT DOING WHATEVER YOU WANT SO LONG AS YOU DON'T HURT ANYONE ELSE.
THE GOAT-BLOOD SEX RUNES ARE THERE FOR PEOPLE WHO FANCY GIVING 'EM A WHIRL.
PERSONALLY, I THINK THEY'RE OVERRATED.

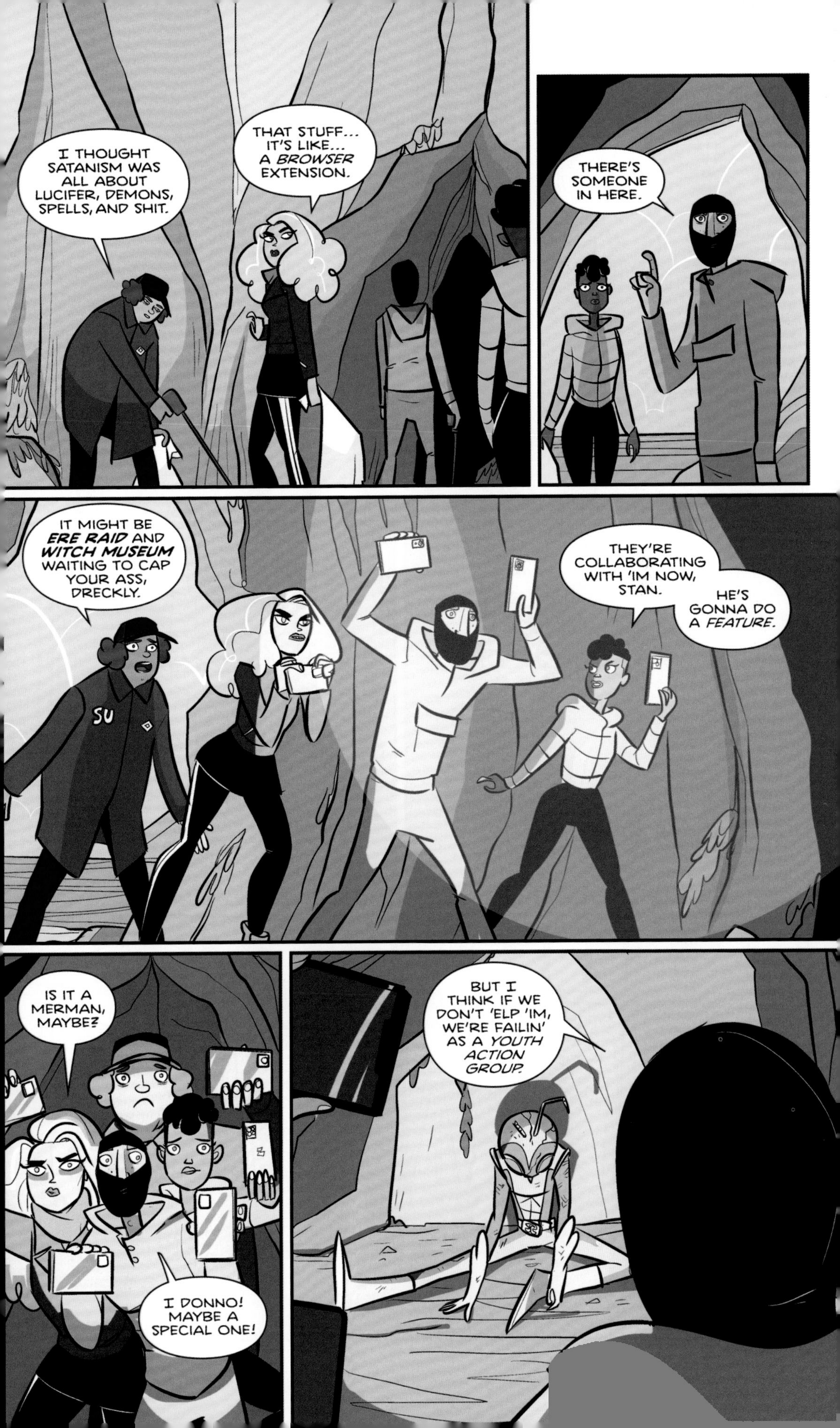

I THOUGHT SATANISM WAS ALL ABOUT LUCIFER, DEMONS, SPELLS, AND SHIT.
THAT STUFF... IT'S LIKE... A *BROWSER* EXTENSION.
THERE'S SOMEONE IN HERE.
IT MIGHT BE ***ERE RAID*** AND ***WITCH MUSEUM*** WAITING TO CAP YOUR ASS, DRECKLY.
THEY'RE COLLABORATING WITH 'IM NOW, STAN.
HE'S GONNA DO A *FEATURE*.
SU
IS IT A MERMAN, MAYBE?
I DONNO! MAYBE A SPECIAL ONE!
BUT I THINK IF WE DON'T 'ELP 'IM, WE'RE FAILIN' AS A *YOUTH ACTION GROUP*.

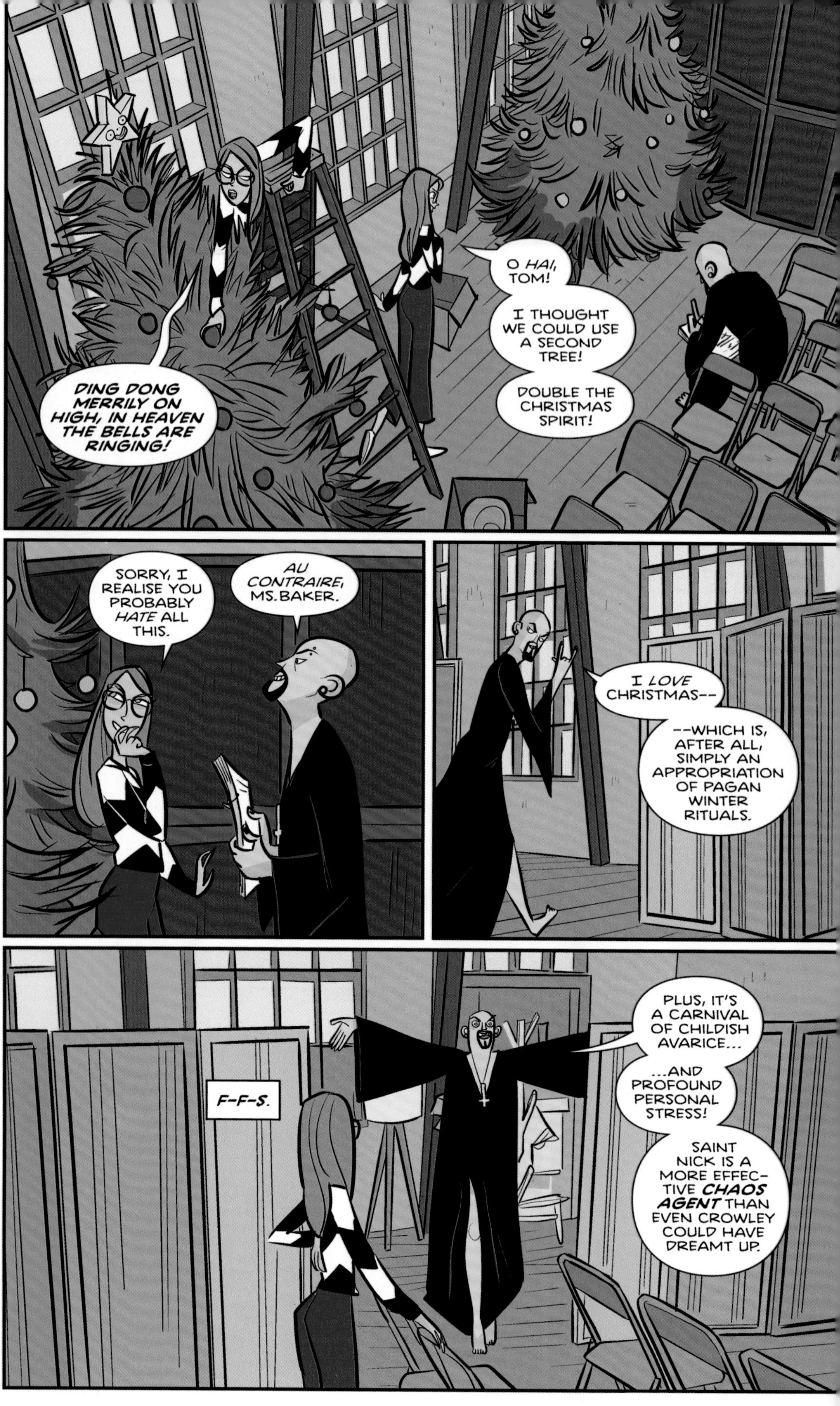
DING DONG MERRILY ON HIGH, IN HEAVEN THE BELLS ARE RINGING!
O HAI, TOM!
I THOUGHT WE COULD USE A SECOND TREE!
DOUBLE THE CHRISTMAS SPIRIT!
SORRY, I REALISE YOU PROBABLY HATE ALL THIS.
AU CONTRAIRE, MS. BAKER.
I LOVE CHRISTMAS--
--WHICH IS, AFTER ALL, SIMPLY AN APPROPRIATION OF PAGAN WINTER RITUALS.
PLUS, IT'S A CARNIVAL OF CHILDISH AVARICE...
...AND PROFOUND PERSONAL STRESS!
SAINT NICK IS A MORE EFFECTIVE CHAOS AGENT THAN EVEN CROWLEY COULD HAVE DREAMT UP.
F-F-S.

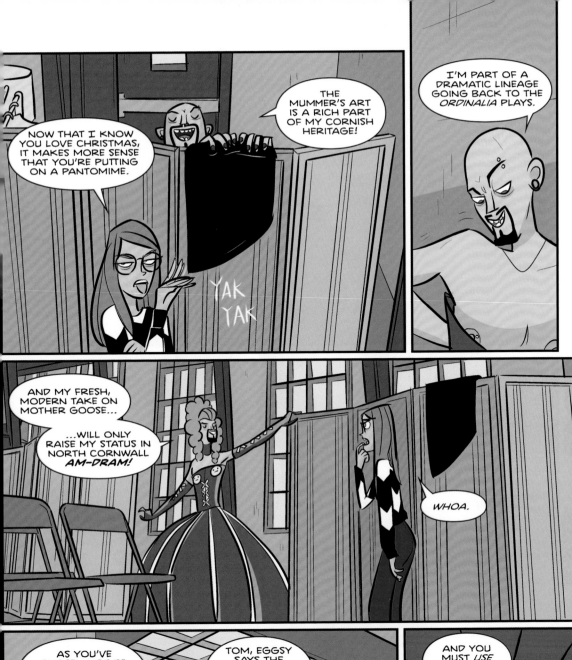

NOW THAT I KNOW YOU LOVE CHRISTMAS, IT MAKES MORE SENSE THAT YOU'RE PUTTING ON A PANTOMIME.

THE MUMMER'S ART IS A RICH PART OF MY CORNISH HERITAGE!

I'M PART OF A DRAMATIC LINEAGE GOING BACK TO THE *ORDINALIA* PLAYS.

YAK YAK

AND MY FRESH, MODERN TAKE ON MOTHER GOOSE...

...WILL ONLY RAISE MY STATUS IN NORTH CORNWALL *AM-DRAM!*

WHOA.

AS YOU'VE CHOSEN NOT TO PARTICIPATE, PLEASE LEAVE US TO OUR DRESS REHEARSAL.

TOM, EGGSY SAYS THE UNDERWIRING IN HIS TAIL IS POKIN' HIM IN THE ARSEHOLE.

AND YOU MUST *USE THAT PAIN,* EGGSY!

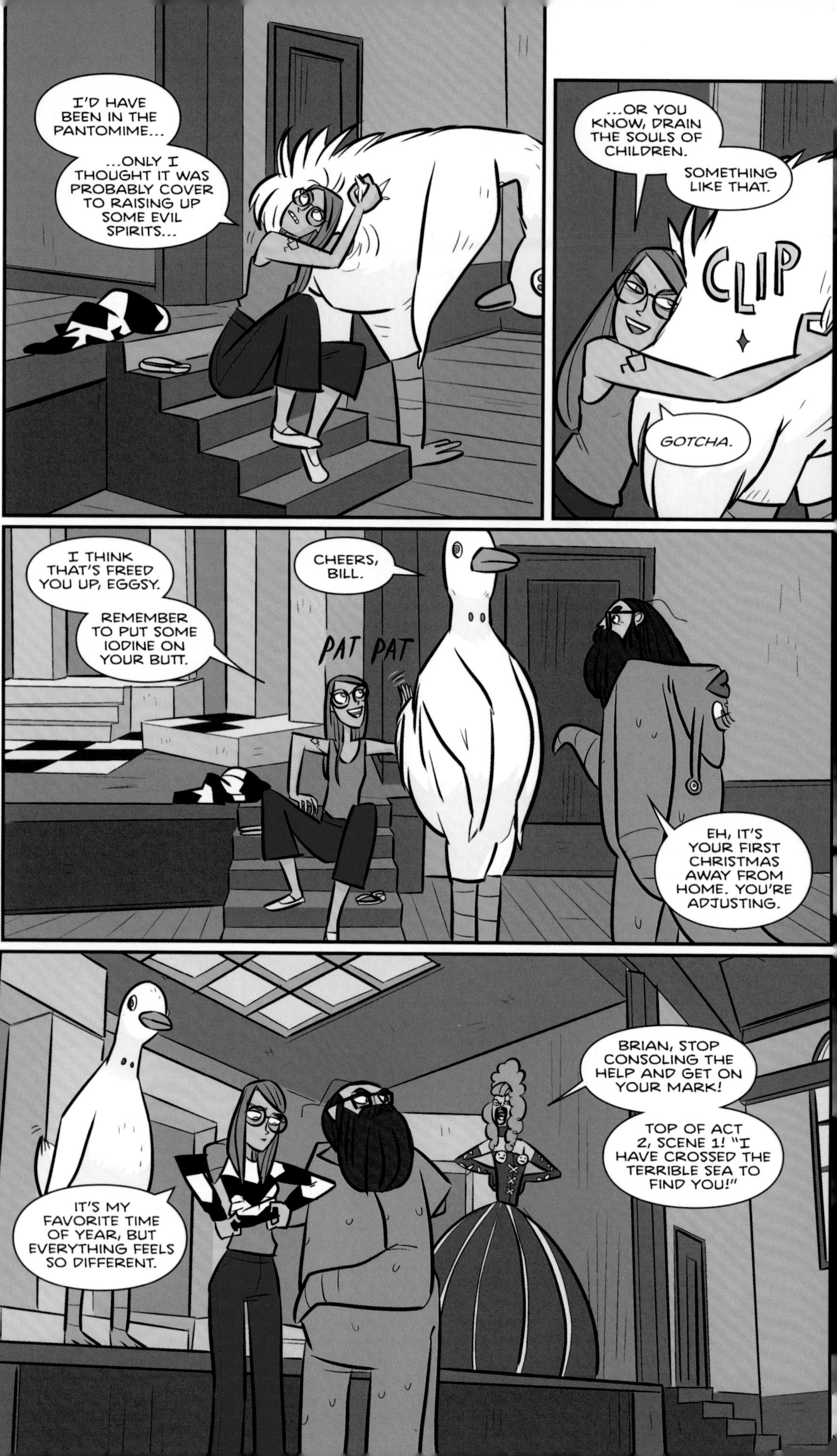
I'D HAVE BEEN IN THE PANTOMIME...
...ONLY I THOUGHT IT WAS PROBABLY COVER TO RAISING UP SOME EVIL SPIRITS...
...OR YOU KNOW, DRAIN THE SOULS OF CHILDREN.
SOMETHING LIKE THAT.
CLIP
GOTCHA.
I THINK THAT'S FREED YOU UP, EGGSY.
REMEMBER TO PUT SOME IODINE ON YOUR BUTT.
CHEERS, BILL.
PAT PAT
EH, IT'S YOUR FIRST CHRISTMAS AWAY FROM HOME. YOU'RE ADJUSTING.
IT'S MY FAVORITE TIME OF YEAR, BUT EVERYTHING FEELS SO DIFFERENT.
BRIAN, STOP CONSOLING THE HELP AND GET ON YOUR MARK!
TOP OF ACT 2, SCENE 1! "I HAVE CROSSED THE TERRIBLE SEA TO FIND YOU!"

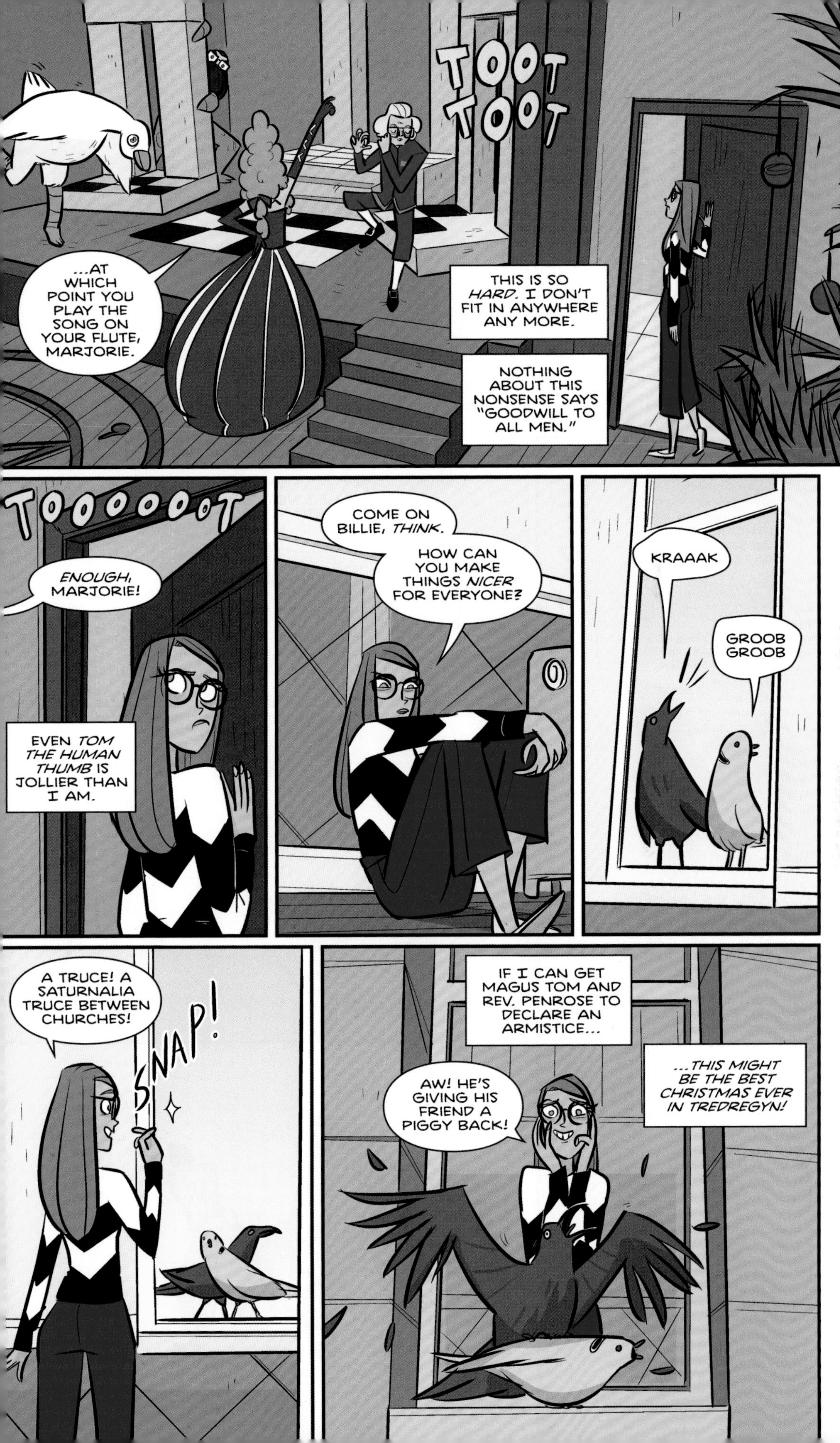
TOOT TOOT
...AT WHICH POINT YOU PLAY THE SONG ON YOUR FLUTE, MARJORIE.
THIS IS SO *HARD*. I DON'T FIT IN ANYWHERE ANY MORE.
NOTHING ABOUT THIS NONSENSE SAYS "GOODWILL TO ALL MEN."
TOOOOOOT
ENOUGH, MARJORIE!
EVEN *TOM THE HUMAN THUMB* IS JOLLIER THAN I AM.
COME ON BILLIE, *THINK*.
HOW CAN YOU MAKE THINGS *NICER* FOR EVERYONE?
KRAAAK
GROOB GROOB
A TRUCE! A SATURNALIA TRUCE BETWEEN CHURCHES!
SNAP!
IF I CAN GET MAGUS TOM AND REV. PENROSE TO DECLARE AN ARMISTICE...
AW! HE'S GIVING HIS FRIEND A PIGGY BACK!
...THIS MIGHT BE THE BEST CHRISTMAS EVER IN TREDREGYN!

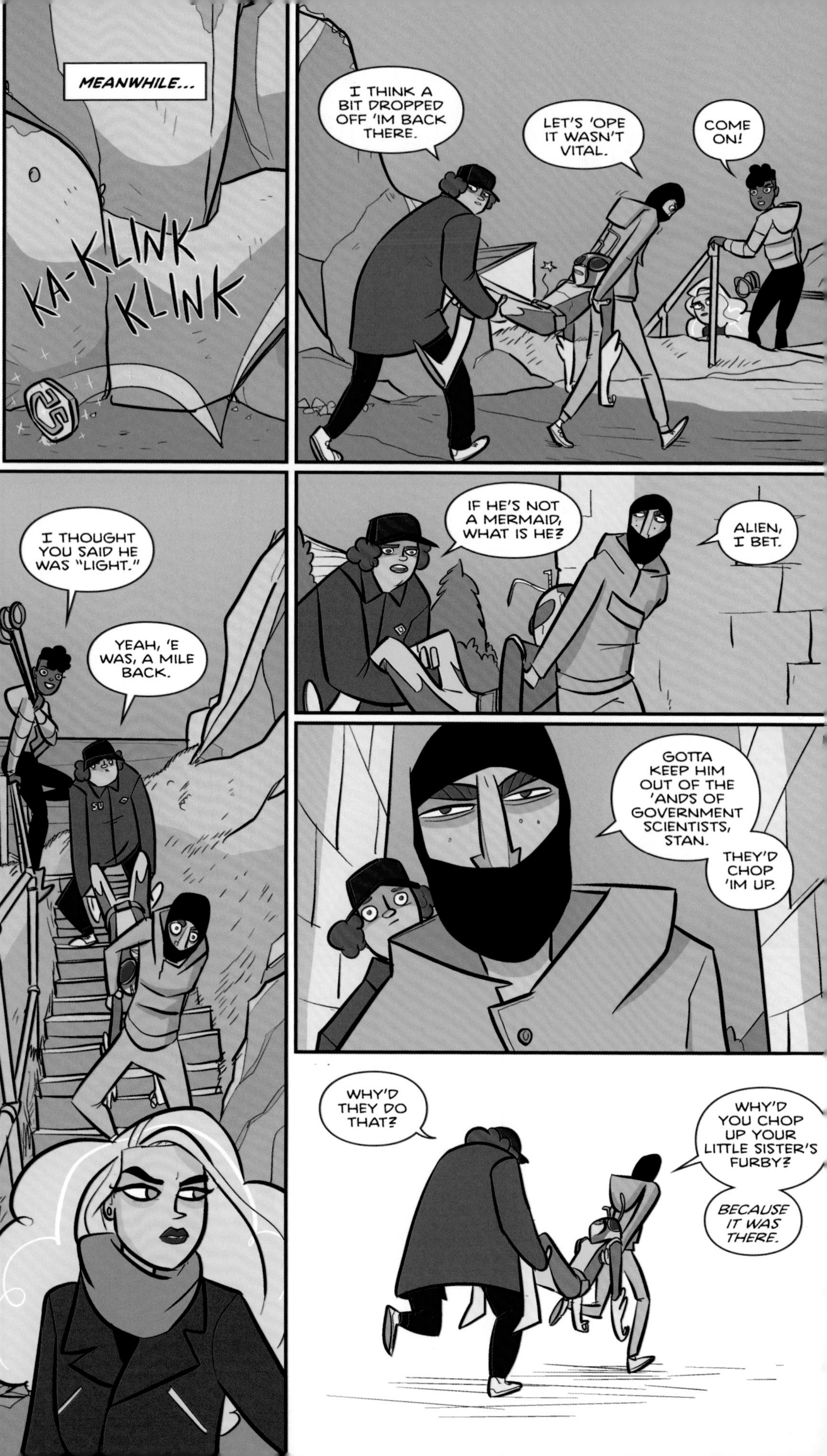
MEANWHILE...
KA-KLINK KLINK
I THINK A BIT DROPPED OFF 'IM BACK THERE.
LET'S 'OPE IT WASN'T VITAL.
COME ON!
I THOUGHT YOU SAID HE WAS "LIGHT."
YEAH, 'E WAS, A MILE BACK.
IF HE'S NOT A MERMAID, WHAT IS HE?
ALIEN, I BET.
GOTTA KEEP HIM OUT OF THE 'ANDS OF GOVERNMENT SCIENTISTS, STAN.
THEY'D CHOP 'IM UP.
WHY'D THEY DO THAT?
WHY'D YOU CHOP UP YOUR LITTLE SISTER'S FURBY?
BECAUSE IT WAS THERE.

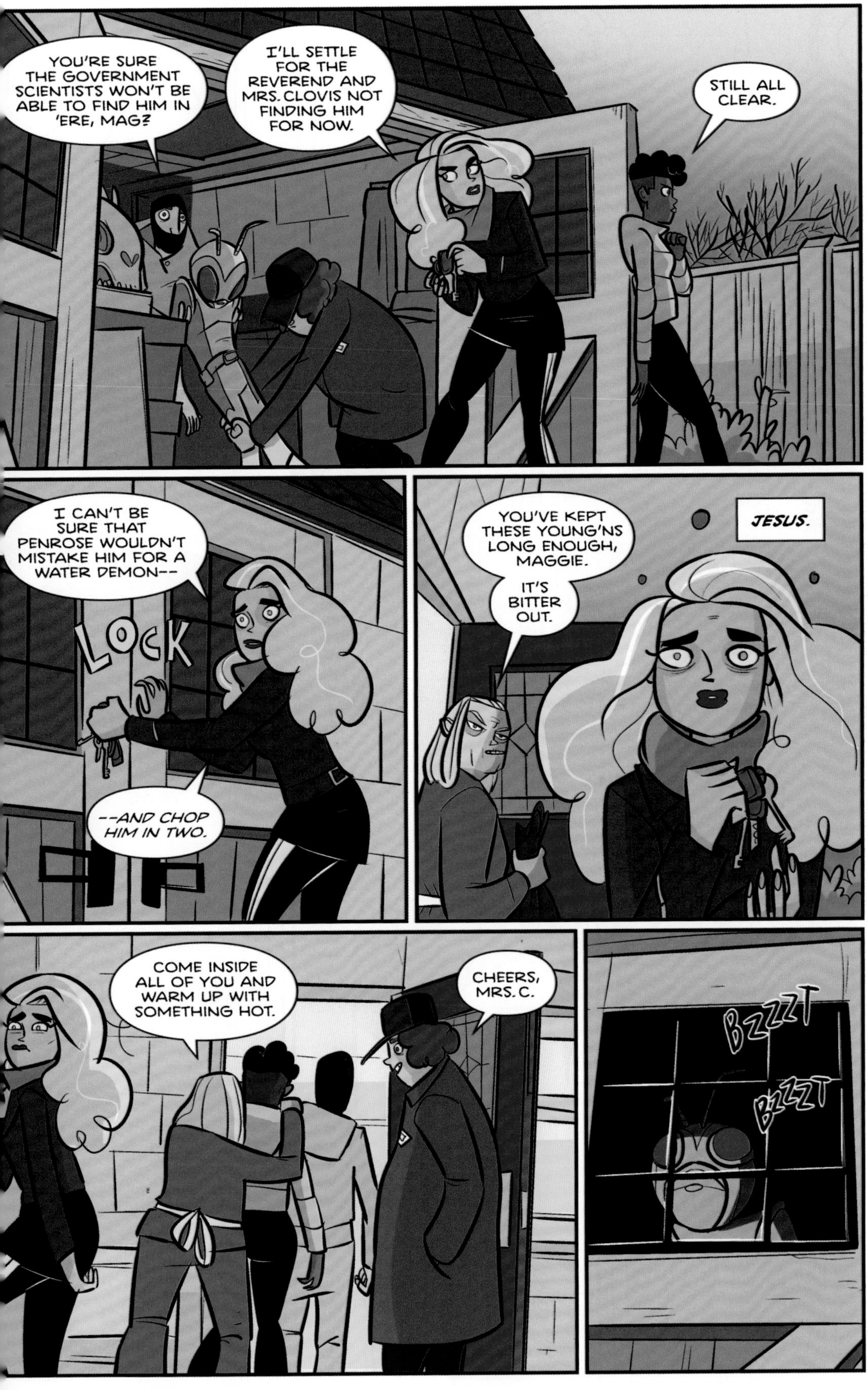
YOU'RE SURE THE GOVERNMENT SCIENTISTS WON'T BE ABLE TO FIND HIM IN 'ERE, MAG?
I'LL SETTLE FOR THE REVEREND AND MRS. CLOVIS NOT FINDING HIM FOR NOW.
STILL ALL CLEAR.
I CAN'T BE SURE THAT PENROSE WOULDN'T MISTAKE HIM FOR A WATER DEMON--
LOCK
--AND CHOP HIM IN TWO.
YOU'VE KEPT THESE YOUNG'NS LONG ENOUGH, MAGGIE.
IT'S BITTER OUT.
JESUS.
COME INSIDE ALL OF YOU AND WARM UP WITH SOMETHING HOT.
CHEERS, MRS. C.
BZZZT
BZZZT

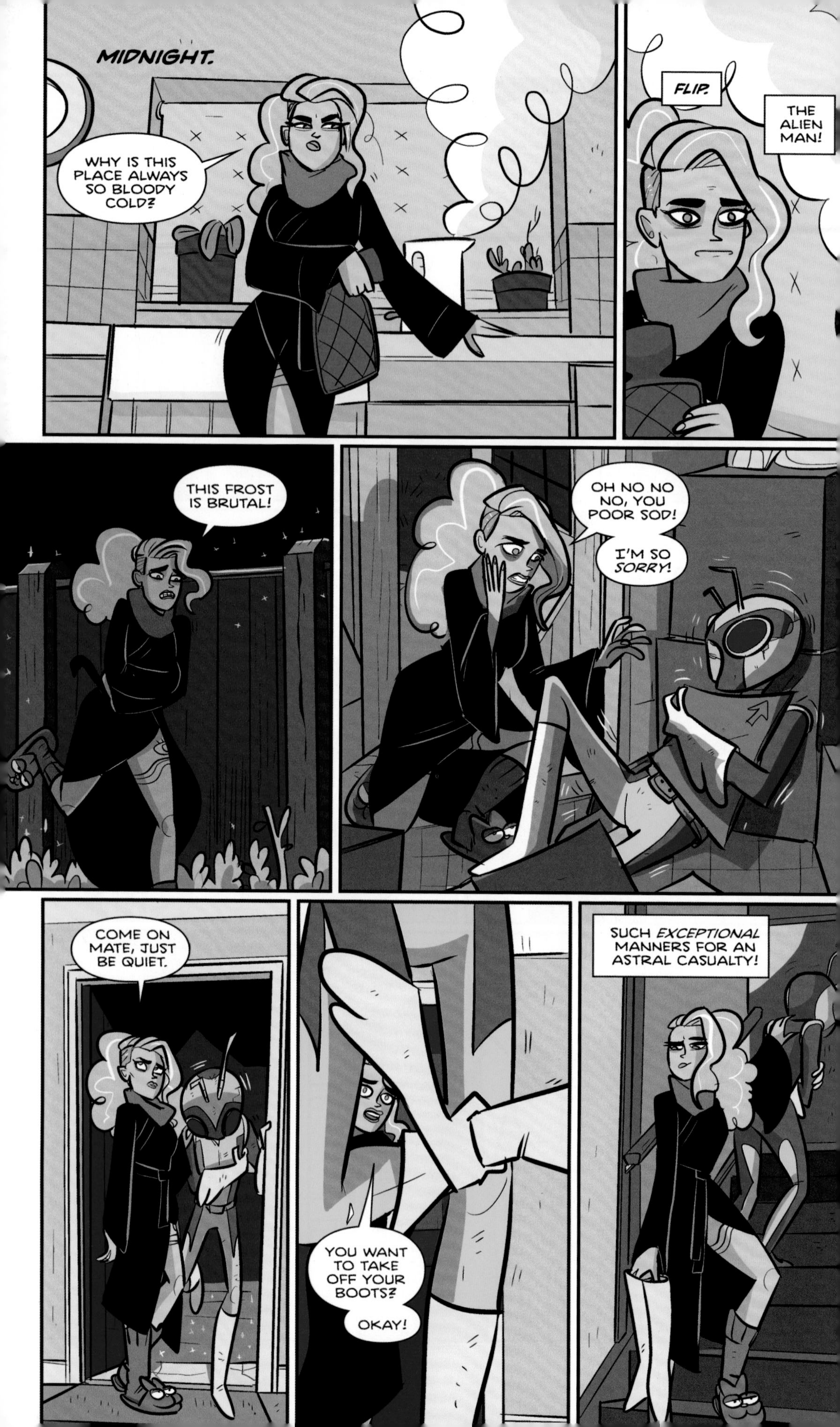

MIDNIGHT.
WHY IS THIS PLACE ALWAYS SO BLOODY COLD?
FLIP.
THE ALIEN MAN!
THIS FROST IS BRUTAL!
OH NO NO NO, YOU POOR SOD!
I'M SO *SORRY*!
COME ON MATE, JUST BE QUIET.
YOU WANT TO TAKE OFF YOUR BOOTS?
OKAY!
SUCH *EXCEPTIONAL* MANNERS FOR AN ASTRAL CASUALTY!

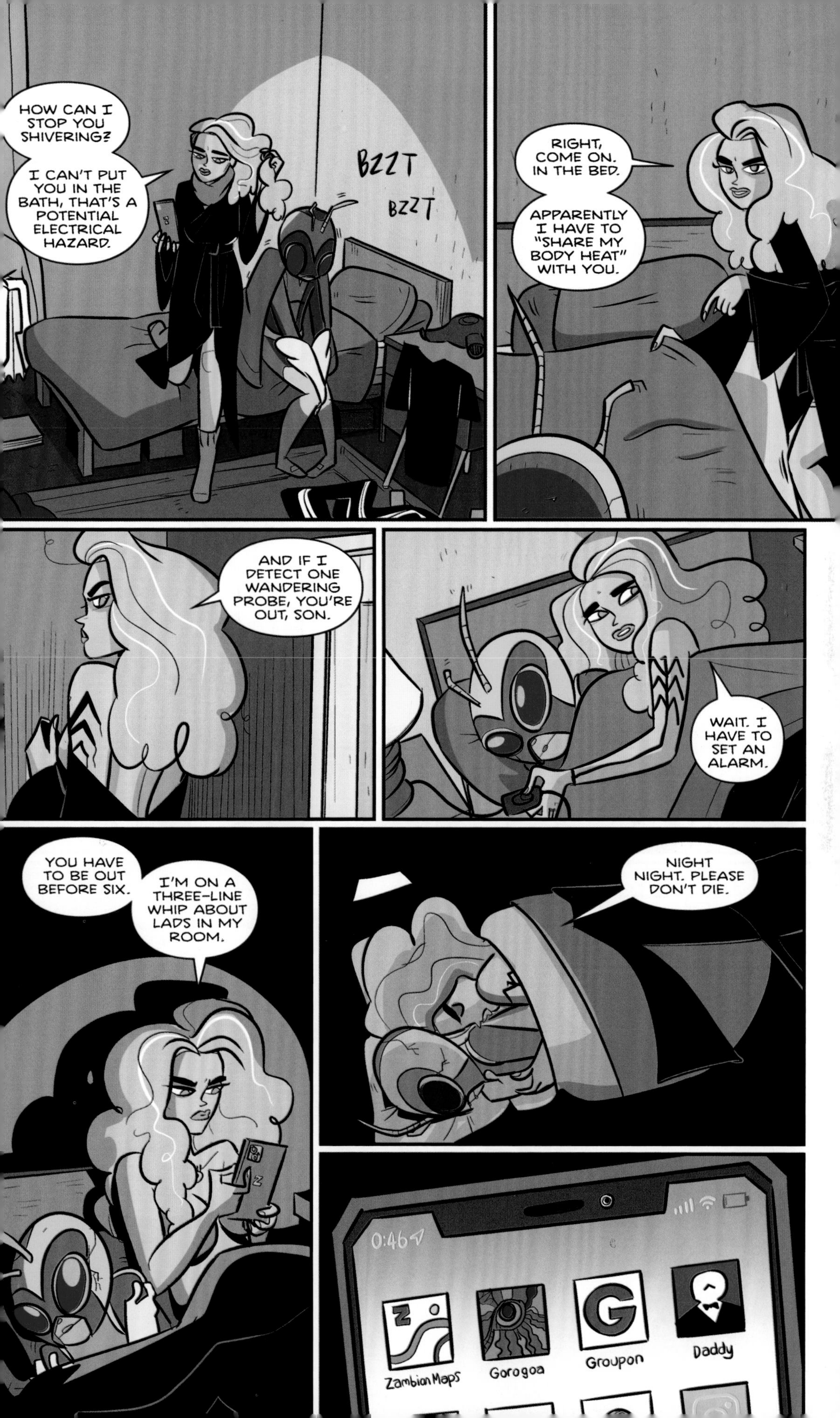

HOW CAN I STOP YOU SHIVERING?
I CAN'T PUT YOU IN THE BATH, THAT'S A POTENTIAL ELECTRICAL HAZARD.
BZZT
BZZT
RIGHT, COME ON. IN THE BED.
APPARENTLY I HAVE TO "SHARE MY BODY HEAT" WITH YOU.
AND IF I DETECT ONE WANDERING PROBE, YOU'RE OUT, SON.
WAIT. I HAVE TO SET AN ALARM.
YOU HAVE TO BE OUT BEFORE SIX.
I'M ON A THREE-LINE WHIP ABOUT LADS IN MY ROOM.
NIGHT NIGHT. PLEASE DON'T DIE.
0:46
Zambian Maps
Gorogoa
Groupon
Daddy

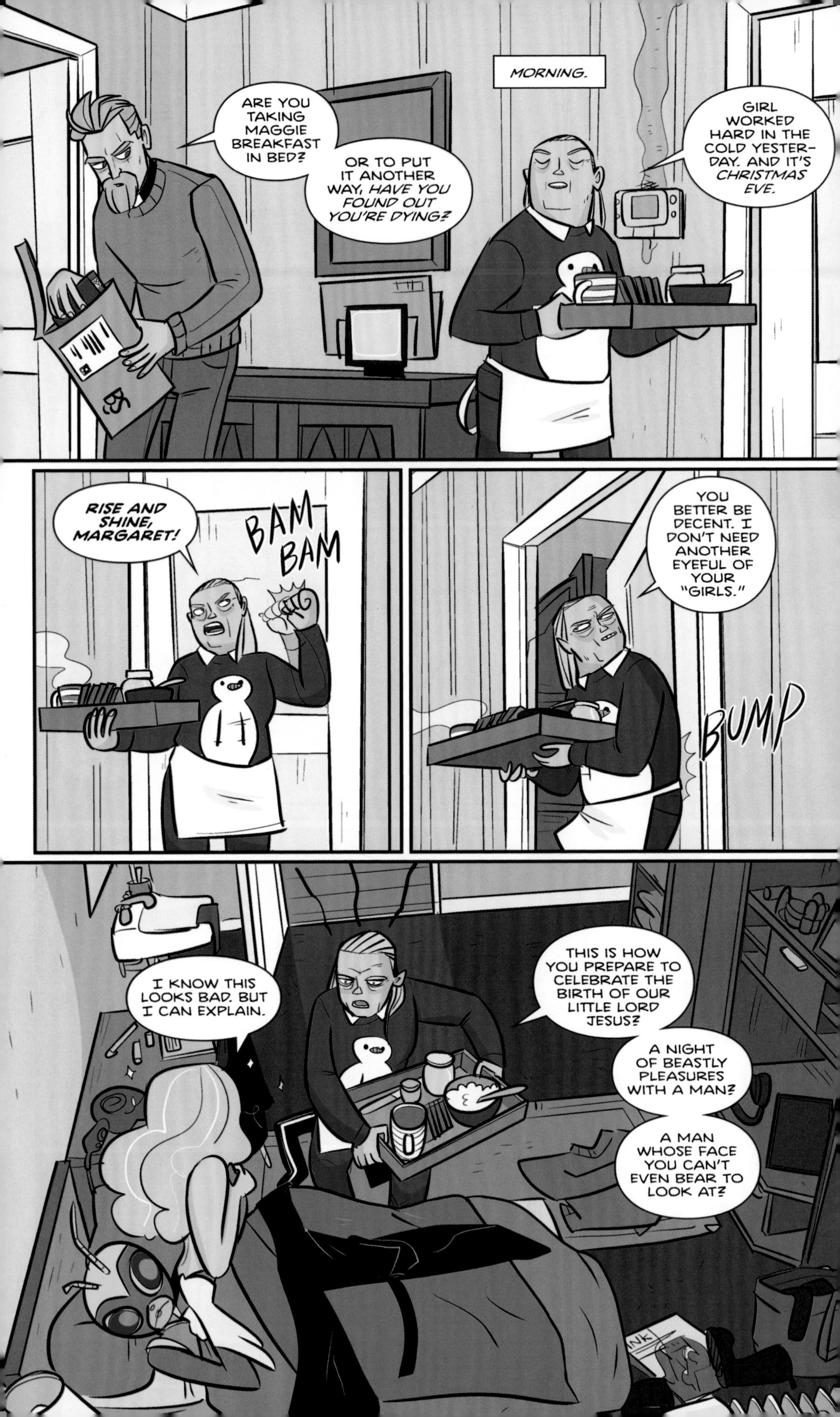
MORNING.
ARE YOU TAKING MAGGIE BREAKFAST IN BED?
OR TO PUT IT ANOTHER WAY, *HAVE YOU FOUND OUT YOU'RE DYING?*
GIRL WORKED HARD IN THE COLD YESTER-DAY. AND IT'S *CHRISTMAS EVE.*
RISE AND SHINE, MARGARET!
BAM BAM
YOU BETTER BE DECENT. I DON'T NEED ANOTHER EYEFUL OF YOUR "GIRLS."
BUMP
I KNOW THIS LOOKS BAD. BUT I CAN EXPLAIN.
THIS IS HOW YOU PREPARE TO CELEBRATE THE BIRTH OF OUR LITTLE LORD JESUS?
A NIGHT OF BEASTLY PLEASURES WITH A MAN?
A MAN WHOSE FACE YOU CAN'T EVEN BEAR TO LOOK AT?

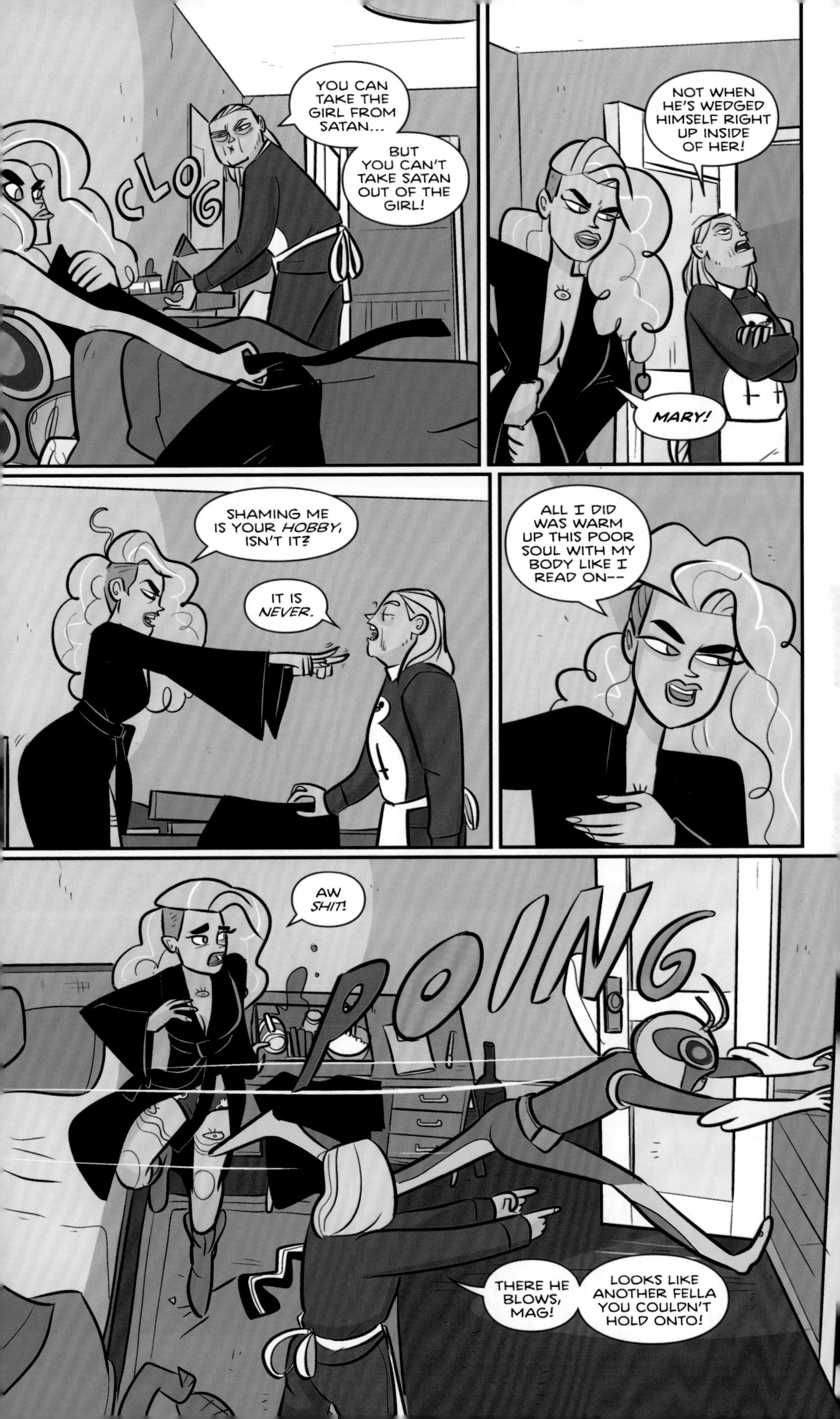
CLOG
YOU CAN TAKE THE GIRL FROM SATAN...
BUT YOU CAN'T TAKE SATAN OUT OF THE GIRL!
NOT WHEN HE'S WEDGED HIMSELF RIGHT UP INSIDE OF HER!
MARY!
SHAMING ME IS YOUR HOBBY, ISN'T IT?
IT IS NEVER.
ALL I DID WAS WARM UP THIS POOR SOUL WITH MY BODY LIKE I READ ON--
AW SHIT!
POING
THERE HE BLOWS, MAG!
LOOKS LIKE ANOTHER FELLA YOU COULDN'T HOLD ONTO!

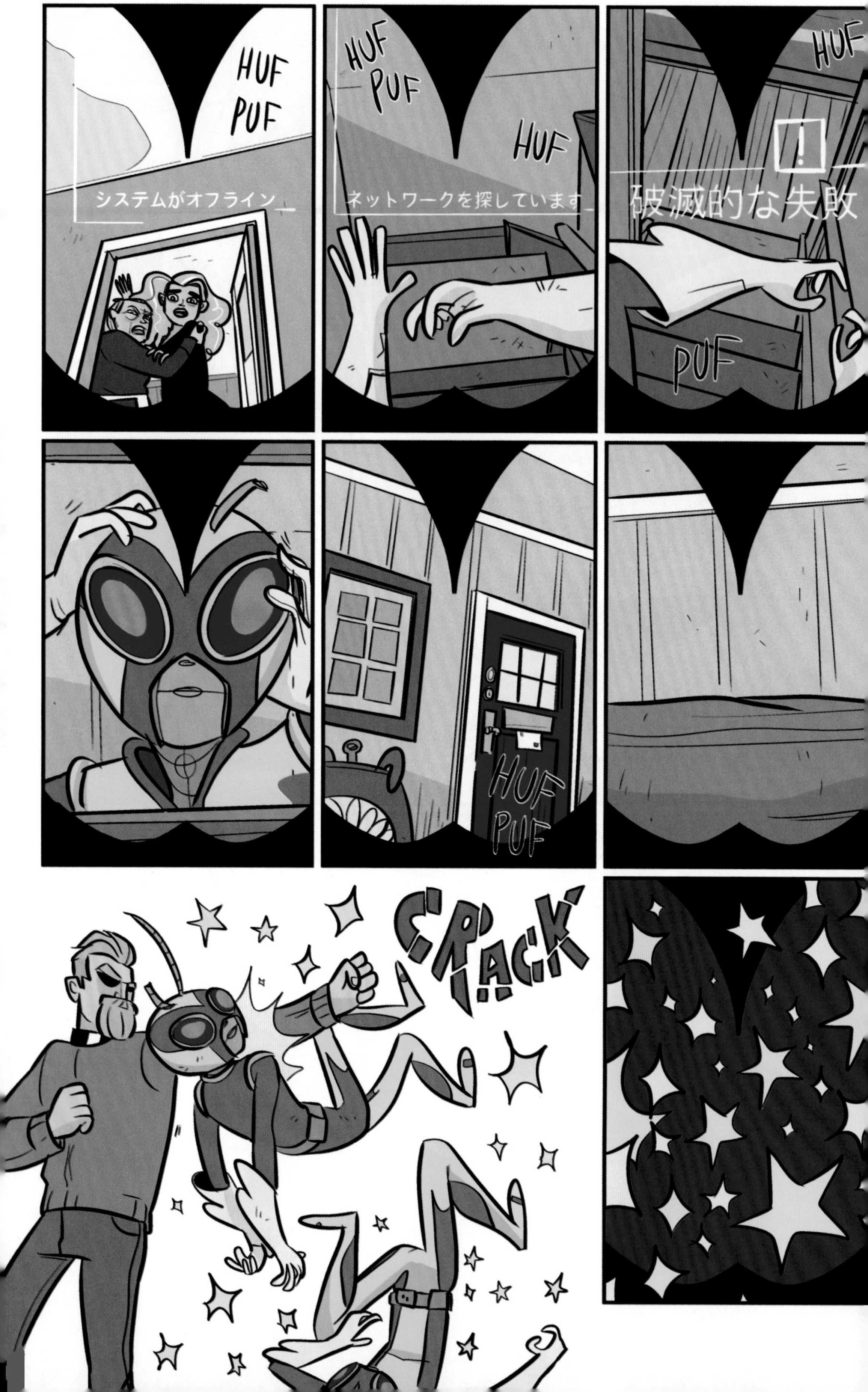
HUF
PUF
システムがオフライン_
HUF
PUF
HUF
ネットワークを探しています_
HUF
!
破滅的な失敗
PUF
HUF
PUF
CRACK

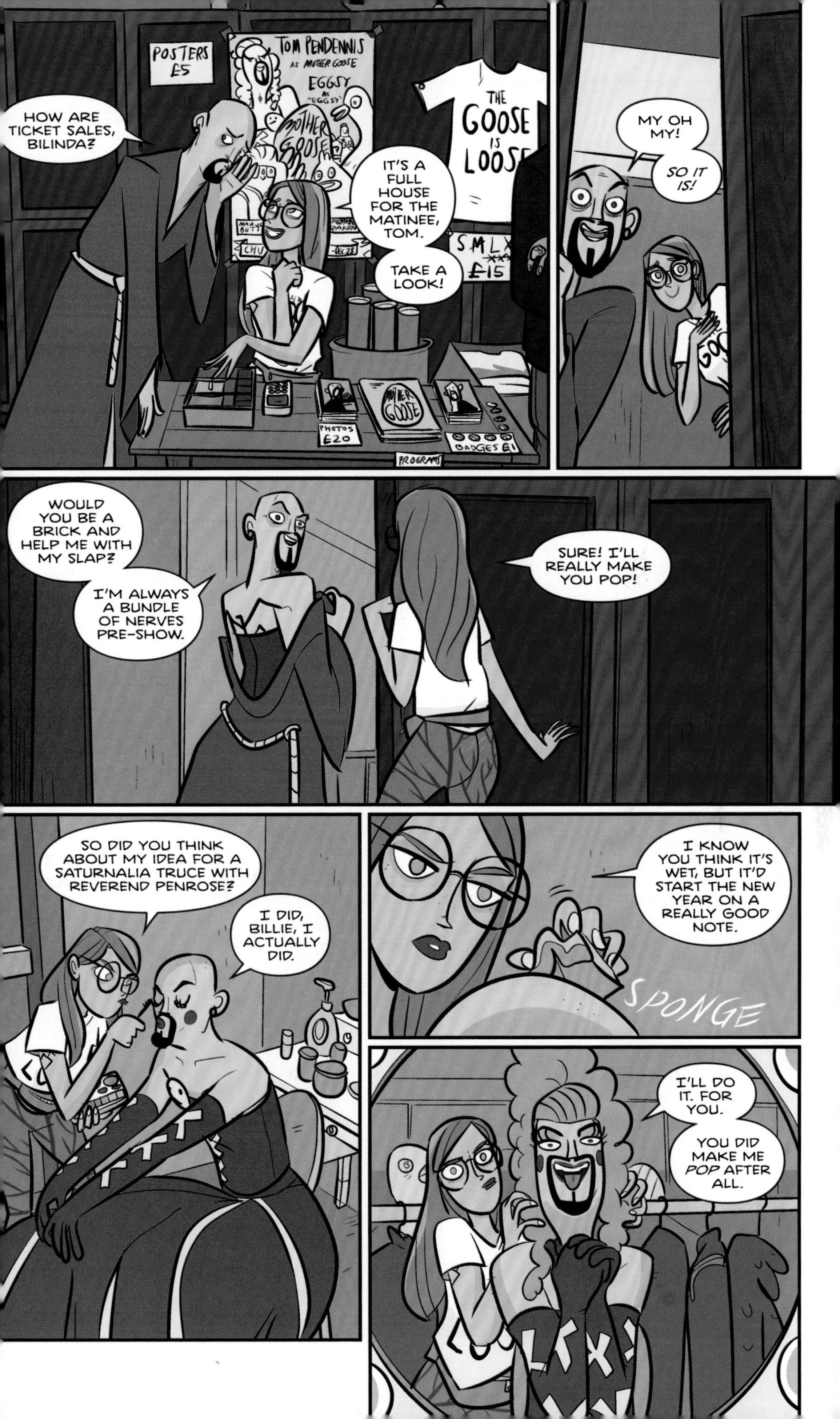
POSTERS £5
TOM PENDENNIS AS MOTHER GOOSE
EGGSY AS "EGGSY"
MOTHER GOOSE
THE GOOSE IS LOOSE
SMLX £15
HOW ARE TICKET SALES, BILINDA?
IT'S A FULL HOUSE FOR THE MATINEE, TOM.
TAKE A LOOK!
PHOTOS £20
BADGES £1
PROGRAMS
MY OH MY!
SO IT IS!
WOULD YOU BE A BRICK AND HELP ME WITH MY SLAP?
I'M ALWAYS A BUNDLE OF NERVES PRE-SHOW.
SURE! I'LL REALLY MAKE YOU POP!
SO DID YOU THINK ABOUT MY IDEA FOR A SATURNALIA TRUCE WITH REVEREND PENROSE?
I DID, BILLIE, I ACTUALLY DID.
I KNOW YOU THINK IT'S WET, BUT IT'D START THE NEW YEAR ON A REALLY GOOD NOTE.
SPONGE
I'LL DO IT. FOR YOU.
YOU DID MAKE ME *POP* AFTER ALL.

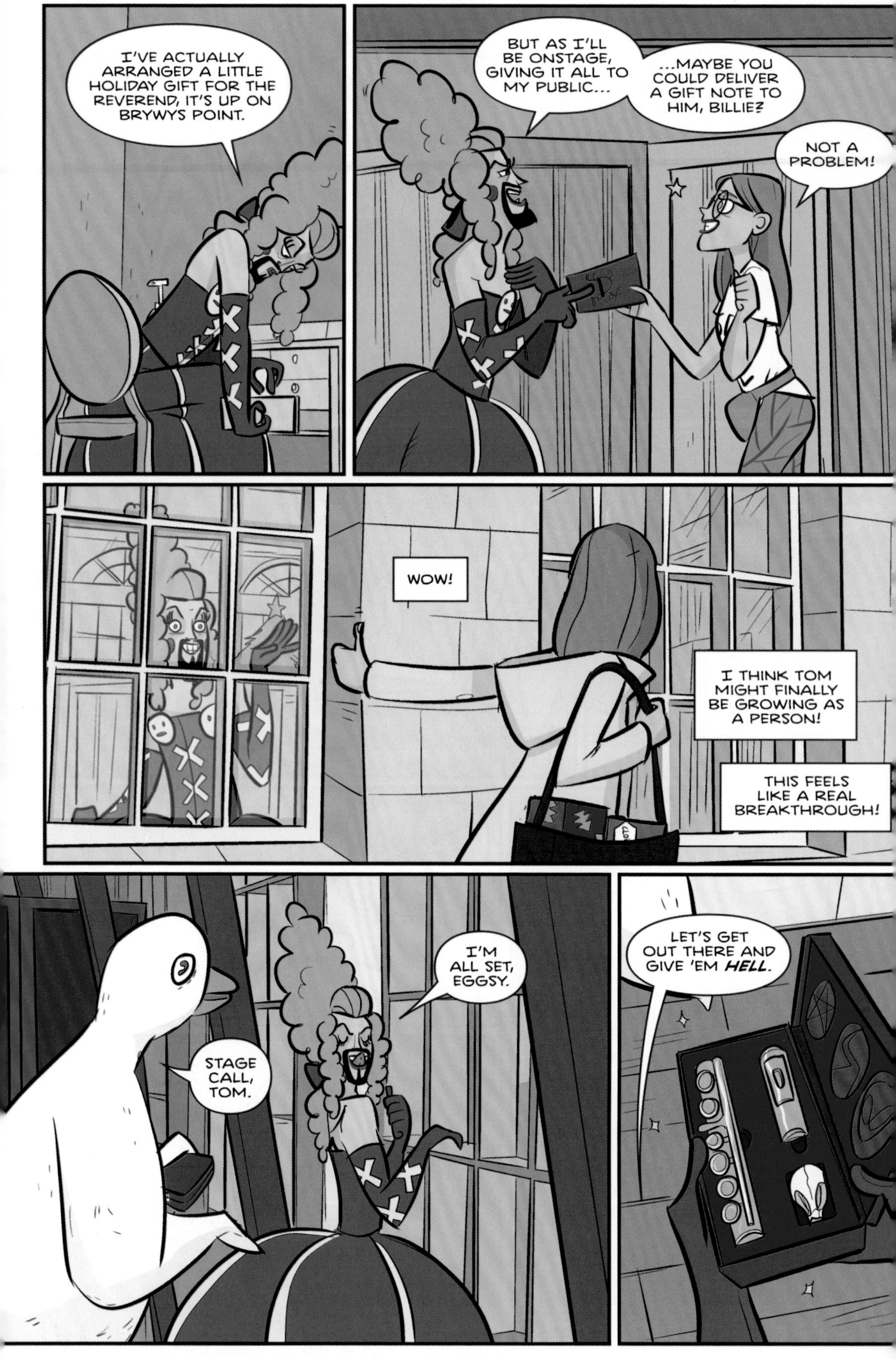
I'VE ACTUALLY ARRANGED A LITTLE HOLIDAY GIFT FOR THE REVEREND, IT'S UP ON BRYWYS POINT.
BUT AS I'LL BE ONSTAGE, GIVING IT ALL TO MY PUBLIC...
...MAYBE YOU COULD DELIVER A GIFT NOTE TO HIM, BILLIE?
NOT A PROBLEM!
WOW!
I THINK TOM MIGHT FINALLY BE GROWING AS A PERSON!
THIS FEELS LIKE A REAL BREAKTHROUGH!
STAGE CALL, TOM.
I'M ALL SET, EGGSY.
LET'S GET OUT THERE AND GIVE 'EM *HELL*.

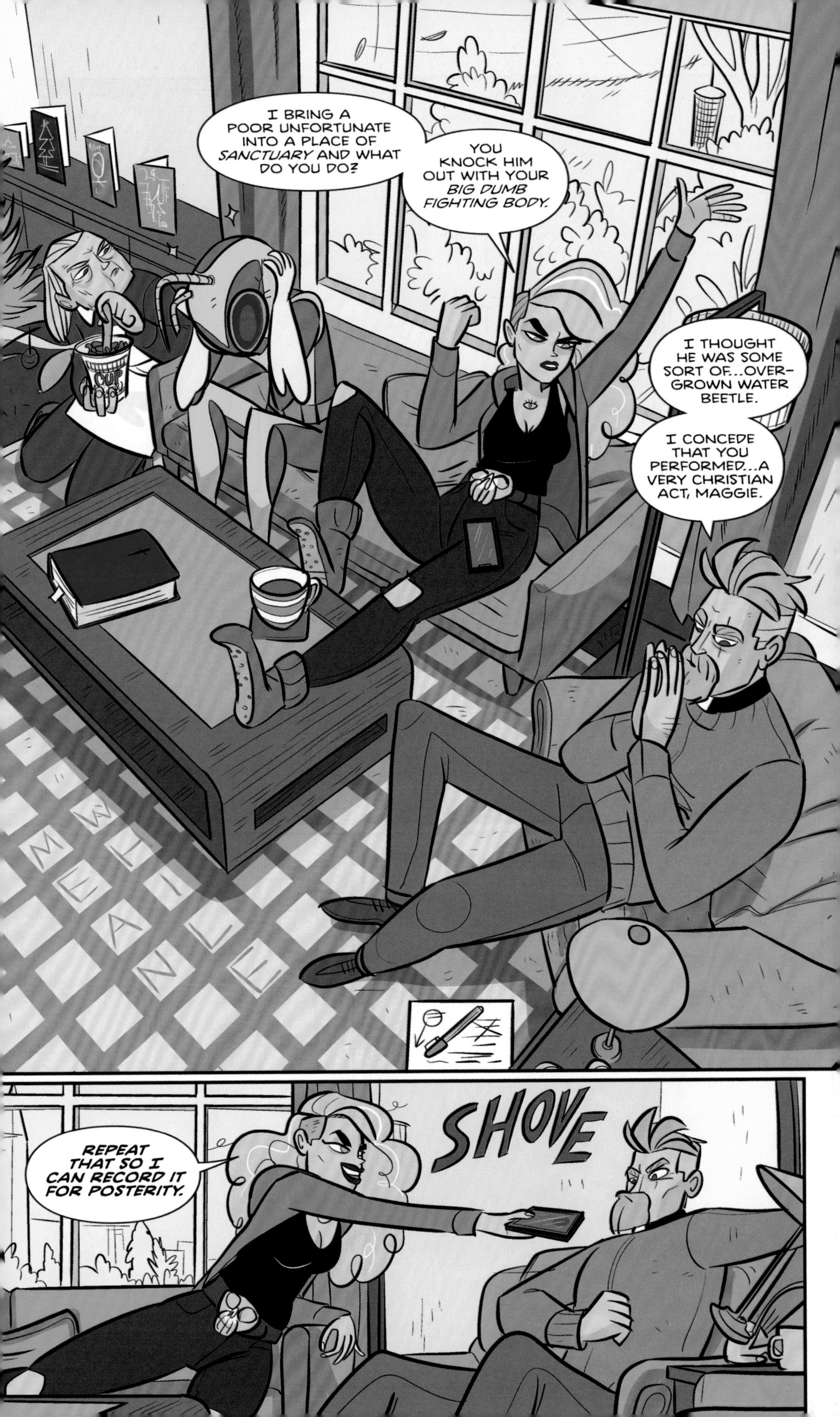
I BRING A POOR UNFORTUNATE INTO A PLACE OF *SANCTUARY* AND WHAT DO YOU DO?
YOU KNOCK HIM OUT WITH YOUR *BIG DUMB FIGHTING BODY.*
I THOUGHT HE WAS SOME SORT OF...OVER-GROWN WATER BEETLE.
I CONCEDE THAT YOU PERFORMED...A VERY CHRISTIAN ACT, MAGGIE.
SHOVE
REPEAT THAT SO I CAN RECORD IT FOR POSTERITY.

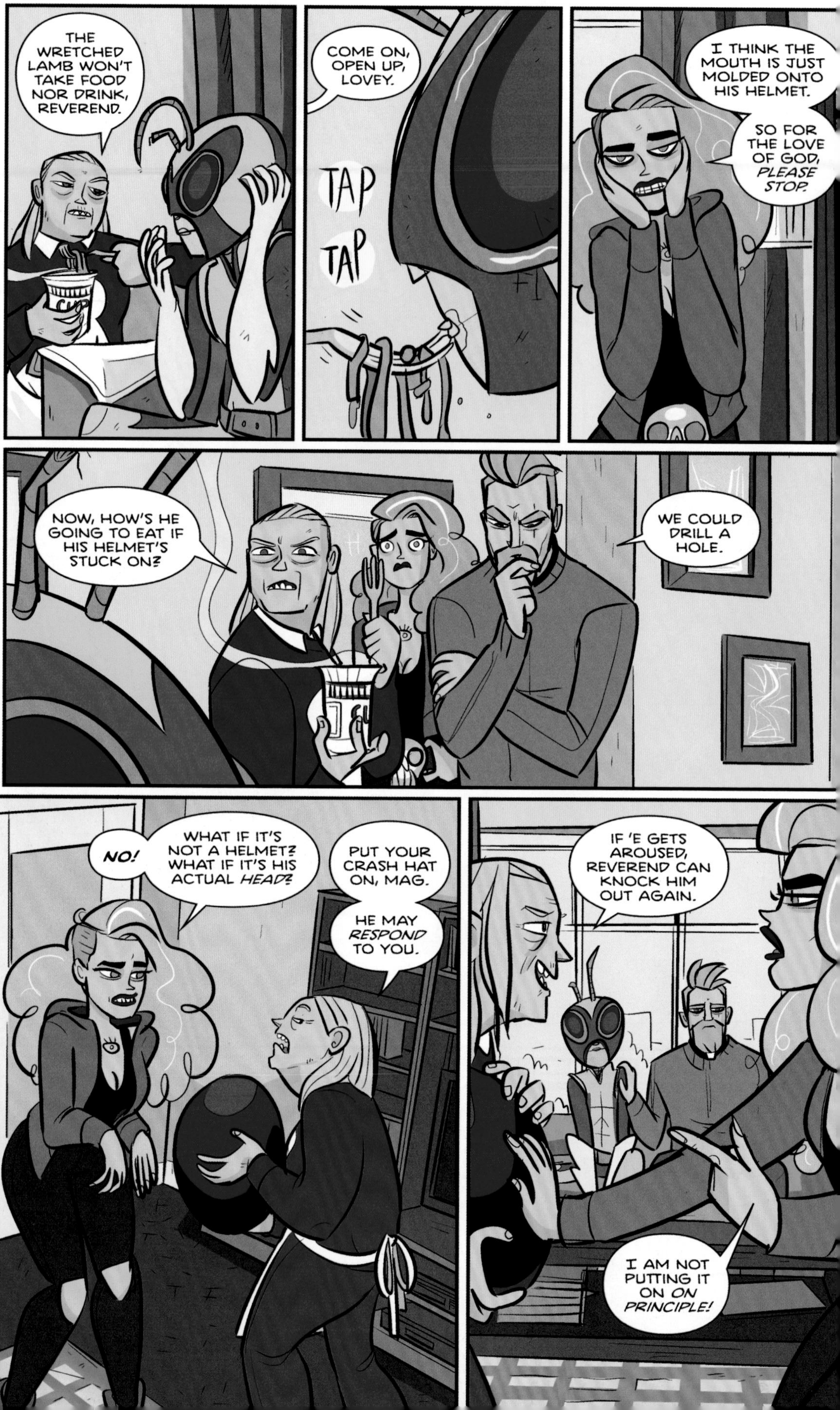
THE WRETCHED LAMB WON'T TAKE FOOD NOR DRINK, REVEREND.
COME ON, OPEN UP, LOVEY.
TAP
TAP
I THINK THE MOUTH IS JUST MOLDED ONTO HIS HELMET.
SO FOR THE LOVE OF GOD, *PLEASE STOP.*
NOW, HOW'S HE GOING TO EAT IF HIS HELMET'S STUCK ON?
WE COULD DRILL A HOLE.
NO!
WHAT IF IT'S NOT A HELMET? WHAT IF IT'S HIS ACTUAL *HEAD?*
PUT YOUR CRASH HAT ON, MAG.
HE MAY *RESPOND* TO YOU.
IF 'E GETS AROUSED, REVEREND CAN KNOCK HIM OUT AGAIN.
I AM NOT PUTTING IT ON *ON PRINCIPLE!*

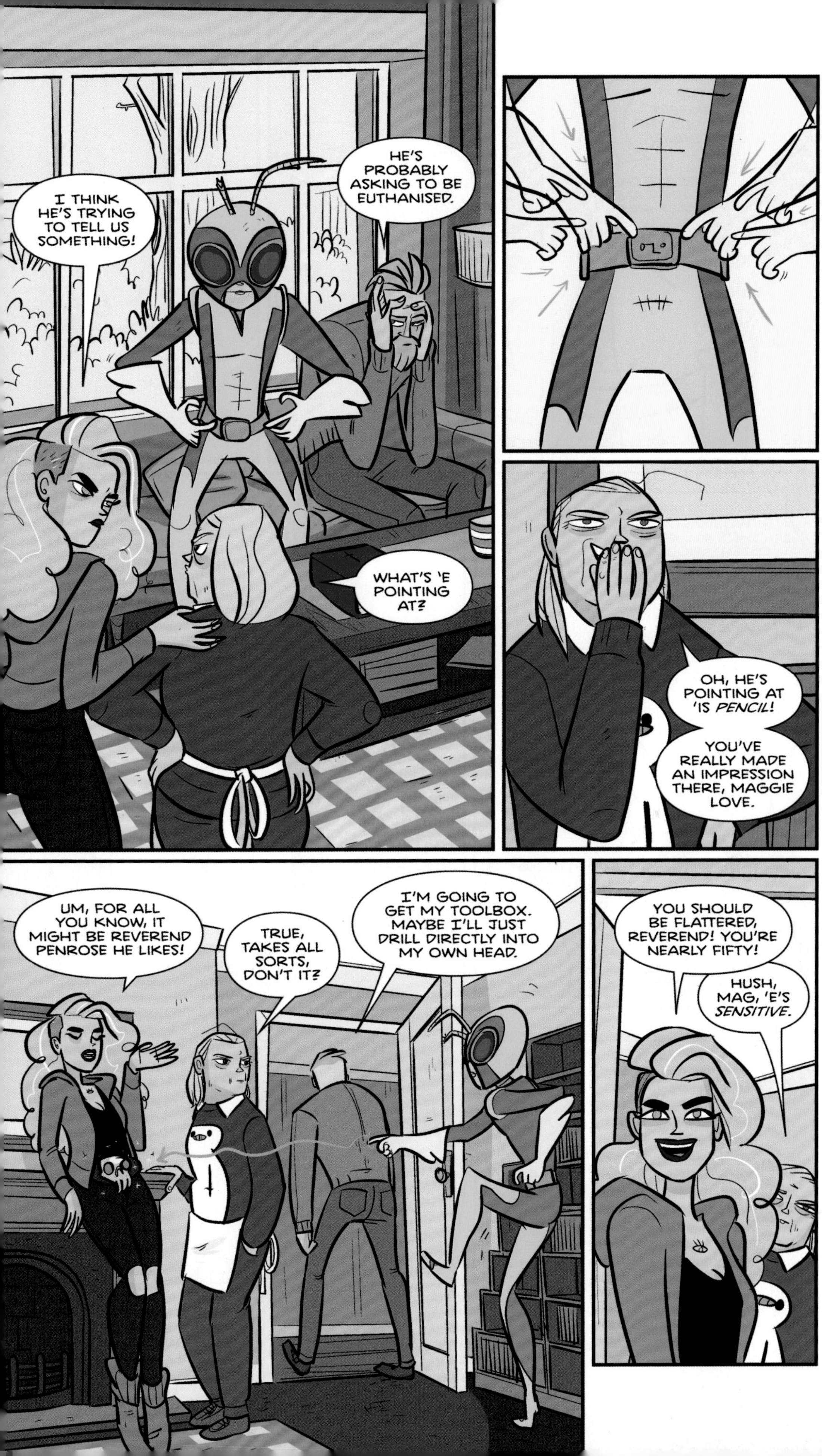
I THINK HE'S TRYING TO TELL US SOMETHING!
HE'S PROBABLY ASKING TO BE EUTHANISED.
WHAT'S 'E POINTING AT?
OH, HE'S POINTING AT 'IS *PENCIL*!
YOU'VE REALLY MADE AN IMPRESSION THERE, MAGGIE LOVE.
UM, FOR ALL YOU KNOW, IT MIGHT BE REVEREND PENROSE HE LIKES!
TRUE, TAKES ALL SORTS, DON'T IT?
I'M GOING TO GET MY TOOLBOX. MAYBE I'LL JUST DRILL DIRECTLY INTO MY OWN HEAD.
YOU SHOULD BE FLATTERED, REVEREND! YOU'RE NEARLY FIFTY!
HUSH, MAG, 'E'S *SENSITIVE*.

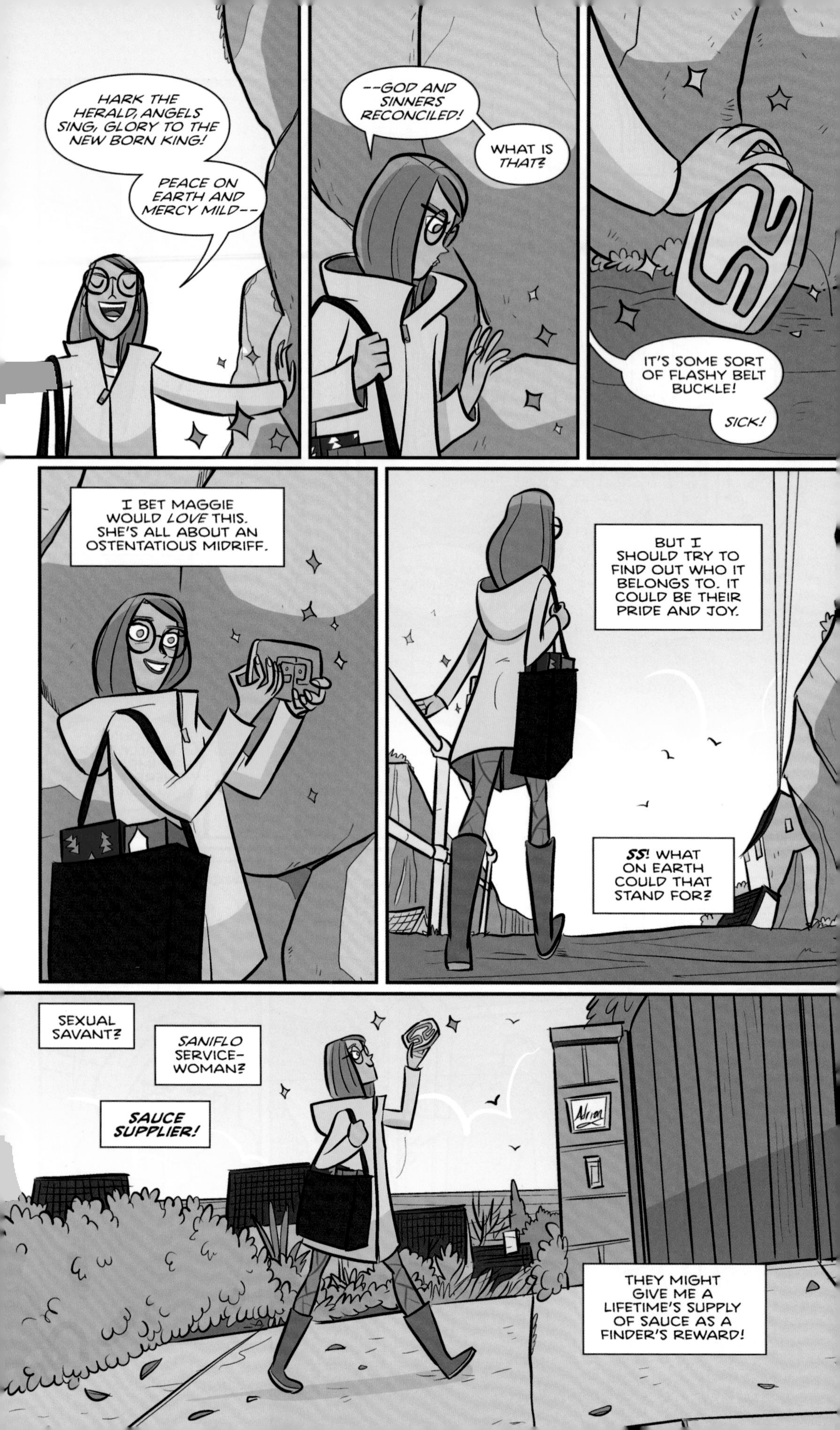
HARK THE HERALD, ANGELS SING, GLORY TO THE NEW BORN KING!
PEACE ON EARTH AND MERCY MILD--
--GOD AND SINNERS RECONCILED!
WHAT IS *THAT*?
IT'S SOME SORT OF FLASHY BELT BUCKLE!
SICK!
I BET MAGGIE WOULD *LOVE* THIS. SHE'S ALL ABOUT AN OSTENTATIOUS MIDRIFF.
BUT I SHOULD TRY TO FIND OUT WHO IT BELONGS TO. IT COULD BE THEIR PRIDE AND JOY.
SS! WHAT ON EARTH COULD THAT STAND FOR?
SEXUAL SAVANT?
SANIFLO SERVICE-WOMAN?
SAUCE SUPPLIER!
Adrian
THEY MIGHT GIVE ME A LIFETIME'S SUPPLY OF SAUCE AS A FINDER'S REWARD!

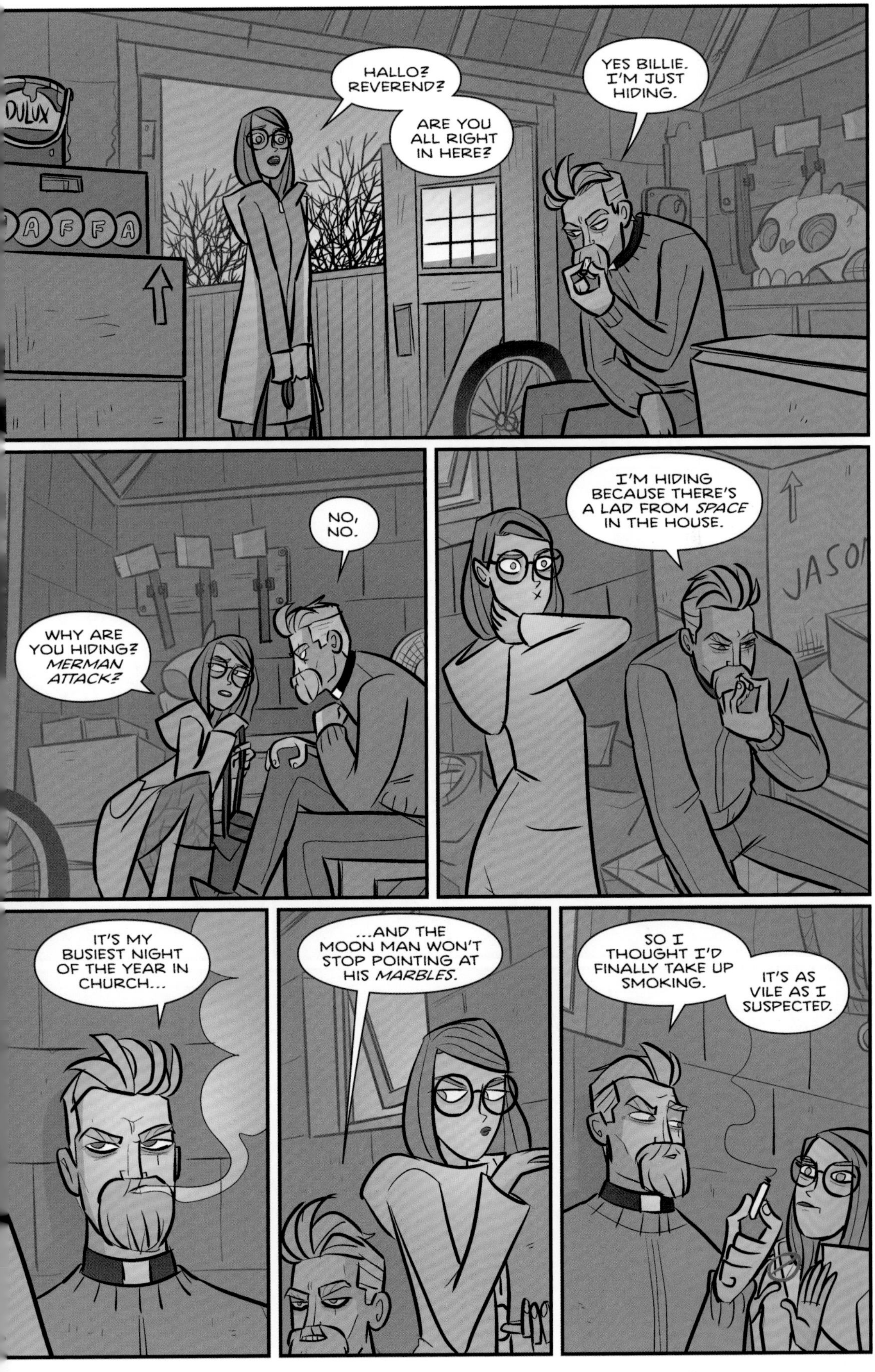
DULUX
DAFFA
HALLO? REVEREND?
ARE YOU ALL RIGHT IN HERE?
YES BILLIE. I'M JUST HIDING.
WHY ARE YOU HIDING? *MERMAN ATTACK?*
NO, NO.
I'M HIDING BECAUSE THERE'S A LAD FROM *SPACE* IN THE HOUSE.
JASON
IT'S MY BUSIEST NIGHT OF THE YEAR IN CHURCH...
...AND THE MOON MAN WON'T STOP POINTING AT HIS *MARBLES.*
SO I THOUGHT I'D FINALLY TAKE UP SMOKING.
IT'S AS VILE AS I SUSPECTED.

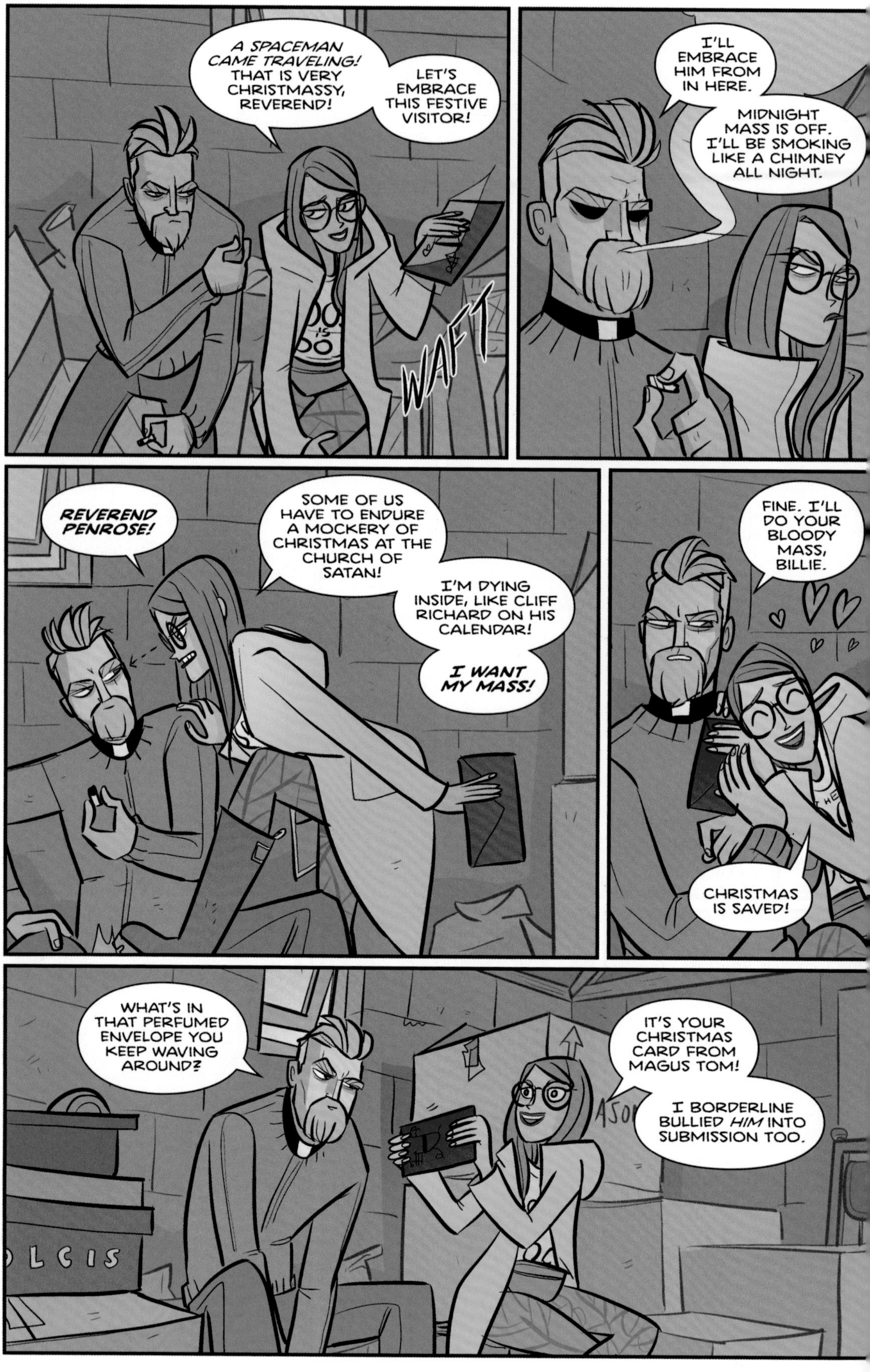
A SPACEMAN CAME TRAVELING! THAT IS VERY CHRISTMASSY, REVEREND!
LET'S EMBRACE THIS FESTIVE VISITOR!
WAFT
I'LL EMBRACE HIM FROM IN HERE.
MIDNIGHT MASS IS OFF. I'LL BE SMOKING LIKE A CHIMNEY ALL NIGHT.
REVEREND PENROSE!
SOME OF US HAVE TO ENDURE A MOCKERY OF CHRISTMAS AT THE CHURCH OF SATAN!
I'M DYING INSIDE, LIKE CLIFF RICHARD ON HIS CALENDAR!
I WANT MY MASS!
FINE. I'LL DO YOUR BLOODY MASS, BILLIE.
CHRISTMAS IS SAVED!
WHAT'S IN THAT PERFUMED ENVELOPE YOU KEEP WAVING AROUND?
IT'S YOUR CHRISTMAS CARD FROM MAGUS TOM!
I BORDERLINE BULLIED HIM INTO SUBMISSION TOO.

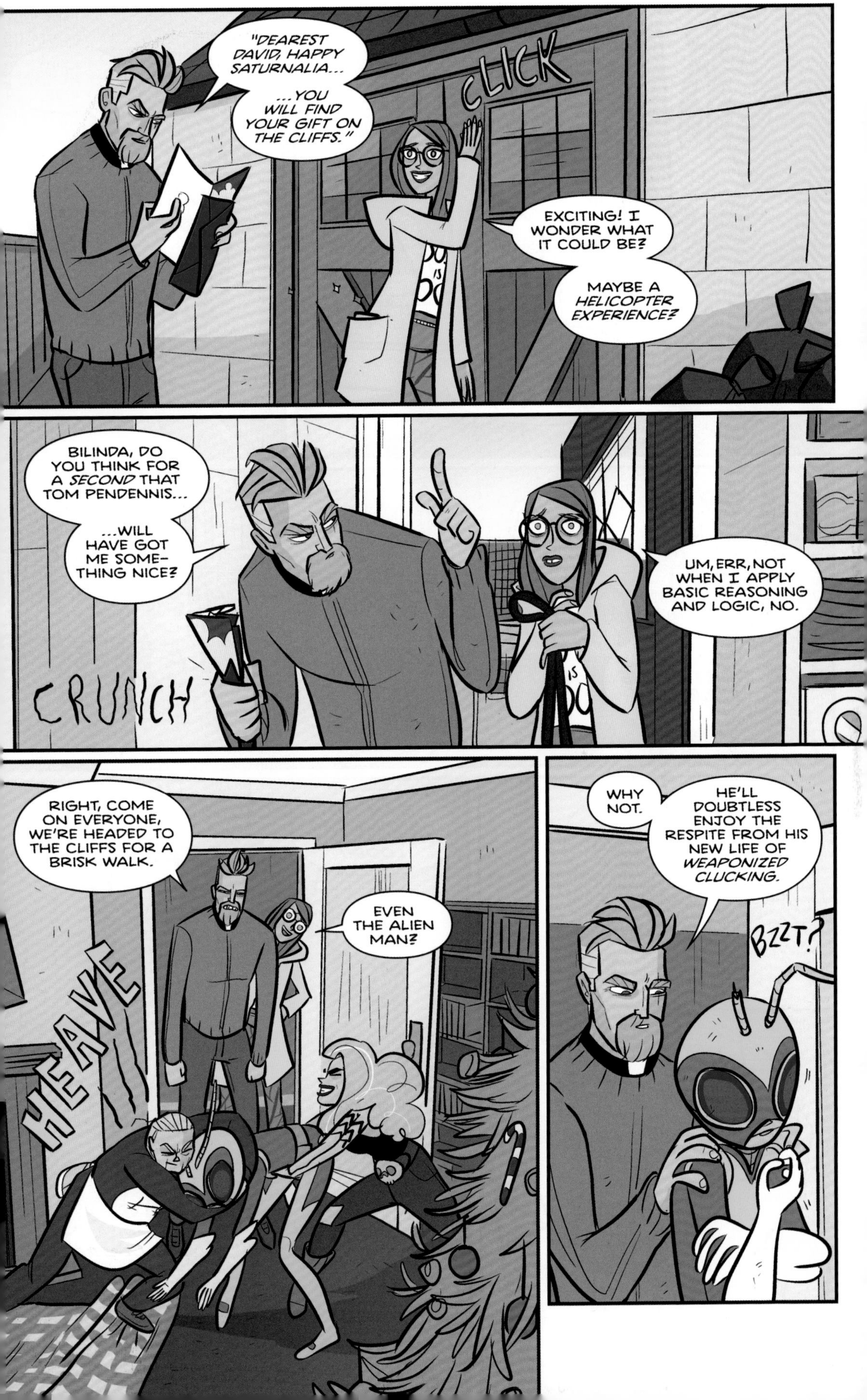
"DEAREST DAVID, HAPPY SATURNALIA...
...YOU WILL FIND YOUR GIFT ON THE CLIFFS."
CLICK
EXCITING! I WONDER WHAT IT COULD BE?
MAYBE A *HELICOPTER EXPERIENCE?*
BILINDA, DO YOU THINK FOR A *SECOND* THAT TOM PENDENNIS...
...WILL HAVE GOT ME SOME-THING NICE?
UM, ERR, NOT WHEN I APPLY BASIC REASONING AND LOGIC, NO.
CRUNCH
RIGHT, COME ON EVERYONE, WE'RE HEADED TO THE CLIFFS FOR A BRISK WALK.
EVEN THE ALIEN MAN?
HEAVE
WHY NOT.
HE'LL DOUBTLESS ENJOY THE RESPITE FROM HIS NEW LIFE OF *WEAPONIZED CLUCKING.*
BZZT?

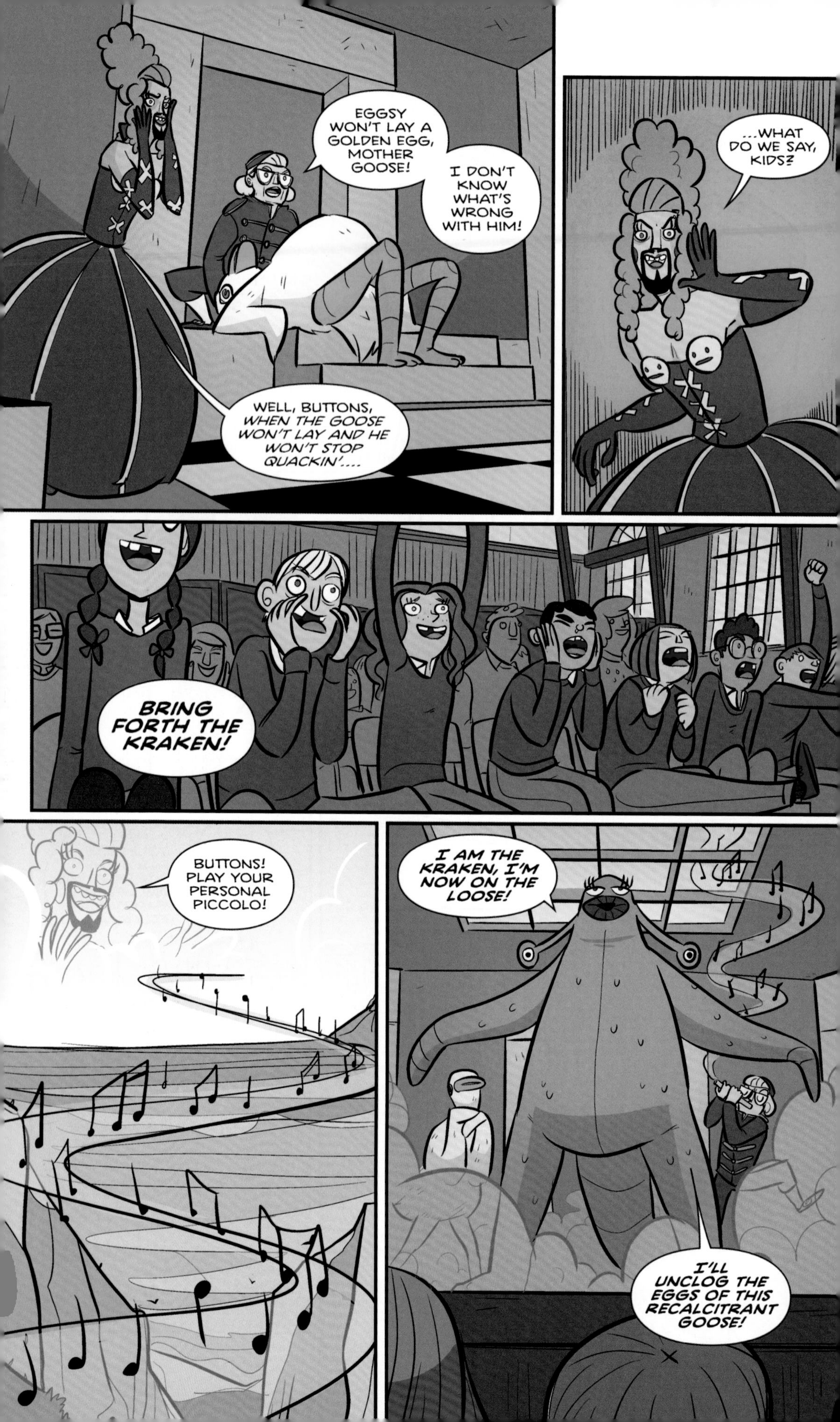
EGGSY WON'T LAY A GOLDEN EGG, MOTHER GOOSE!
I DON'T KNOW WHAT'S WRONG WITH HIM!
WELL, BUTTONS, *WHEN THE GOOSE WON'T LAY AND HE WON'T STOP QUACKIN'....*
...WHAT DO WE SAY, KIDS?
BRING FORTH THE KRAKEN!
BUTTONS! PLAY YOUR PERSONAL PICCOLO!
I AM THE KRAKEN, I'M NOW ON THE LOOSE!
I'LL UNCLOG THE EGGS OF THIS RECALCITRANT GOOSE!

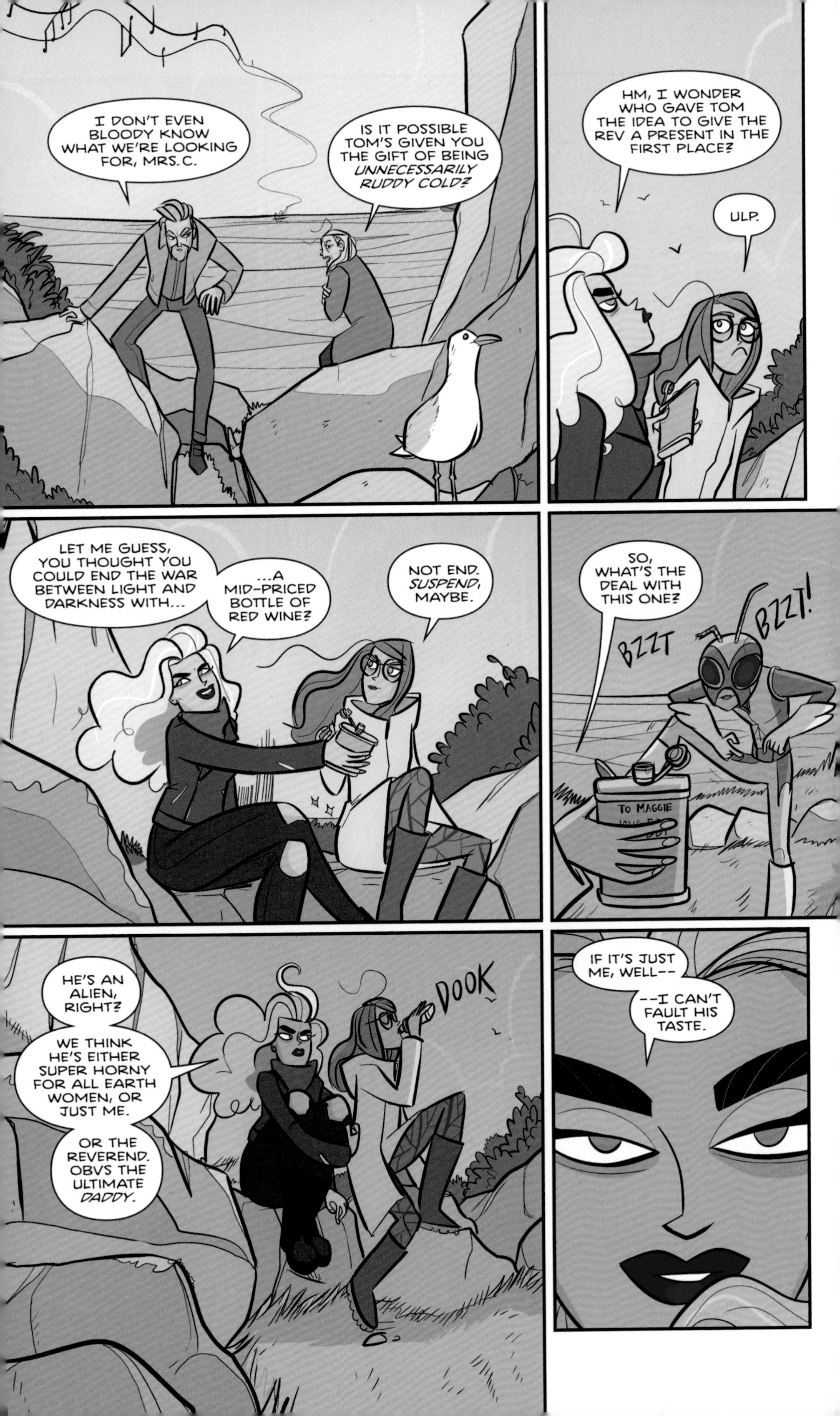
I DON'T EVEN BLOODY KNOW WHAT WE'RE LOOKING FOR, MRS. C.
IS IT POSSIBLE TOM'S GIVEN YOU THE GIFT OF BEING *UNNECESSARILY RUDDY COLD?*
HM, I WONDER WHO GAVE TOM THE IDEA TO GIVE THE REV A PRESENT IN THE FIRST PLACE?
ULP.
LET ME GUESS, YOU THOUGHT YOU COULD END THE WAR BETWEEN LIGHT AND DARKNESS WITH...
...A MID-PRICED BOTTLE OF RED WINE?
NOT END. *SUSPEND*, MAYBE.
SO, WHAT'S THE DEAL WITH THIS ONE?
BZZT
BZZT!
TO MAGGIE
HE'S AN ALIEN, RIGHT?
WE THINK HE'S EITHER SUPER HORNY FOR ALL EARTH WOMEN, OR JUST ME.
OR THE REVEREND. OBVS THE ULTIMATE *DADDY*.
DOOK
IF IT'S JUST ME, WELL--
--I CAN'T FAULT HIS TASTE.

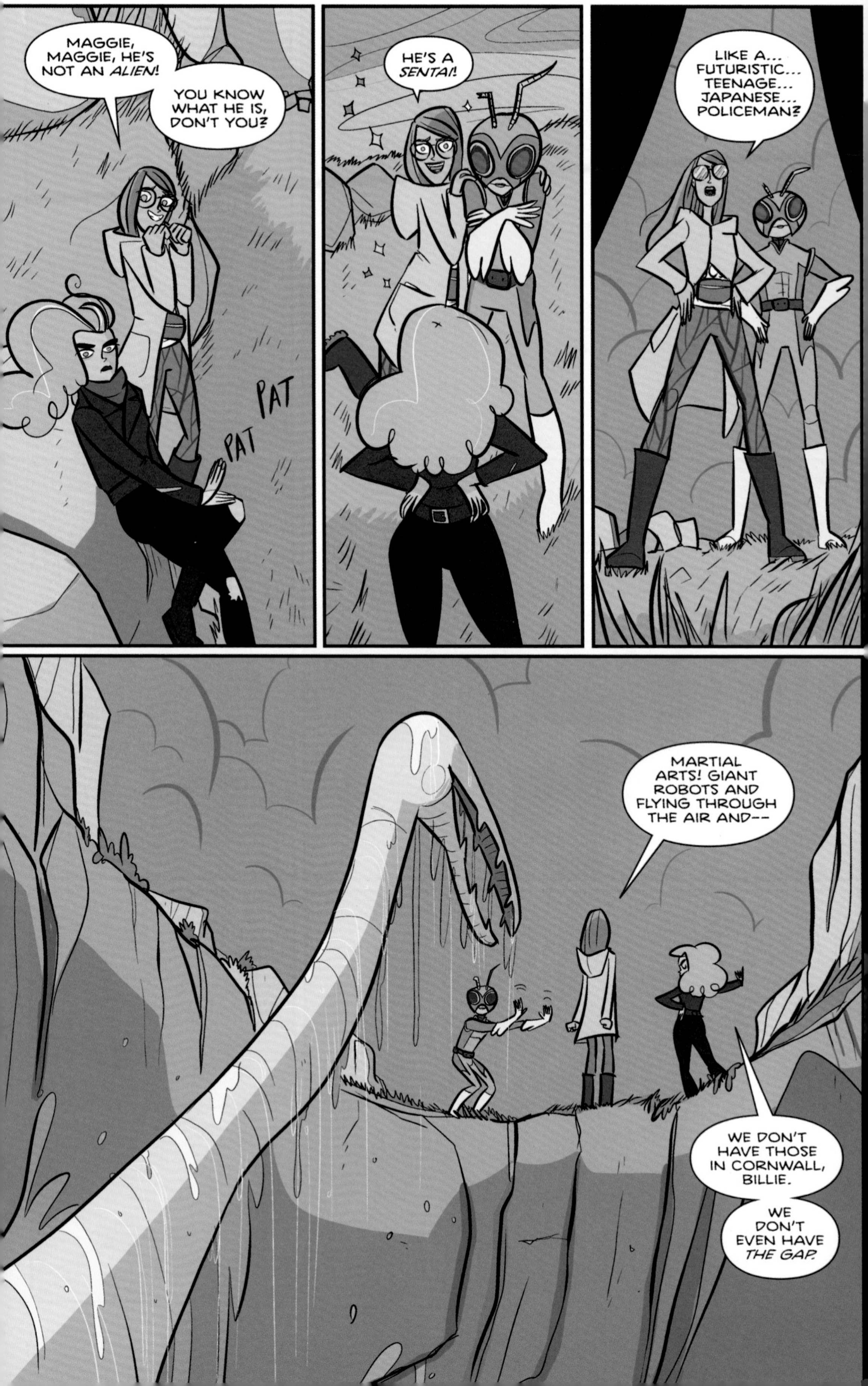
MAGGIE, MAGGIE, HE'S NOT AN *ALIEN*!
YOU KNOW WHAT HE IS, DON'T YOU?
PAT
PAT
HE'S A *SENTAI*!
LIKE A... FUTURISTIC... TEENAGE... JAPANESE... POLICEMAN?
MARTIAL ARTS! GIANT ROBOTS AND FLYING THROUGH THE AIR AND--
WE DON'T HAVE THOSE IN CORNWALL, BILLIE.
WE DON'T EVEN HAVE *THE GAP*.

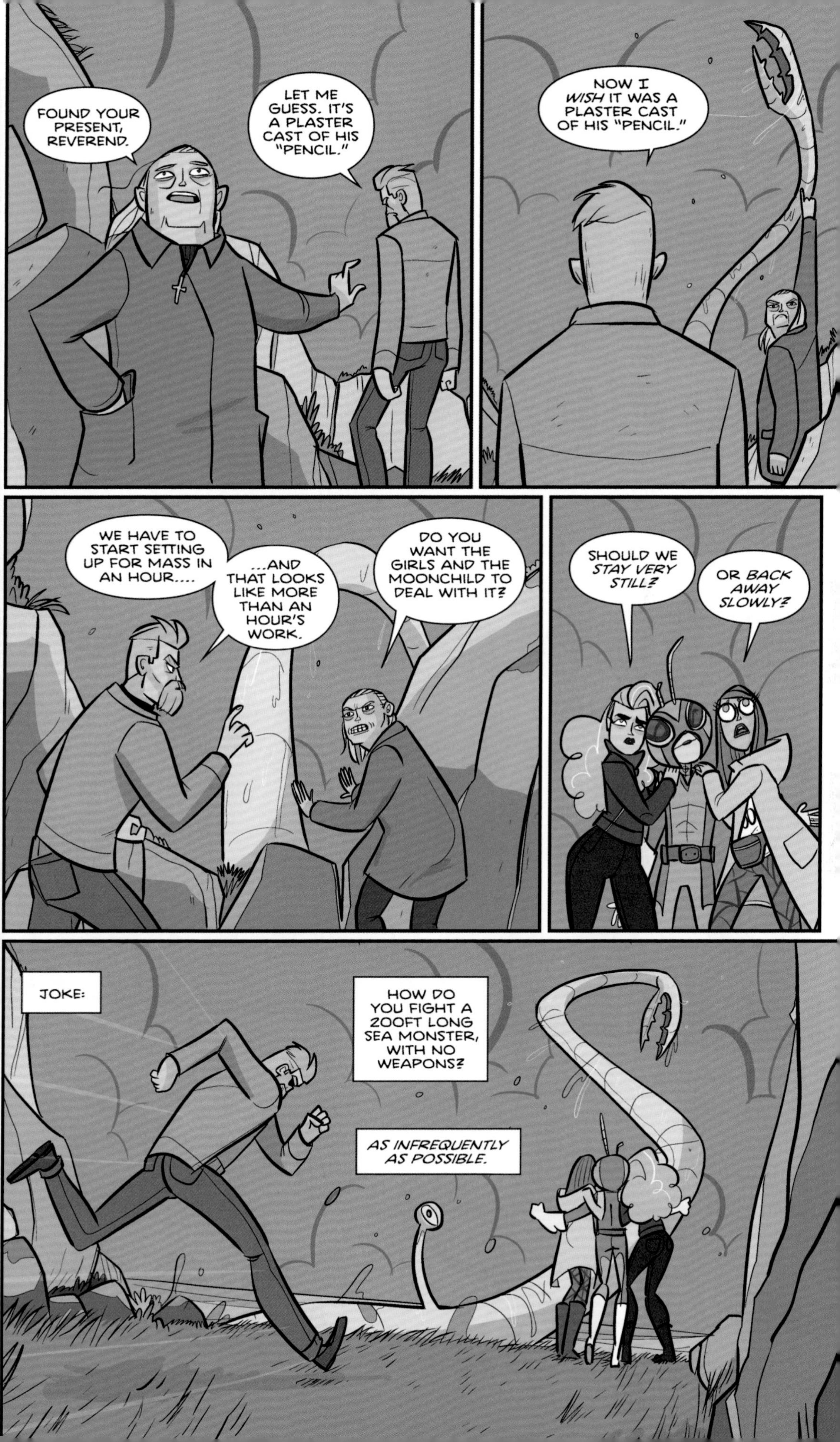
FOUND YOUR PRESENT, REVEREND.
LET ME GUESS. IT'S A PLASTER CAST OF HIS "PENCIL."
NOW I *WISH* IT WAS A PLASTER CAST OF HIS "PENCIL."
WE HAVE TO START SETTING UP FOR MASS IN AN HOUR....
...AND THAT LOOKS LIKE MORE THAN AN HOUR'S WORK.
DO YOU WANT THE GIRLS AND THE MOONCHILD TO DEAL WITH IT?
SHOULD WE *STAY VERY STILL?*
OR *BACK AWAY SLOWLY?*
JOKE:
HOW DO YOU FIGHT A 200FT LONG SEA MONSTER, WITH NO WEAPONS?
AS INFREQUENTLY AS POSSIBLE.

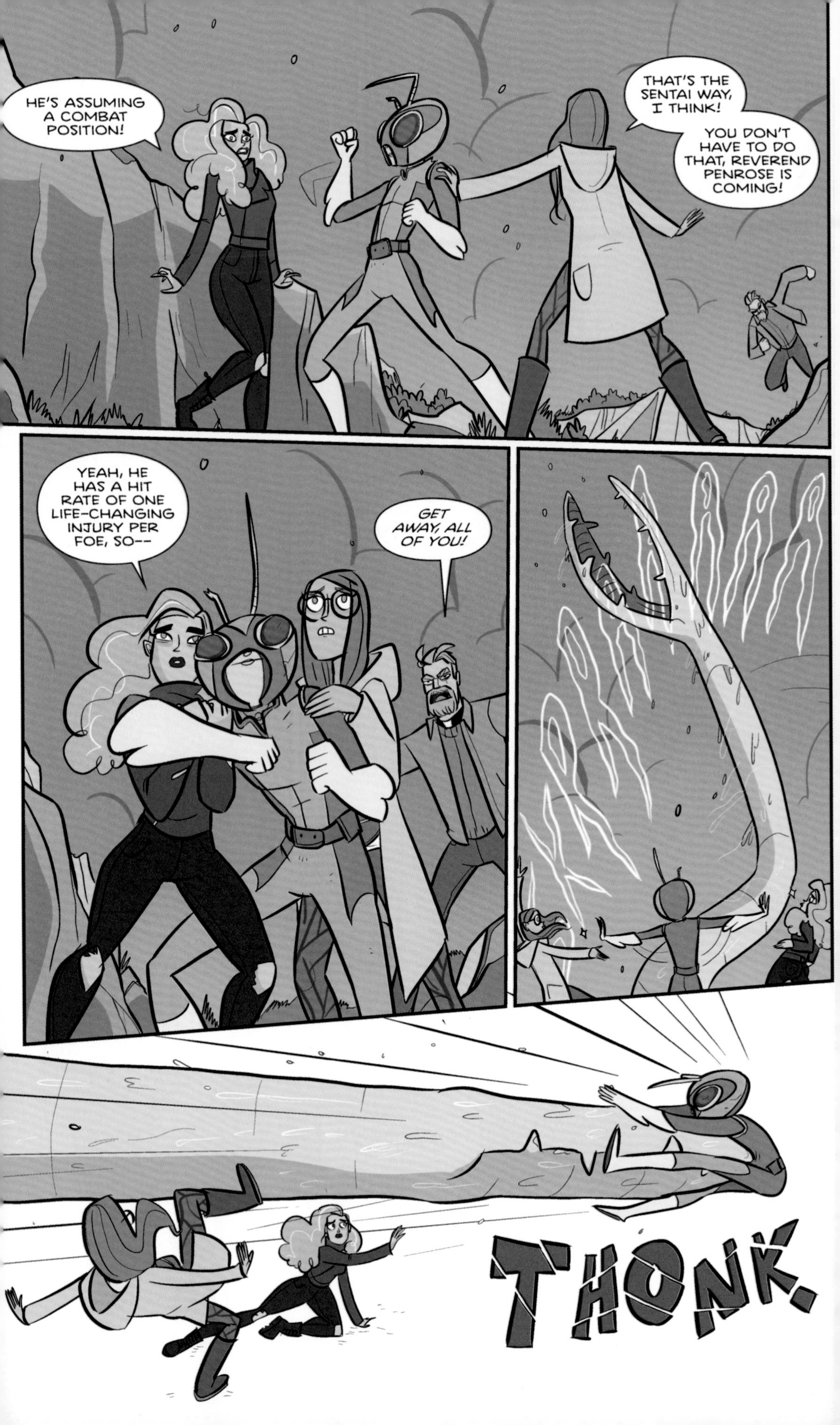
HE'S ASSUMING A COMBAT POSITION!
THAT'S THE SENTAI WAY, I THINK!
YOU DON'T HAVE TO DO THAT, REVEREND PENROSE IS COMING!
YEAH, HE HAS A HIT RATE OF ONE LIFE-CHANGING INJURY PER FOE, SO--
GET AWAY, ALL OF YOU!
THONK.

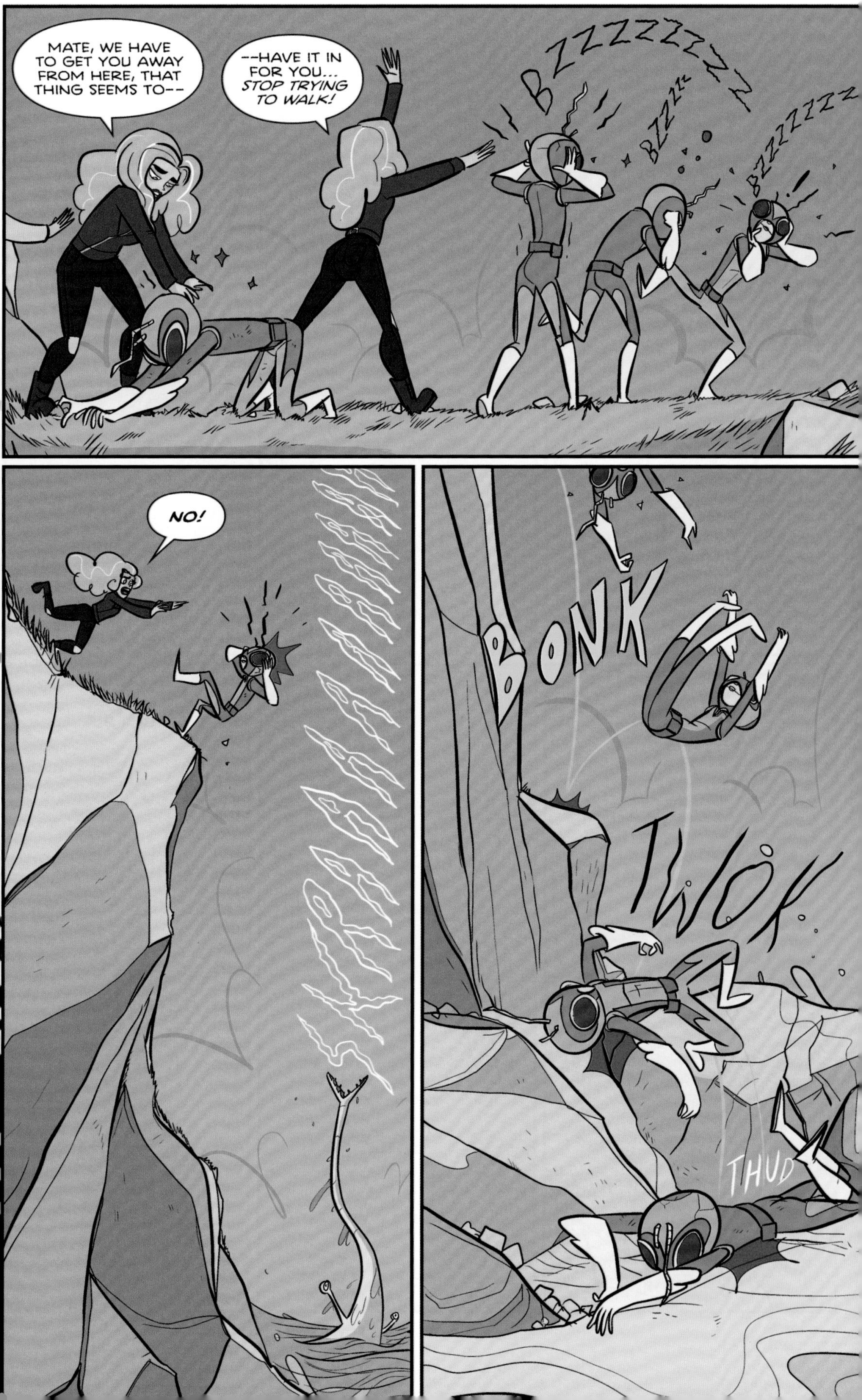

MATE, WE HAVE TO GET YOU AWAY FROM HERE, THAT THING SEEMS TO--
--HAVE IT IN FOR YOU... *STOP TRYING TO WALK!*
BZZZZZZZZZ
BZZZZ
BZZZZZZZZ
NO!
BONK
TWOK
THUD

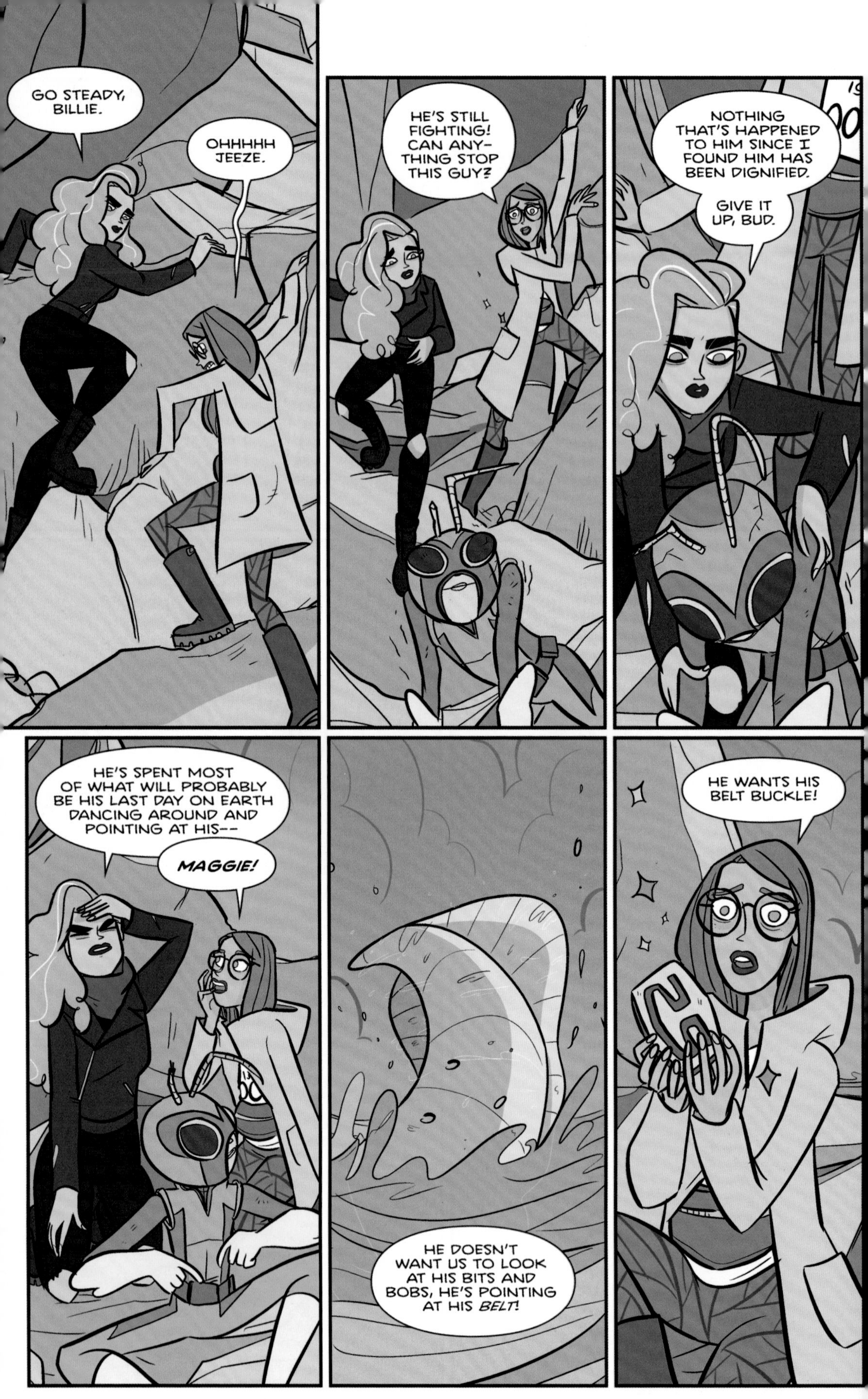
GO STEADY, BILLIE.
OHHHHH JEEZE.
HE'S STILL FIGHTING! CAN ANYTHING STOP THIS GUY?
NOTHING THAT'S HAPPENED TO HIM SINCE I FOUND HIM HAS BEEN DIGNIFIED.
GIVE IT UP, BUD.
HE'S SPENT MOST OF WHAT WILL PROBABLY BE HIS LAST DAY ON EARTH DANCING AROUND AND POINTING AT HIS--
MAGGIE!
HE DOESN'T WANT US TO LOOK AT HIS BITS AND BOBS, HE'S POINTING AT HIS BELT!
HE WANTS HIS BELT BUCKLE!

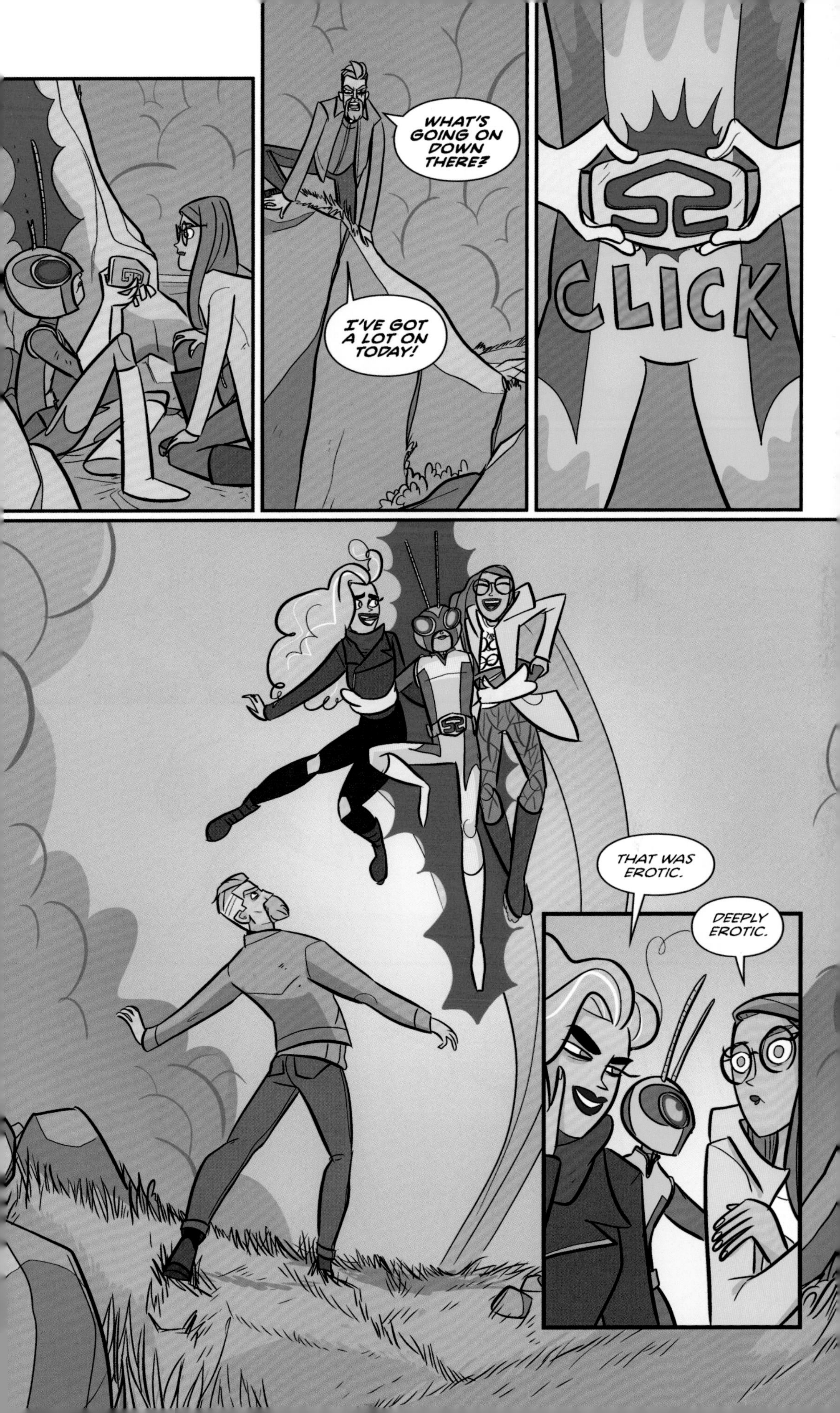
WHAT'S GOING ON DOWN THERE?
I'VE GOT A LOT ON TODAY!
CLICK
THAT WAS EROTIC.
DEEPLY EROTIC.

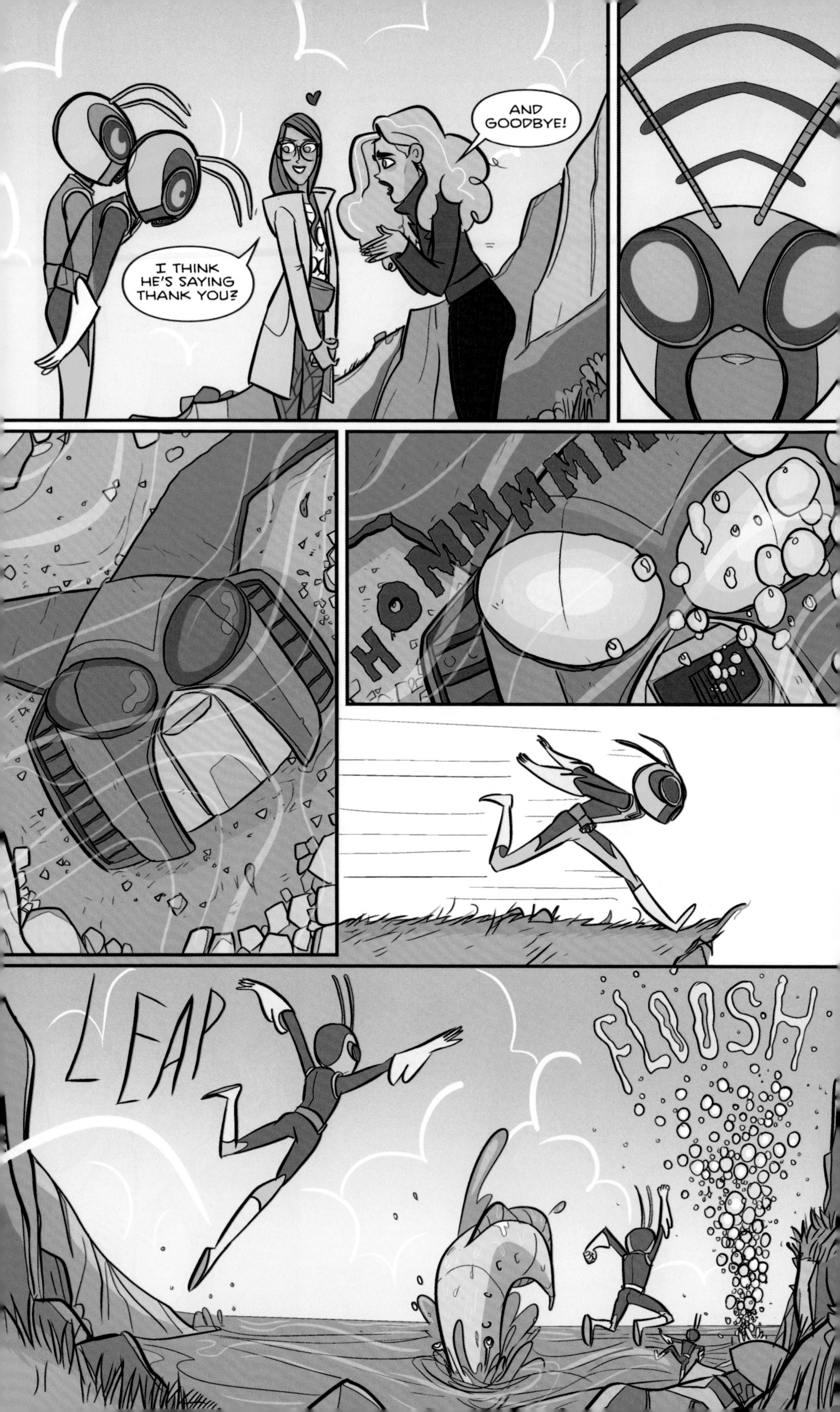
I THINK HE'S SAYING THANK YOU?
AND GOODBYE!
HOMMMMM
LEAP
FLOOSH

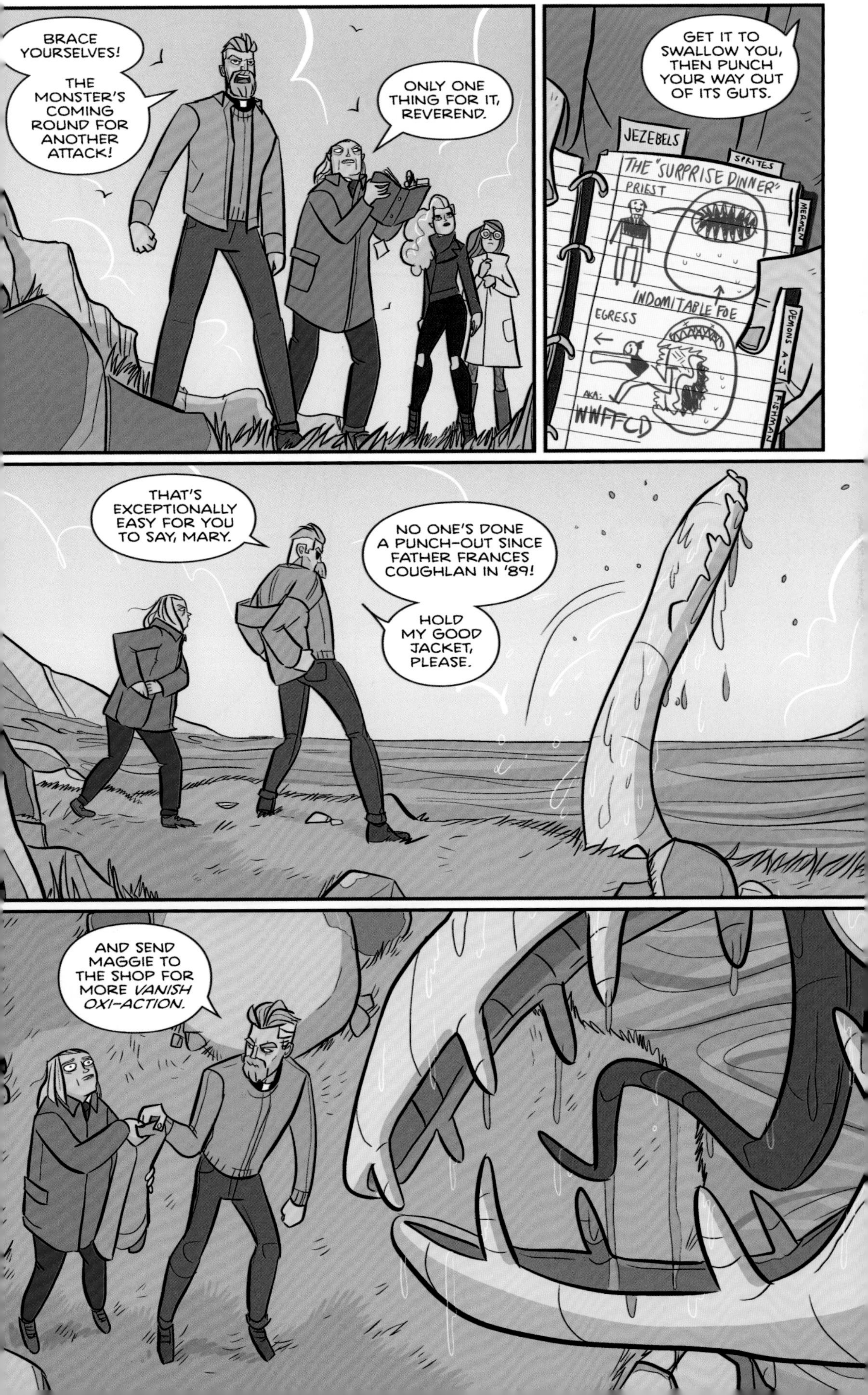
BRACE YOURSELVES!
THE MONSTER'S COMING ROUND FOR ANOTHER ATTACK!
ONLY ONE THING FOR IT, REVEREND.
GET IT TO SWALLOW YOU, THEN PUNCH YOUR WAY OUT OF ITS GUTS.
JEZEBELS
SPRITES
MERMEN
THE "SURPRISE DINNER"
PRIEST
INDOMITABLE FOE
EGRESS
DEMONS A-J
FISHMAN
AKA:
WWFFCD
THAT'S EXCEPTIONALLY EASY FOR YOU TO SAY, MARY.
NO ONE'S DONE A PUNCH-OUT SINCE FATHER FRANCES COUGHLAN IN '89!
HOLD MY GOOD JACKET, PLEASE.
AND SEND MAGGIE TO THE SHOP FOR MORE VANISH OXI-ACTION.

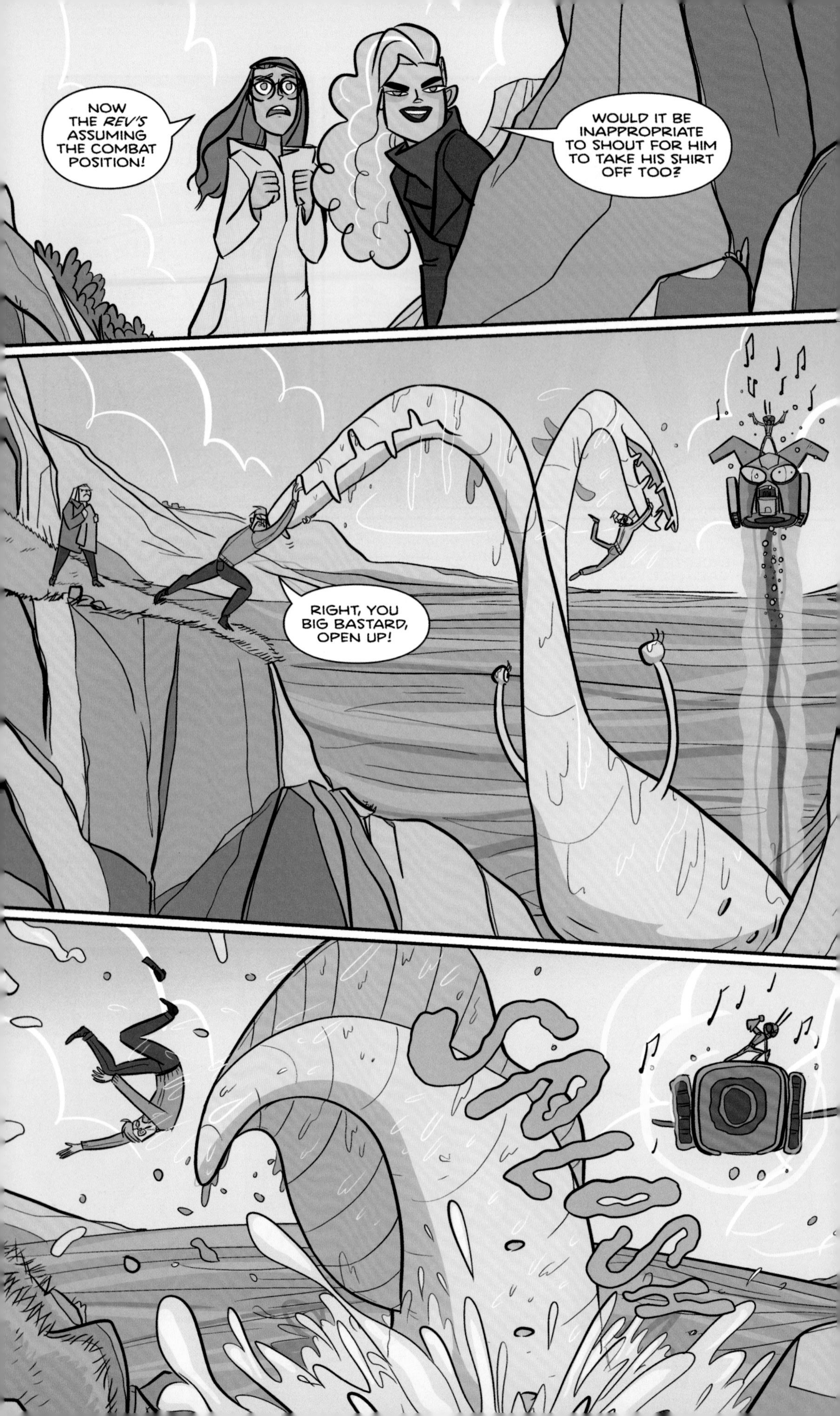
NOW THE *REV'S* ASSUMING THE COMBAT POSITION!
WOULD IT BE INAPPROPRIATE TO SHOUT FOR HIM TO TAKE HIS SHIRT OFF TOO?
RIGHT, YOU BIG BASTARD, OPEN UP!

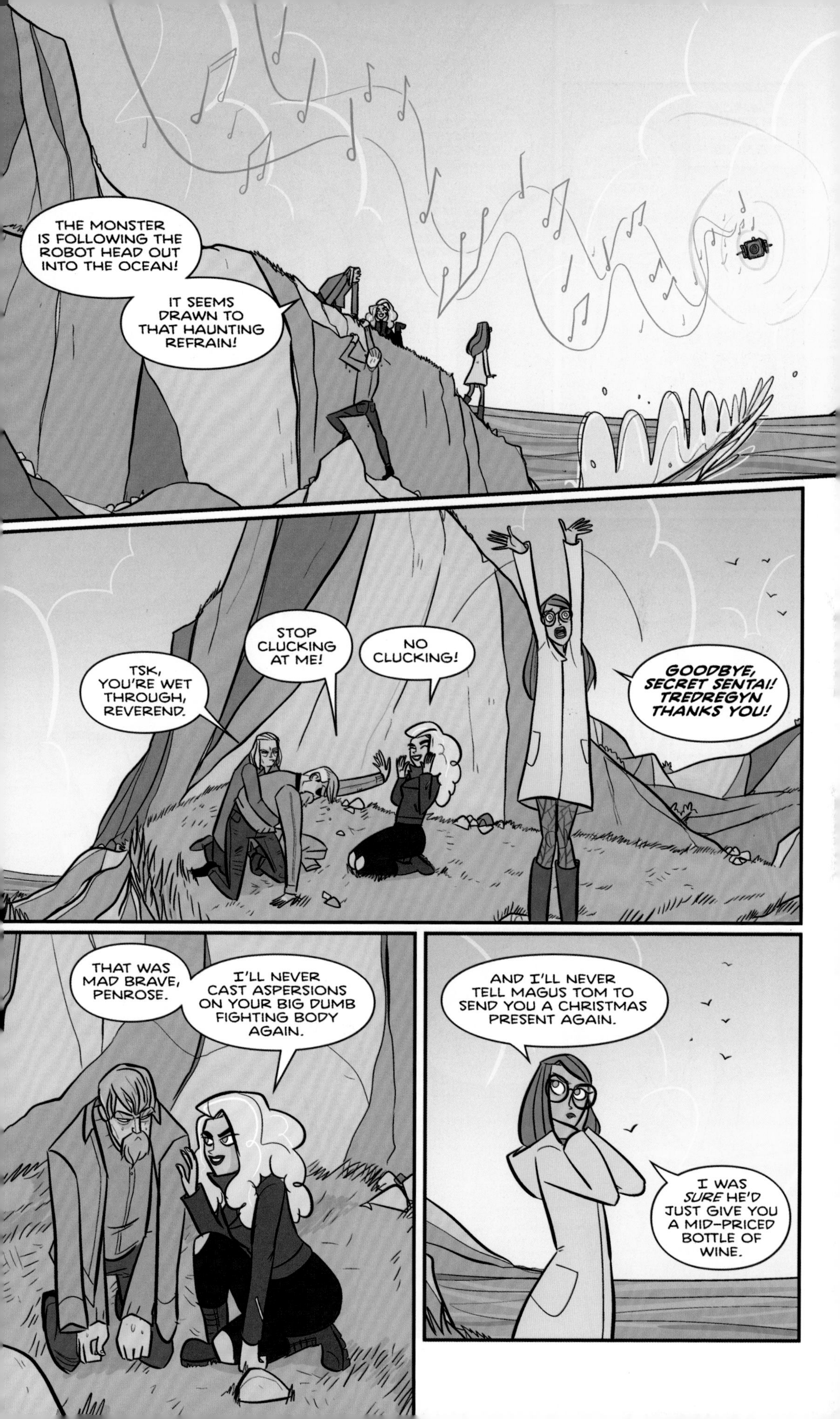
THE MONSTER IS FOLLOWING THE ROBOT HEAD OUT INTO THE OCEAN!
IT SEEMS DRAWN TO THAT HAUNTING REFRAIN!
TSK, YOU'RE WET THROUGH, REVEREND.
STOP CLUCKING AT ME!
NO CLUCKING!
GOODBYE, SECRET SENTAI! TREDREGYN THANKS YOU!
THAT WAS MAD BRAVE, PENROSE.
I'LL NEVER CAST ASPERSIONS ON YOUR BIG DUMB FIGHTING BODY AGAIN.
AND I'LL NEVER TELL MAGUS TOM TO SEND YOU A CHRISTMAS PRESENT AGAIN.
I WAS SURE HE'D JUST GIVE YOU A MID-PRICED BOTTLE OF WINE.

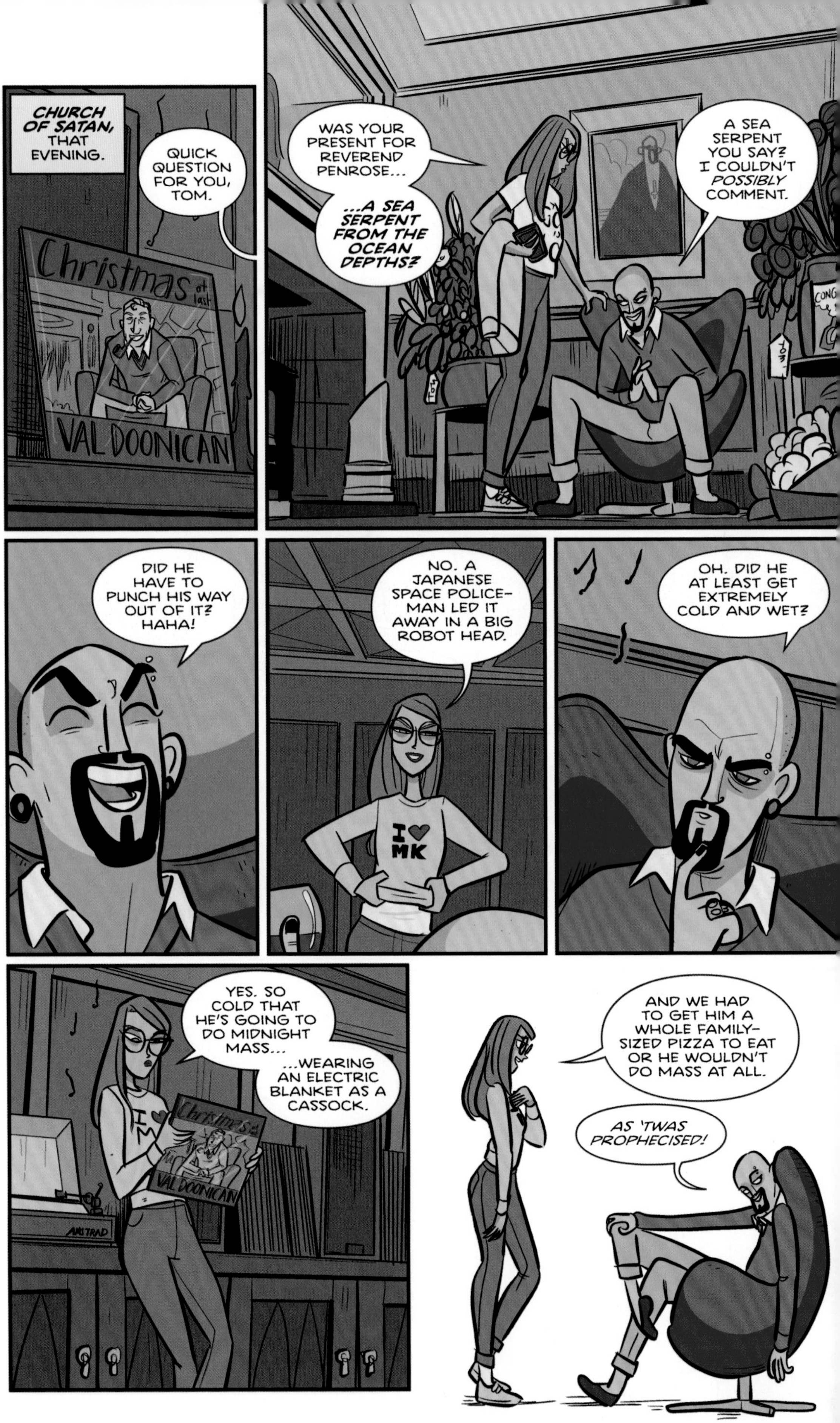

CHURCH OF SATAN, THAT EVENING.
QUICK QUESTION FOR YOU, TOM.
Christmas at last
VAL DOONICAN
WAS YOUR PRESENT FOR REVEREND PENROSE...
...A SEA SERPENT FROM THE OCEAN DEPTHS?
A SEA SERPENT YOU SAY? I COULDN'T POSSIBLY COMMENT.
DID HE HAVE TO PUNCH HIS WAY OUT OF IT? HAHA!
NO. A JAPANESE SPACE POLICE-MAN LED IT AWAY IN A BIG ROBOT HEAD.
I ♥ MK
OH. DID HE AT LEAST GET EXTREMELY COLD AND WET?
YES. SO COLD THAT HE'S GOING TO DO MIDNIGHT MASS...
...WEARING AN ELECTRIC BLANKET AS A CASSOCK.
VAL DOONICAN
AMSTRAD
AND WE HAD TO GET HIM A WHOLE FAMILY-SIZED PIZZA TO EAT OR HE WOULDN'T DO MASS AT ALL.
AS 'TWAS PROPHECISED!

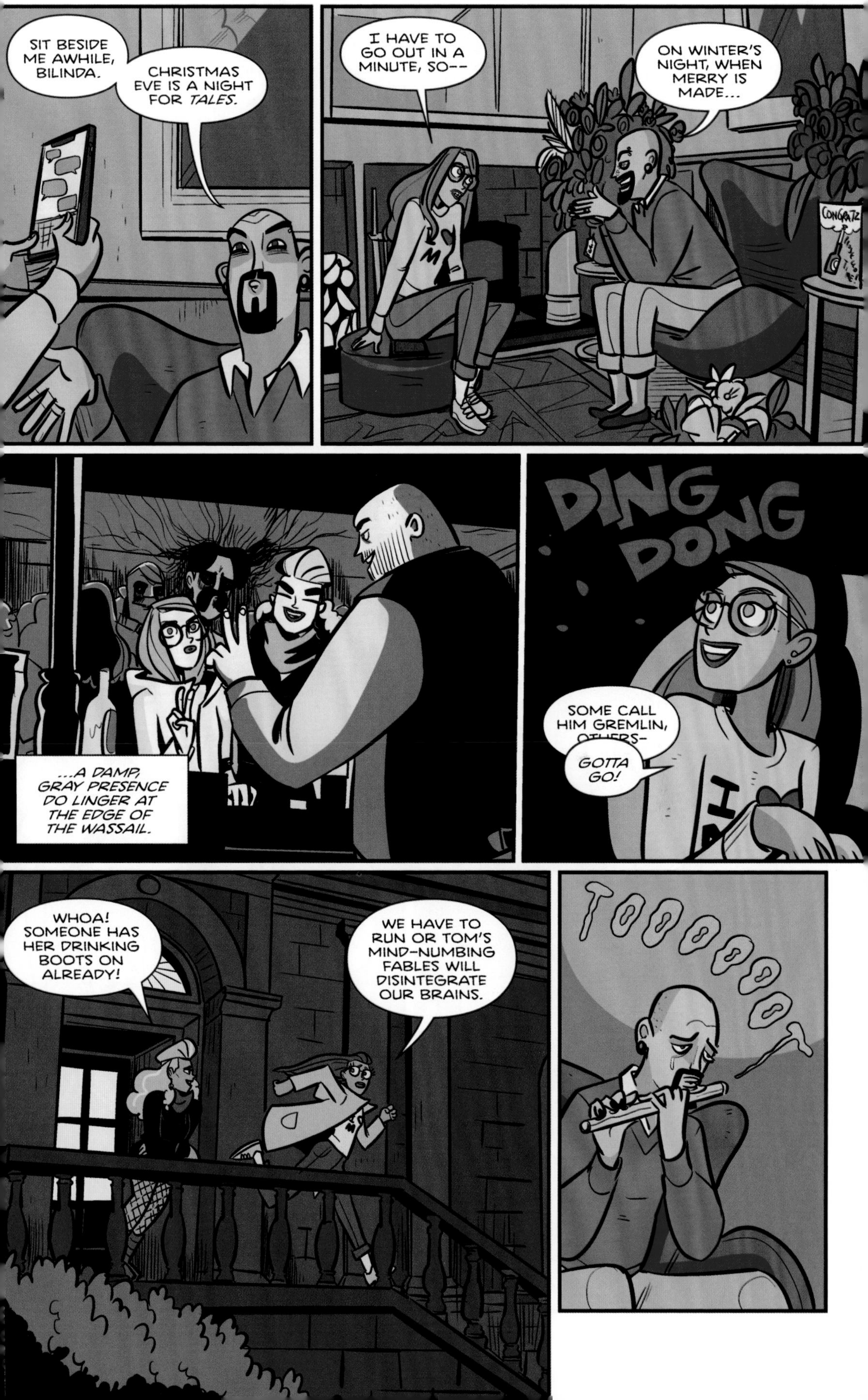
SIT BESIDE ME AWHILE, BILINDA.
CHRISTMAS EVE IS A NIGHT FOR *TALES*.
I HAVE TO GO OUT IN A MINUTE, SO--
ON WINTER'S NIGHT, WHEN MERRY IS MADE...
CONGRATZ
...A DAMP, GRAY PRESENCE DO LINGER AT THE EDGE OF THE WASSAIL.
DING DONG
SOME CALL HIM GREMLIN,
GOTTA GO!
WHOA! SOMEONE HAS HER DRINKING BOOTS ON ALREADY!
WE HAVE TO RUN OR TOM'S MIND-NUMBING FABLES WILL DISINTEGRATE OUR BRAINS.
TOOOOOOT

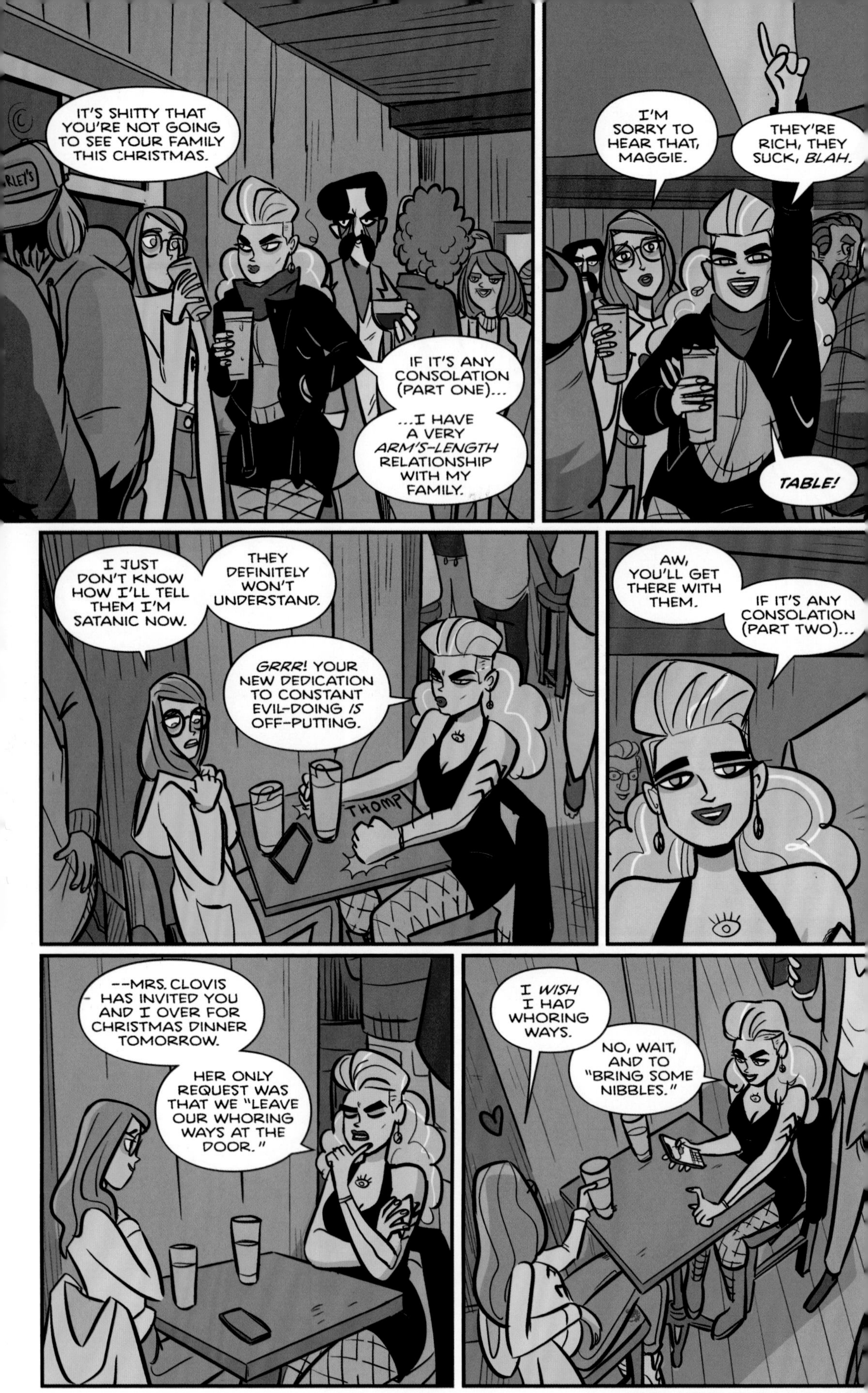
IT'S SHITTY THAT YOU'RE NOT GOING TO SEE YOUR FAMILY THIS CHRISTMAS.
IF IT'S ANY CONSOLATION (PART ONE)...
...I HAVE A VERY *ARM'S-LENGTH* RELATIONSHIP WITH MY FAMILY.
I'M SORRY TO HEAR THAT, MAGGIE.
THEY'RE RICH, THEY SUCK, *BLAH*.
TABLE!
I JUST DON'T KNOW HOW I'LL TELL THEM I'M SATANIC NOW.
THEY DEFINITELY WON'T UNDERSTAND.
GRRR! YOUR NEW DEDICATION TO CONSTANT EVIL-DOING *IS* OFF-PUTTING.
THOMP
AW, YOU'LL GET THERE WITH THEM.
IF IT'S ANY CONSOLATION (PART TWO)...
--MRS. CLOVIS HAS INVITED YOU AND I OVER FOR CHRISTMAS DINNER TOMORROW.
HER ONLY REQUEST WAS THAT WE "LEAVE OUR WHORING WAYS AT THE DOOR."
I *WISH* I HAD WHORING WAYS.
NO, WAIT, AND TO "BRING SOME NIBBLES."

UNTIL NEXT TIME...THE END!

STEEPLE™

SKETCHBOOK

NOTES BY

JOHN ALLISON

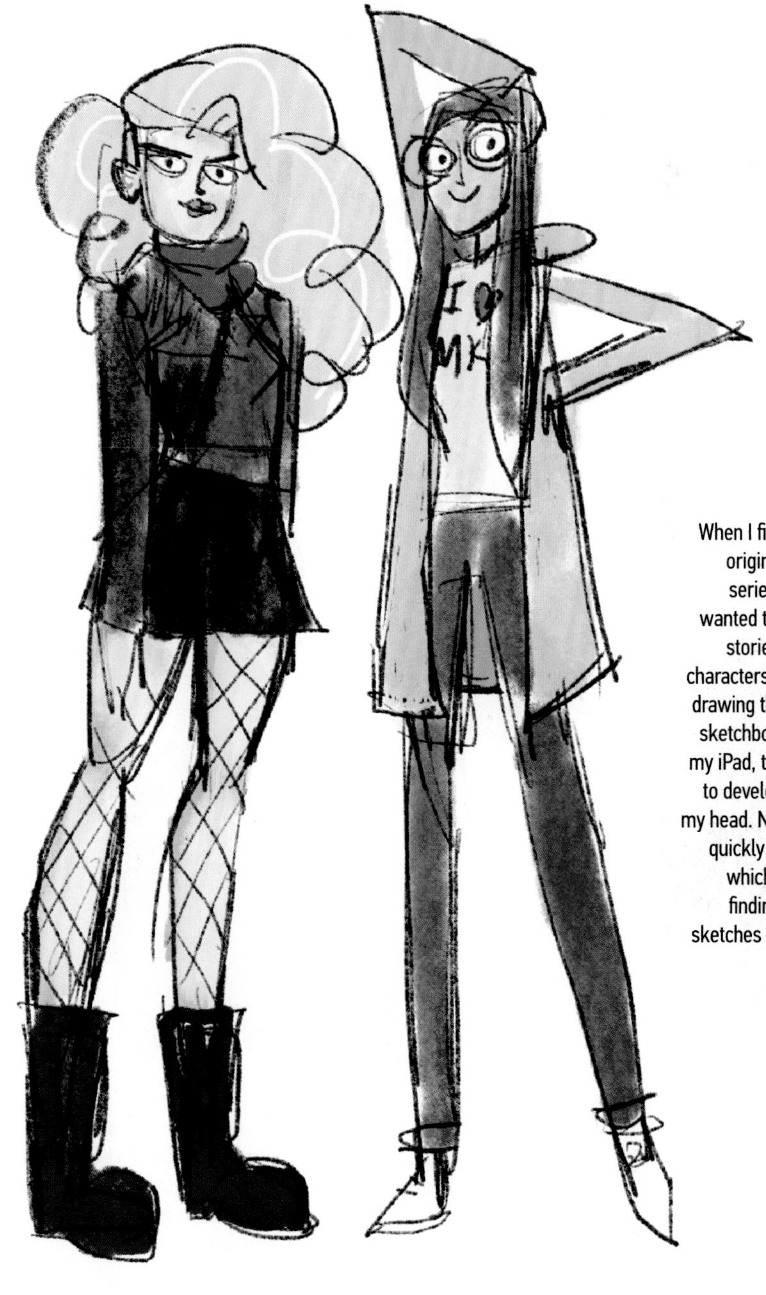

I ♥
MX

When I finished the original *Steeple* series, I knew I wanted to do more stories with the characters. So I kept drawing them in my sketchbook and on my iPad, to continue to develop them in my head. New quirks quickly appeared, which I enjoyed finding in loose sketches like these.

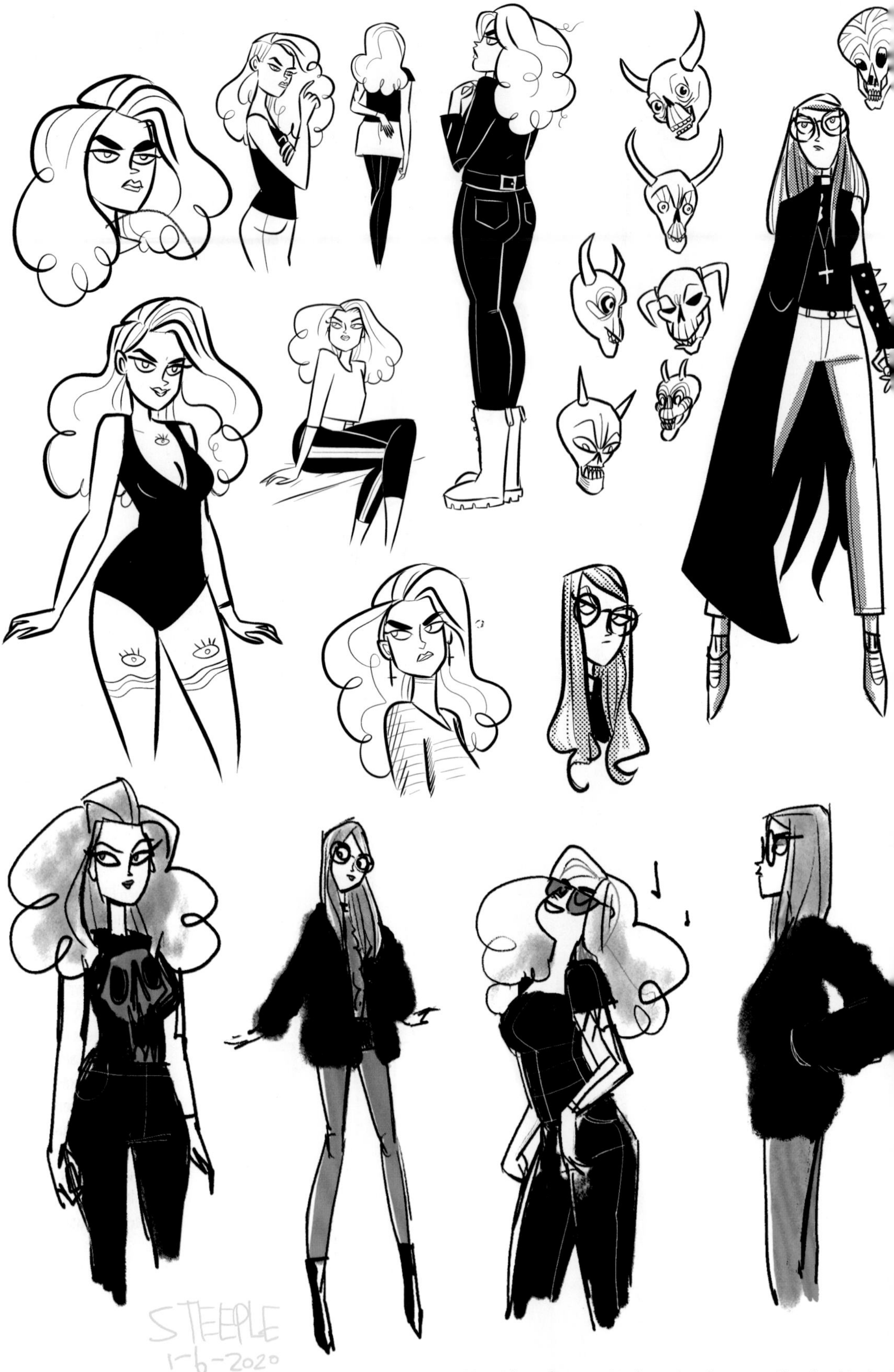
STEEPLE
1-6-2020

Fashion is an important part of my character design process. In volume 1, Billie had lost most of her clothes when her car blew up. With her move to the Church of Satan, and with a few more weeks gone, she's started to build a slightly anarchic new look.

Maggie's outfits are critical, too, in volume two. There's a bit of "athleisure" and a bit of a biker hangover, she wears a bit of the old Cornish standby, "ratty old sweaters." At first I thought she might try to dress more conservatively, living at the rectory. But that seemed unlikely.

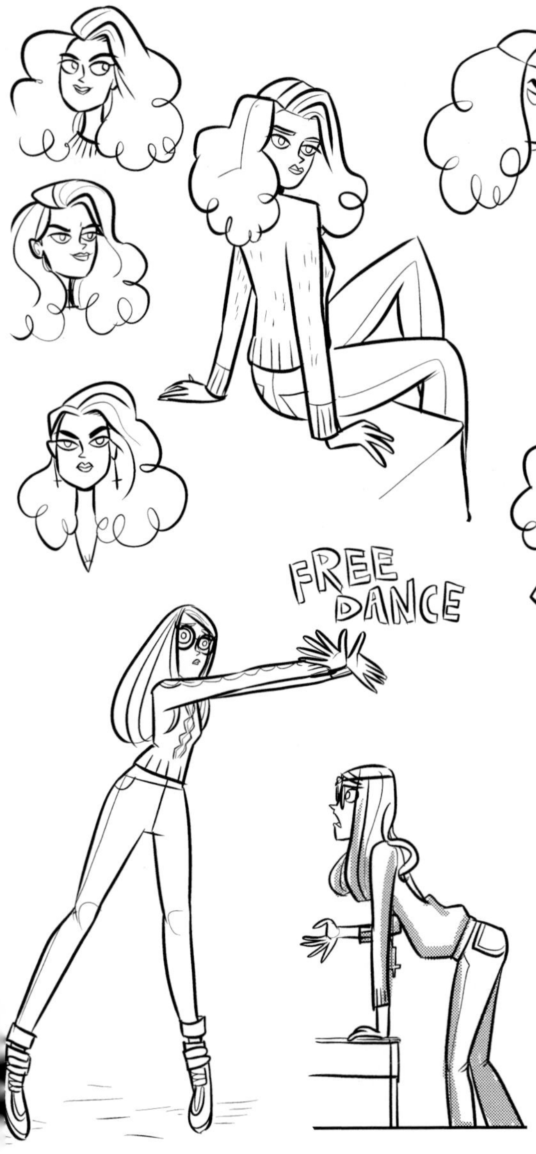
FREE
DANCE

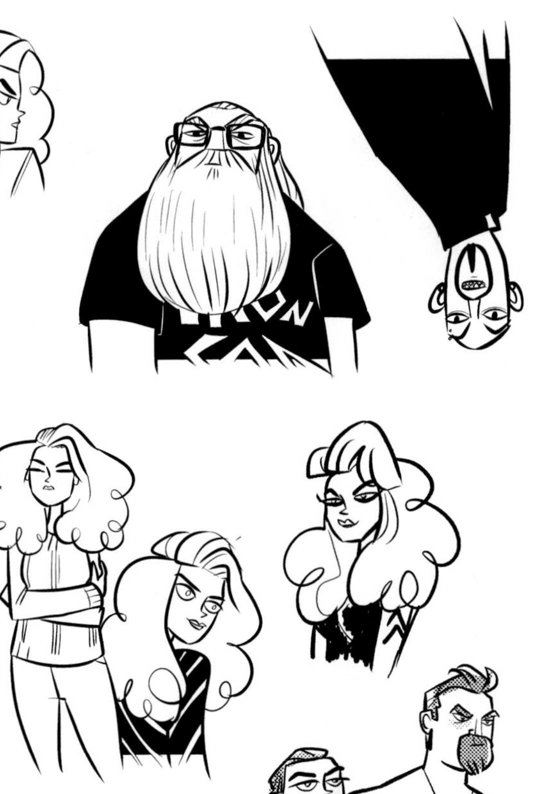

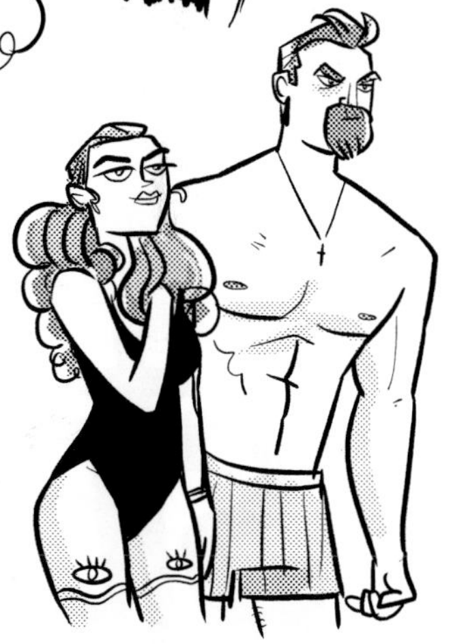

Volume 2 features some of Billie's "arts in the community" ideas. I didn't get to include her journeys in "free dance" in these stories. Next time!

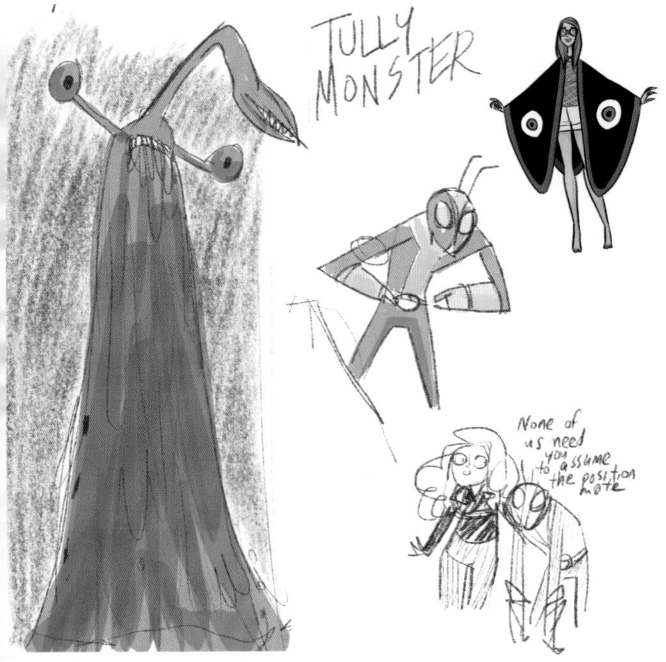
TULLY
MONSTER
None of us need you to assume the position mate

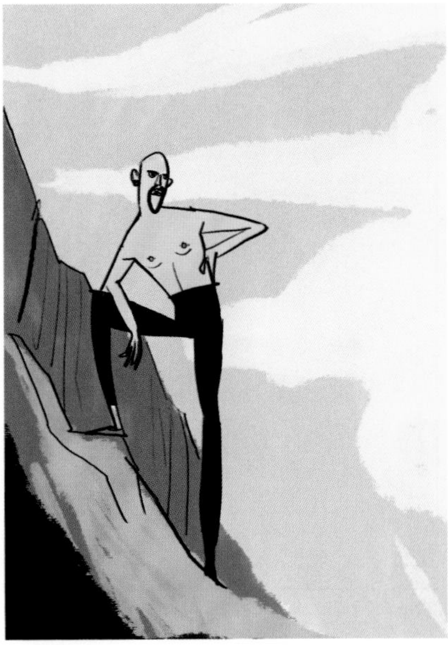

Magus Tom is comfortable with his body. And why shouldn't he be? It's the only one he's got. Here he is, shirtless on a clifftop.

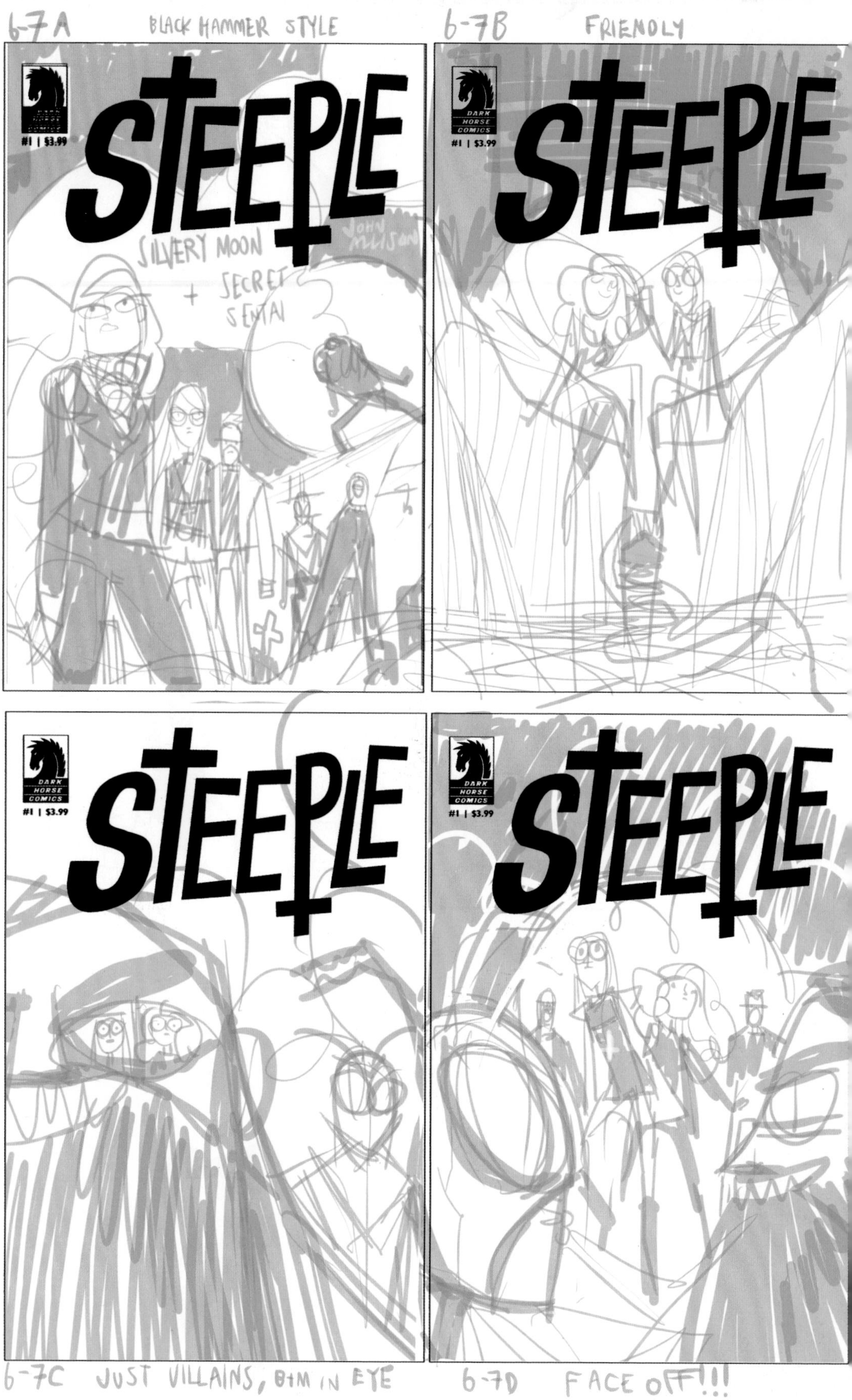
6-7A
BLACK HAMMER STYLE
STEEPLE
DARK HORSE COMICS
#1 | $3.99
SILVERY MOON + SECRET SENTAI
JOHN ALLISON
6-7B
FRIENDLY
STEEPLE
DARK HORSE COMICS
#1 | $3.99
STEEPLE
DARK HORSE COMICS
#1 | $3.99
STEEPLE
DARK HORSE COMICS
#1 | $3.99
6-7C
JUST VILLAINS, B+M IN EYE
6-7D
FACE OFF!!!

Four cover ideas for Max Sarin. I often rough out an alluring design featuring an angle I can't actually draw neatly. But with Max in charge, I had no fear of the "under-chin conundrum," the "top-down foreshortening quandary," or the "dangerous multi-character composition." Visual irresponsibility was my *modus operandi*.